Abstracting and Indexing Services in Perspective:

Miles Conrad Memorial Lectures 1969-1983

Commemorating the Twenty-fifth Anniversary of the National Federation of Abstracting and Information Services

Edited by M. LYNNE NEUFELD
MARTHA CORNOG
INEZ L. SPERR

INFORMATION RESOURCES PRESS
Arlington, Virginia
1983

© 1983 by Information Resources Press, a division of Herner & Company.
All rights reserved.
Printed in the United States of America. No part of this publication may be reproduced, stored in a retrieval system, or transmitted, in any form or by any means, electronic, mechanical, photocopying, recording, or otherwise, without the prior written permission of the publisher.

Available from
Information Resources Press
1700 North Moore Street
Arlington, Virginia 22209

Library of Congress Catalog Card Number 82-084484
ISBN 0-87815-043-9

Contents

The Editors	vii
Introduction and Dedication *M. Lynne Neufeld*	ix
PART I BACKGROUND AND HISTORY	1
Introduction: Dedication to Dedication! *Malcolm Rigby*	3
1. The History of NFAIS 1958–1971 *Malcolm Rigby*	9
2. The History of NFAIS 1972–1982 *Lois Granick and Martha Cornog*	21
The Miles Conrad Memorial Lectures: Background and Significance *Inez L. Sperr*	27
PART II PERSPECTIVES	31
In the Beginning *Raymond A. Jensen*	33
Signposts of the Past and Future *Stella Keenan*	37
Toward the Fourth Era of Information Services *Toni Carbo Bearman*	41

Abstracting and Indexing Services —
Past, Present, and Future ... 45
  Dale B. Baker
From Isolation to a Community ... 47
  Carolyn M. Flanagan
A View of Things in Their True Relations ... 49
  Kenneth C. Spengler
The User — Once and for All ... 51
  Everett H. Brenner
A Hexadecimal Dump Is Not a Greenwich Village Dive ... 55
  Joel J. Lloyd
A Perspective on Fifteen Years in the Abstracting
and Indexing Field ... 57
  H. E. Kennedy
Will Abstracts Survive Technological Developments?
And Will "Cheaper Is Better" Win Out? ... 61
  Ben H. Weil
NFAIS: Some Thoughts ... 63
  John E. Creps, Jr.
Information Dissemination: Evolution or Creationism? ... 67
  Russell J. Rowlett, Jr.
The Key Role of NFAIS to Information Services:
Past and Future ... 71
  H. William Koch
Perspective of a Humanist ... 73
  Richard H. Lineback
Proposed: A Code of Ethics for the Information Community ... 75
  Lois Granick
Change and Renewal ... 77
  E. K. Gannett
Influences for the Future ... 79
  Ronald L. Wigington

PART III   THE MILES CONRAD MEMORIAL LECTURES ... 83

Merging Operations Internationally ... 85
  J. R. Smith
The Changing Roles of Information Services ... 93
  Robert M. Hayes
After Organization X — What Next? ... 97
  Burton W. Adkinson
The Canadian National Scientific and Technical
Information System: A Progress Report ... 105
  Jack E. Brown
Science Information Services in an Environment of Change ... 117
  Phyllis V. Parkins

6	USSR/USA Scientific and Technical Information in Perspective *Dale B. Baker*	129
7	Sharing — The Hope of the Seventies *Melvin S. Day*	143
8	Comparative Development of Abstracting and Indexing, and Monograph Cataloging *Frederick G. Kilgour*	151
9	Progress in a Profession *William O. Baker*	157
10	Information Transfer in a Time of Transition: The Need for Community, Organizational, and Individual Empathy and Ethics *Ben H. Weil*	197
11	The Information Community: Its Dilemma, Opportunities, and Challenges *Donald W. King*	211
12	Surviving the Eighties: New Roles for Publishers, Information Service Organizations, and Users *Carlos A. Cuadra*	231
13	Abstracts, Who Needs Them? *Russell J. Rowlett, Jr.*	253
14	Abstracting and Indexing Services: The Business and the Science *Saul Herner*	269
15	STI, A Psychohistorical Evaluation 1983: "CHIMO" *John E. Creps, Jr.*	279

SUMMARY 291

BIBLIOGRAPHY 293

PUBLICATIONS BY AND ABOUT NFAIS 299

INDEX (Inside Back Cover)

The Editors

M. LYNNE NEUFELD is Executive Director of the National Federation of Abstracting and Information Services (NFAIS) in Philadelphia. Before joining the Federation in 1979, Ms. Neufeld was Deputy Group Manager for the Information Storage and Retrieval Group at Calculon Corporation (formerly Auerbach Associates). She has also served as Director of Library Operations at the Institute for Scientific Information.

Ms. Neufeld graduated magna cum laude from the University of Alberta, Canada, with a B.Sc. degree in chemistry and was the recipient of the Gold Medal in Science. She holds an M.S. degree in information science from Drexel University.

The author of nearly 20 publications and presentations, Ms. Neufeld is active in the American Society for Information Science and has served on its Awards, Education, and Marketing committees.

MARTHA CORNOG is currently Special Projects Coordinator for NFAIS. Her responsibilities focus on planning and writing Federation publications and assisting in research projects and programs. She is also Associate Editor for the *NFAIS Newsletter*. Prior to her involvement with NFAIS, Ms. Cornog was a consultant in information systems at Calculon Corporation. While there, she also served as head of the corporate information center. Previously, she held positions in the Haddonfield Public

Library in New Jersey and in the Paley Library at Temple University.

Ms. Cornog holds B.A. and M.A. degrees in linguistics from Brown University and an M.L.S. degree from Drexel University.

INEZ L. SPERR is Executive Director of Migration Information & Abstracts Service and President-Elect of NFAIS. From 1969 to 1982, she edited *Social Work Abstracts*, and, during that time, has been involved in a number of research-related activities. Dr. Sperr conducted postdoctoral research in ethology at Fordham University, was project director and project consultant on research methodology for a variety of projects at Fordham and several social agencies, and is currently directing a study on the "Information Needs of Decision Makers" for the Social Sciences Committee of the International Federation for Documentation.

Dr. Sperr serves on the Board of Directors of the American Theological Libraries Association–Indexes and is Chairman of the Special Interest Group/Behavioral and Social Sciences of the American Society for Information Science. She has served on the NFAIS Board of Directors since 1975 and was secretary of the Federation from 1977 to 1981.

Dr. Sperr holds an M.S.W. degree in psychiatric social work from Fordham University and a D.S.W. degree in social work research methods from Columbia University.

Introduction and Dedication

M. LYNNE NEUFELD, *Executive Director, NFAIS, 1979–*

In this volume, we have collected a state-of-the-art review of the secondary services, both from various points in the past 25 years through the Miles Conrad Lectures and from the present through the perspectives. The major issues and concerns that have emerged within the information community during the existence of the National Federation of Abstracting and Information Services (NFAIS) are well documented.

Much more than simply a state-of-the-art review, the following pages constitute a very personal family history, written about NFAIS by NFAIS members — its leaders over the past 25 years. This history was conceived as a means of commemorating, in a permanent way, the silver anniversary of NFAIS. Because this collection has been written by ourselves and about ourselves, personal opinion is mixed with professional comment — "in-group" wit with serious policy observations. If some references seem obscure to the outsider, no matter; the writings reflect the individualism and diversity of the members of a unique organization, an organization that has been able to respond rapidly to its members' needs because of its nonbureaucratic nature and cooperative spirit.

Although NFAIS is a federation of organizations, it has a highly individualistic quality. This stems from the strong and varied personalities of its leaders, reflected in their individual statements. It is this quality, despite its small size and financial vicissitudes, that has made the Federation such a dominant and respected force in the development of the information community during the last quarter century.

This volume consists of three sections: a two-part history of NFAIS from its founding and renaissance to its modern role; the perspectives of the past presidents and executive directors of NFAIS; and the 15 Miles Conrad Memorial Lectures, which were preserved in recorded form. The history, which provides both the facts and the flavor, places these issues in the context of the current events surrounding the times in which the lectures were given. The perspectives are just that—refreshing and highly individual in style, they indicate the personal and professional concerns of their contributors. The Miles Conrad Lectures have taken the pulse of the information community at various points during the past 15 years.

What emerges is a picture wherein much has changed and much has remained constant. NFAIS was, and is today, a *traditional* organization by virtue of the long-standing involvements of its members and the balanced and consensual approach it has taken to matters involving change. Sometimes organizations are created to address a pressing problem or deal with current issues. Other organizations of permanence and substance find ways to absorb change at a measured pace, a pace always too rapid for the conservative element and too slow for the more radical. Yet these organizations do change, while still remaining true to the principals on which they were founded. NFAIS has demonstrated this type of viability.

The current issues facing NFAIS and the community it speaks for are broader in scope and much less parochial than 25 years ago, limited as they were at that time to scientific and technical information (STINFO was the catchword). Many of today's members integrate the functions of the various discrete organizations that have traditionally made up the information-transfer chain: primary journal publishers, secondary or abstracting and indexing services, and end users.

In recent years, we have interposed the "vendor" and the "telecommunications network" between the secondary service and the user to facilitate access to the online version of the product. As the secondary services have matured in the business sense, however, they have undergone "vertical integration," reaching forward and backward along the information chain to expand their services and perform some of the functions formerly thought to be the domain of other organizations. Thus, one of the larger services has begun providing access to some of its own specialized files directly, bypassing the vendor; another is providing the documents cited in its files; and yet another is making specialized file subsets available (on floppy disk) to the end user, once again restoring the more intimate relationship that existed 25 years ago between the individual user and the producer of the index or abstract journal.

These changing roles have been brought about by economics and technology; although better service is promised, various other concerns are raised. Will the migration from print to online erode the subscription base for the printed product, which has provided the financial underpinnings for most bibliographic services? What of the reuse and repackaging of this online version, since the advent of microprocessors makes it possible for end users to remove and construct, in digitized form, their own particular subfiles for future repetitive searching? There are many issues of copyright and ownership of data that must be examined to ensure the maximum dissemination of information without a weakening of the economic foundations of the producer organizations.

Intertwined with these factors is a redefinition of the user. Microprocessors and home video technology are shifting the emphasis from the intermediary or librarian to the end user. It is clear that the end users will soon have access to a wealth of information reference resources in their own homes.

Whether these resources will be highly used remains to be seen. Regardless, these new technologies per se are not nearly as important as their impact on the user. Changes will occur in the behavior and use patterns of researchers, legislators, and ordinary citizens, allowing greater awareness, input, and interaction in the decision-making processes—both large and small, local and national, and scientific and social—from all segments of society.

Finally, we must not overlook our relationships with others in this "global village." Information is viewed variously as a right, a means of advancing the human condition, a commodity, and an instrument of foreign policy. Transborder data flow, technology export regulations, security restrictions, and market competition among nations and the need for specialized coverage in Third World countries are problems vying for solutions in the international arena. In acknowledgement of the importance of these problems and to promote cooperation and the unrestricted flow of information on our continent, NFAIS has broadened its full membership requirements to span all of North America.

This volume has been a pleasure to edit. The timeliness and liveliness of contributions have exceeded my expectations and provided me with greater insights into the people and the past of NFAIS. I am deeply indebted to the contributors and my coeditors, Martha Cornog and Inez L. Sperr. Their efforts provide another example of the dedication of the NFAIS membership. It is to that membership, in turn, that this book is dedicated.

PART I

Background and History

Introduction:
Dedication to Dedication!

MALCOLM RIGBY, *National Oceanographic and Atmospheric Administration, Washington, D.C.*

In my 25 years of association with NFAIS and its officers, board members, and staffs of the member services, the one characteristic that has been overwhelmingly evident to me is the sense of dedication — almost of mission — that has motivated nearly every person involved. This dedication has carried with it a sense of optimism or faith that what is being done is worthwhile and that the mistakes — if any — will be self-correcting. Another article of faith born of this devotion is that there is strength not only in union, but also in diversity. Finally, there is the belief that much is gained through serendipity when a number of dedicated people with common interests but diverse backgrounds come together and stimulate the minds of each other through detailed goals, objectives, programs, and plans (the end-all and the be-all of our late-20th-century western society).

The fact that the Federation has survived a turbulent era and grown steadily since the late 1960s is as much due to the faith, genius, and dedication of the leaders (and their many active assistants and associates) of the 14 original services and those that have since become involved as it is to any of the planning or surveys and studies from both inside and outside NFAIS. In the long run, of course, the planning and studies have been valuable in many ways — namely, they have supported intuitive judgments or have given a better perspective to growth and progress.

This historical review of NFAIS is divided into two parts:

1. I will cover the turbulent years of the Federation's formation and maturation (1957 – 1971), during which I was deeply and continually involved as a founding board member, treasurer, vice president, and chairman of a number of committees.

2. The years of maturity, steady growth, and broadened scope (1972–1982) will be reviewed by Lois Granick, an involved board member throughout this time and president from 1980 to 1981, and Martha Cornog, a Federation staff member.

Probably the most succinct introduction to the history of NFAIS, however, can be found in the following press release from *Biological Abstracts (BA)*. *BA's* Director, Miles Conrad, provided the impetus and facilities for the informal planning meeting held in December 1957 and for the three-day meeting in January 1958 at which the Federation was founded and its course chartered.

Issued by *Biological Abstracts*, 3815 Walnut St., Philadelphia, Pa.
For immediate release.
January 31, 1958

NATIONAL FEDERATION OF SCIENCE ABSTRACTING
AND INDEXING SERVICES FORMED

A National Federation of Science Abstracting and Indexing Services has been formed by representatives of the larger United States services at a three-day meeting in Philadelphia that ended today. The new Federation will endeavor through cooperative measures, education and research to improve the abstracting, indexing and analysis of scientific information so that such information will be more readily available to all scientists and technologists in this country and throughout the English-speaking world.

The conference, which was organized by *Biological Abstracts* and supported by the National Science Foundation, was attended by 34 representatives of the following 14 abstracting and indexing services:

Aeronautical Reviews (Institute of the Aeronautical Sciences, Inc.)
Applied Mechanics Reviews (Southwest Research Institute)
Bibliography of Agriculture (U.S. Department of Agriculture)
Biological Abstracts
Chemical Abstracts (American Chemical Society)
Current List of Medical Literature (U.S. National Library of Medicine)
Engineering Index
Mathematical Reviews (American Mathematical Society)
Meteorological Abstracts (American Meteorological Society)
Nuclear Science Abstracts (U.S. Atomic Energy Commission)
Psychological Abstracts (American Psychological Association)
Review of Metal Literature (American Society for Metals)

Technical Abstract Bulletin (Armed Services Technical Information Agency)
United States Government Research Reports (Office of Technical Services,
   Department of Commerce)

In addition, 11 representatives of the following organizations, which are concerned with the problems of science abstracting and indexing, were present:

American Association for the Advancement of Science
American Geological Institute
American Geophysical Union
National Science Foundation
UNESCO
U.S. Joint Publications Research Service

The opening session of the conference was addressed by Dr. Detlev W. Bronk, President of the Rockefeller Institute and President of the National Academy of Sciences. He commented that this conference provided an example of American institutions working at their best, the participants having come together in an informal way to see how by cooperation they could improve their services and work together toward common goals. He deplored the growing tendency to believe that large and difficult tasks should be relegated to the Federal government. The great strength of the American nation has been the sense of responsibility on the part of individuals, private organizations and local communities. Because the conference was being held with the support of the National Science Foundation, Dr. Bronk, who is also Chairman of the National Science Board of the Foundation, emphasized that one of the principles of the Foundation is to assist science through existing agencies and institutions and to help to make them more effective.

In the area of scientific information services, Dr. Bronk said that he does not think it necessary to create a large national scientific information center just because the Soviet Union has such a center. We should set our own goals and objectives and choose the methods we believe best for our purposes.

Although science and technology foster growth and change, Dr. Bronk admitted that scientists do not always welcome change. He expressed the hope that we can recognize the problems of the present and modify many of our traditional procedures to satisfy better our present and future requirements. It is possible, for example, that there are other, more efficient ways of storing and retrieving scientific information than in the form of books and journals. We now have high-speed computers that extend the powers of the human mind. The utilization of such devices in the realm of information processing, however, requires adaptability on the part of the users.

If we are to forge ahead in science, as Dr. Bronk believes we must and will, the task of abstracting and indexing scientific information will become even greater. The problem of dealing effectively with the great and rapidly growing body of scientific knowledge is one of the gravest facing science today. Some who have recognized the problem have said that we cannot afford to deal with it; but, he insisted, we can and must pay the bill to do whatever needs to be done to make scientific knowledge more available and useful if scientists are not to be submerged and overwhelmed by the sheer volume of it.

The stated objective of the newly formed Federation is to improve the documentation (abstracting, indexing and analyzing) of the scientific and technological literature of the world in such a manner as to make it readily available to all scientists and technologists: (a) by encouraging the development of abstracting and indexing for those specialized subject fields not at present covered by such services and the further development of existing services; (b) by seeking greater uniformity in such matters as journal citations and abbreviations, and transliteration of foreign language titles; (c) by cooperation, education, research, and the pursuit of mutually useful enterprises, to strive for the best possible research information services for science and technology in the United States and abroad.

Each of the abstracting and indexing services represented at the Conference will name a representative to a temporary council to serve until the new Federation is formally organized, at which time other eligible abstracting and indexing services will be invited to join the Federation. An interim executive committee of three will act for the temporary council in taking the necessary steps leading to the formal organization and incorporation of the Federation. The members of the executive committee are G. Miles Conrad of *Biological Abstracts*, Chairman; Dale B. Baker of *Chemical Abstracts;* and John C. Green of the Office of Technical Services, Department of Commerce. Funds for setting up a secretariat of the Federation will be contributed on a voluntary basis by services represented at the conference as an expression of their interest in the development of the new organization. It is expected that grants and donations will help to maintain and to expand the activities of the Federation.

During the Conference, the participants discussed a number of problem areas which will be given continuing attention by the new Federation. Among the matters discussed were the possibility of establishing standards in form, classification, abbreviations, and transliteration that could be adopted by the member services; improved means of learning about new scientific publications; cooperative methods for insuring optimum coverage of scientific literature by the abstracting and indexing services of the U.S.; ways and means to provide user access to the primary publications abstracted and/or indexed by the various services; the need for research and studies directed toward better indexing techniques that would help all the services to improve the quality of their indexes and the speed with which they are issued; the development and adaptation of new methods and equipment for printing, particularly for printing indexes and bibliographic listings, more economically and more promptly; and the development and evaluation of new types of services for users.

The support of the National Science Foundation that helped start and, through payment of dues for the five government member services until 1964, kept the Federation Secretariat in Washington running for the first seven years was greatly appreciated. When this support was withdrawn due to changing government policy regarding organizations devoted to the "support of science," the Federation underwent several years of agonizing reappraisal of its role, scope of membership, dues structure, role and strength of the secretariat (which, in 1965, was moved from Washington to the BioSciences Information Service [BIOSIS] in Philadelphia), and its projects, seminars, and voting rights.

Most of these problems had been ironed out by 1970, after numerous board meetings and even "retreats," where directors came to grips with costs and policy (such as admission of secondary services in the social sciences and humanities and, later, international and for-profit organizations). Fortunately, the major services, who paid the highest dues, had very capable financial and technical assistants who could manage budgets two orders of magnitude greater than NFAIS's budget.

Overall, the challenges of diversity, standardization, automation, online network and commercial competition, user and publications explosion, growth, and inflation have been dealt with effectively (even if they have not been totally solved). Most important, the world information community knows the strengths and weaknesses of American abstracting and indexing services better than it did in the late 1950s.

1. The History of NFAIS 1958–1971

MALCOLM RIGBY, *National Oceanographic and Atmospheric Administration, Washington, D.C.*

FOUNDING

The National Federation of Science Abstracting and Indexing Services (NFSAIS) was conceived at an informal meeting in December 1957 convened by G. Miles Conrad, Director of *Biological Abstracts (BA)* (now BIOSIS), with the full cooperation of the major U.S. abstracting and indexing services and the National Science Foundation. Nearly all the 14 founding services were represented at that meeting. Notable among those present were Dr. E. Crane, Director of Chemical Abstracts Service; his capable assistant, Dale Baker, who soon became director of that service; Miles Conrad and his top assistants at *BA*: Foster Mohrhardt of the U.S. Department of Agriculture Library; Carolyn Flanagan of *Engineering Index*; and a number of others who later became active leaders of the Federation. All agreed that there was a need for an organization of abstracting and indexing (A&I) services, but the need for a strong, unified, corporate body such as some had proposed was highly controversial. A meeting embracing all A&I services was supported, however, and plans were made immediately.

The founding meeting was held in Philadelphia on January 29–31, 1958 and was attended by members of the founding services, listed in the press release on pages 4–6.

BACKGROUND

The impetus toward forming a federation was a response by the nonprofit A&I services to the challenge of the Soviet Union's VINITI (All Union Scientific and Technical Institute). VINITI had expanded greatly in the mid-1950s and was publishing 40 *Referntivnyi Zhurnal* series covering most of the fields of pure and applied science and technology. This effort by the USSR was interpreted by some in the United States to be the ideal solution to our chaotic system, which involved duplication and lack of standardization and left gaps in the overall coverage of science and technology. But, the fulfillment of this idealistic (or bureaucratic) dream entailed resources—estimated at that time at $50–$100 million—not to mention procurement of hardware and personnel, as well as several years to become operational and up-to-date. It would also destroy the usefulness and continuity of existing services (according to several studies of the U.S. information system published in 1958, 1962, and 1963). After the Federation was founded, it was able to respond to these challenges and to prove that much strength lies in diversity and voluntary cooperation. The past 25 years of growth and experience with automation have borne out this proposition.

PURPOSES

The stated goals or purposes of the Federation were to

–provide a communication forum for the membership and the information community
–develop standards, where necessary, for interchange of products
–encourage special services for interdisciplinary and mission-oriented requirements
–work together in developing machine-readable databases and techniques for producing them
–help provide access to primary documents cited through the Federation or through libraries and document centers, both government and nongovernment.

MEMBERSHIP AND COVERAGE

Originally, 14 members (9 not-for-profit services and 5 government agencies) comprised the Federation. During the turbulent years from 1958 to 1970, that number ranged from 14 to 22. The year 1965 enjoyed the largest membership; after that, government members were excluded, owing to a self imposed conflict-of-interest criterion.

When the Federation reorganized in 1966 and 1967, the government agencies were invited to join and participate as affiliate members, and membership gradually was broadened to include nontechnical fields, foreign affiliates, and, finally, profit-making organizations. Since 1970, the membership has grown steadily from 25 services in 1971 to 36 in 1976, 44 in 1980, and, at present, nearly 50.

The coverage of the world's literature has grown even more spectacularly during the past 25 years, as shown in Table 1, which has been extracted from the Federation's annual "Member Service Statistics" report.

Table 1 Annual Output of Abstracted or Indexed Items

	1957	1967	1977	1982
Voting member services of NFAIS	225,000	560,000	1,200,000	1,500,000
Gross for all NFAIS services	350,000	800,000	2,100,000	3,400,000

Source: "Member Service Statistics." *NFAIS Newsletter*, 24(1), February 1982.

The number of full voting members has increased threefold in 25 years, while the production of these members had increased sixfold. The productivity of the entire NFAIS membership (voting members and affiliates) has grown 10-fold (350,000 to 3.4 million), with three times as many member services. Interestingly, the total productivity of the three largest full membership services has also increased sixfold (169,000 in 1957 to 1.04 million in 1982 for Chemical Abstracts Service [CAS], BIOSIS, and *Engineering Index* [*Ei*]), showing that the coverage of the overall membership has grown at the same rate as that of the largest and most sophisticated services.

PERSONALITIES

The benefits of membership in the Federation (and to a great extent, the benefits of the Federation for the scientific information processing community) stem as much from the serendipitous contacts with the most dedicated leaders of the member services as from the products and accomplishments of the Federation. Who is not richer from having rubbed shoulders with such giants (or characters) as E. J. Crane, Miles Conrad, Dale Baker, Foster Mohrhardt, Phyllis Parkins, Bill Woods, Ev Brenner, Ben Weil, Lois Granick, Mel Day, Burt Adkinson, or Steve Juhasz? The

12 *Abstracting and Indexing Services in Perspective*

Table 2 Presidents and Executive Directors of NFAIS

Presidents

1958–1961	G. Miles Conrad *(Biological Abstracts)*
1961–1963	Dale B. Baker (Chemical Abstracts Service)
1963–1964	John Green (U.S. Department of Commerce, Office of Technical Services)
1964–1965	Foster Mohrhardt (U.S. Department of Agriculture, National Agricultural Library)
1965–1966	Carolyn Flanagan *(Engineering Index)*
1966–1968	Phyllis V. Parkins (BioSciences Information Service)
1968–1970	Gordon L. Walker (American Mathematical Association)
1970–1971	Kenneth Spengler (American Meteorological Society)
1971–1972	William M. Woods *(Engineering Index)*
1972–1973	Everett H. Brenner (American Petroleum Institute)
1973–1974	Joel J. Lloyd (American Geological Institute)
1974–1975	H. E. Kennedy (BioSciences Information Service)
1975–1976	Ben H. Weil (Exxon Research and Engineering)
1976–1977	John E. Creps, Jr. *(Engineering Index)*
1977–1978	Russell J. Rowlett, Jr. (Chemical Abstracts Service)
1978–1979	H. W. Koch (American Institute of Physics)
1979–1980	Richard H. Lineback (Philosophy Documentation Center)
1980–1981	Lois W. Granick (American Psychological Association)
1981–1982	E. K. Gannett (Institute of Electrical and Electronics Engineers)
1982–1983	Ronald L. Wigington (Chemical Abstracts Service)
1983–1984	Inez L. Sperr (Migration Information & Abstracts Service)

Executive Directors

1959–1966	Raymond A. Jensen
1968–1974	Stella Keenan
1974–1979	Toni Carbo Bearman
1979–	M. Lynne Neufeld

Federation's most memorable officers, board members, committee members, keynote speakers, and staff members are only partially represented in Tables 2 and 3.

ACCOMPLISHMENTS

In its one-quarter century of active life, the Federation has not accomplished all the goals that some members or interested parties thought

Table 3 Miles Conrad Memorial Lecturers

1968	Robert Cairns (National Academy of Sciences/National Academy of Engineering, Committee on Scientific and Technical Communication)
1969	J. R. Smith (formerly with INSPEC)
1970	Robert M. Hayes (University of California at Los Angeles)
1971	Burton W. Adkinson (American Geographical Society)
1972	Jack E. Brown (National Research Council of Canada)
1973	Phyllis V. Parkins (BioSciences Information Service)
1974	Dale B. Baker (Chemical Abstracts Service)
1975	Melvin S. Day (National Library of Medicine)
1976	Frederick G. Kilgour (Ohio College Library Center)
1977	William O. Baker (Bell Laboratories)
1978	Ben H. Weil (Exxon Research and Engineering)
1979	Donald W. King (King Research, Inc.)
1980	Carlos Cuadra (Cuadra Associates, Inc.)
1981	Russell J. Rowlett, Jr. (Chemical Abstracts Service)
1982	Saul Herner (Herner and Company)
1983	John E. Creps, Jr. (formerly with *Engineering Information*)

it should (such as elimination of overlap, standardization of elements for publication, and implementation of "Organization X"). But it has achieved most, if not all, of the major aims or goals set by the founding services in January 1958 and reaffirmed some 10 years later when it entered a more mature and independent phase of its existence. These accomplishments fall into six categories—conferences, workshops or seminars, publications, surveys, participation in national information activities, and participation in international exchanges and bodies—which I will discuss briefly.

ANNUAL CONFERENCES

The annual conferences have been held from "year zero" (1958) to present (1983), except for the year 1966, when only a few strong "believers" attended a meeting of the Federation and board at *Engineering Index* headquarters in New York. At that meeting, Carolyn Flanagan, Phyllis Parkins, H. E. Kennedy, Dale Baker, and a few others, including myself, fought bravely to keep the Federation alive against heavy odds, convinced that there was as great a need for the Federation then as in the future. We also believed that the interaction with government services could be kept alive by allowing their representatives to attend meetings and conferences even though they could not legally pay the greatly increased dues needed to maintain a good secretariat. Table 4 lists the places, dates, and themes of these annual conferences, which were held in conjunction with the annual membership meeting required by the constitution and bylaws.

Table 4 Federation Meetings

Date	Location	Theme
Dec. 9, 1957	Philadelphia	
Jan. 29–31, 1958	Philadelphia	
Feb. 26–27, 1959	Washington, D.C.	
March 17–18, 1960	Washington, D.C.	
March 9–11, 1961	Cleveland, Ohio	
March 28–30, 1962	Boston	
March 20–22, 1963	Washington, D.C.	
March 11–13, 1964	San Antonio	
March 25–26, 1965	Columbus, Ohio	
March 23–25, 1966	New York	
March 29–30, 1967	Philadelphia	
March 12–13, 1968	Providence	
March 18–20, 1969	Raleigh	
March 10–12, 1970	Boston	
Feb. 22–24, 1971	Arlington, Virginia	
March 6–8, 1972	New York	
March 6–8, 1973	Philadelphia	"User/Producer Forum"
March 11–13, 1974	Chicago	"Information as a Resource"
March 4–5, 1975	Arlington, Virginia	"Information Interfaces"
March 9–10, 1976	Columbus, Ohio	"Information: Dilemmas, Decisions, Directions"
March 8–9, 1977	Arlington, Virginia	"Information Changes, Concerns, Challenges: Changing Role of Government, Changes & Challenges in Indexing, Concerns in Research, Challenges of Deposited Documents"
March 7–8, 1978	Philadelphia	"A&I Perspective: A Look Ahead"
March 6–7, 1979	Arlington, Virginia	"Today's Challenges for Information Services"
March 3–6, 1980	Arlington, Virginia	"New Technology in the 1980's"
March 2–4, 1981	Arlington, Virginia	"Strategies for Change"
March 1–3, 1982	Arlington, Virginia	"Conflict in the Information Environment: Risks and Opportunities"
Feb. 28–March 2, 1983	Arlington, Virginia	"Information Transfer: Incentives for Innovation"

MILES CONRAD LECTURES

Miles Conrad was the "father" of NFAIS, and his untimely death in 1964 saddened all who had known him, worked with him, or traveled with him. To honor his memory, the board and membership voted in 1966 to establish the Miles Conrad Memorial Lecture, to be delivered by some notable person inside or outside the Federation as the keynote address at every annual conference. This plan has been strictly adhered to and is one of the most attractive features of the conferences, honoring as it does both the speaker and the memory of Miles Conrad. Most lectures have been published separately or in annual reports, but this book collects in one place the best perspectives of the state of the art at the time of the speech, as well as predictions for the future.

INDEXING IN PERSPECTIVE SEMINARS

Since 1969, a series of seminars on abstracting and indexing and related topics has been held under the auspices of the Federation and organized by the executive director, with the able assistance of experts from Federation services. Seminars have been held throughout the United States and in Europe and Canada (see Table 5).

These seminars have been quite popular and have helped greatly in educating both the producers and the users of information services, especially in this age of automation.

PUBLICATIONS

The Federation's broadest impact probably comes from its many publications, all of which receive wide distribution among library and documentation circles, as well as among NFAIS member services here and abroad. Not the least among these is the bimonthly *NFAIS Newsletter*, which not only carries short articles of current interest from the various member services, but which also represents pertinent international news items regarding A&I activities, new publications, guides, glossaries, and conference notices.

The earliest and most widely circulated NFSAIS publications were the *Guide to U.S. Indexing and Abstracting Services in Science and Technology*, prepared in cooperation with the Library of Congress, Science and Technology Division, in June 1960, and the expanded *Guide to the World's Abstracting and Indexing Services in Science and Technology*, published in 1963. A compilation of primary journals or serials covered by

Table 5 Federation Seminars

Date	Location	Number of Registrants
December 8–10, 1969	Penn Center Inn Philadelphia	24
May 18–20, 1970	Sheraton-Lincoln Hotel Houston	not avail.
June 12–14, 1970	Sheraton-Cadillac Hotel Detroit	not avail.
February 3–5, 1971	Pratt Manhattan Center New York	71
May 24–26, 1971	American Dental Association Chicago	25
April 24–26, 1972	University of Maryland College Park	87
February 7–9, 1973	Pratt Manhattan Center New York	28
June 27–29, 1973	INSPEC London	31
June 5–7, 1974	University of Toronto Toronto	100
June 5–7, 1975	American Dental Association Chicago	24
October 6–10, 1975	NFAIS/ASIDIC, Chemists' Club New York	38
June 21–26, 1976	Warsaw	30
October 12–14, 1976	University of Alberta Edmonton, Canada	42
June 14–16, 1977	American Chemical Society Washington, D.C.	20
January 30–February 1, 1978	The Catholic University of America Washington, D.C.	37
June 8–10, 1978	University of Missouri Kansas City, Missouri	34
January 24–26, 1979	United Engineering, Inc. New York	23
May 9–11, 1979	University of California Berkeley	31
December 3–5, 1979	Drexel University Philadelphia	28
June 23–25, 1980	Solar Energy Research Institute Denver	18
November 12–14, 1980	Ramada Inn Durham, North Carolina	21
June 10–12, 1981	Atlanta Hilton Atlanta	25

Table 5 (Continued)

November 5–6, 1981	Holiday Inn–Market Center Dallas	10
July 21–23, 1982	National Library of Canada Ottawa	41
	Other Seminars	
October 5, 1980	"Information Resources in the Behavioral and Social Sciences and Humanities" Disneyland Hotel Anaheim, California	11
June 24–26, 1981	"Online and Otherwise: Energy and Environment Information" University of Alberta Edmonton, Canada	18

member services was also produced during those early years. This compilation was too bulky to publish, but it was reproduced and circulated among member services and the National Science Foundation for planning purposes.

The Federation also participated with The International Federation for Documentation (FID) in compiling and publishing two updated editions of the *Guide to the World's Abstracting and Indexing Services in Science and Technology* during 1969 and 1975. The 1969 edition was printed (with help from Unesco); the 1975 version appeared in machine-readable form only (with help from NSF).

RESEARCH PROJECTS

The most interesting study, commissioned for the Federation by Robert Heller and Associates in 1962, led to the so-called *Heller Report*, which recommended an "Organization X" for repackaging and marketing the products of the A&I services to help support and improve the unsubsidized but essential services. Both the Federation and NSF recognized the need for upgrading the discipline-oriented services to provide full international coverage but took a dim view of the cost-effectiveness of such an organization in the light of the problems of standardization (necessary for repackaging) and of proprietary interests of publishers of primary and secondary services.

The *System Study of Abstracting and Indexing in the United States*, compiled by the System Development Corporation for the National

Science Foundation and the Committee on Scientific and Technical Information (COSATI), with the full cooperation of NFSAIS, had great impact on the Federation's future. It gave a clear perspective of the status of A&I production in 1962 when scientific societies were producing 58 percent of the one million abstracts and 38 percent of the 1.9 million indexed items published in the United States. (Those numbers increased by more than 40 percent by 1966.)

Another survey was made during 1969–1971 and reported during 1972–1973 in the *Journal of the American Society for Information Science* by James Wood, Carolyn Flanagan, and H. E. Kennedy. This was a study of overlap in coverage among *Chemical Abstracts*, *Biological Abstracts*, and *Engineering Index*. It was pointed out that some overlap is in the user's interest and hence beneficial when two distinct communities have some common interests (e.g., chemistry and biology for biochemists or physics and biology for biophysicists).

AUTOMATION

When the Federation was founded in 1958, a number of services realized that automation in one phase or another of A&I was inevitable, but it was not until 1959–1960 that any actual attempts were made to use mechanical or electronic devices for maintaining files, such as subject heading lists, or publishing KWIC (keyword-in-context) or KWOC (keyword-out-of-context) indexes.

By 1960, BIOSIS, *Meteorological Abstracts*, Armed Services Technical Information Agency (ASTIA), and others were experimenting with or operational in publishing permuted title indexes using IBM 1401 computers and other tabulators or computers. Bibliographies were also being prepared with automated equipment. By 1973, almost all the member services were using electronic equipment to produce many printed products and authority files of subjects, chemicals, and authors. NFAIS did not demand or organize such automation, but Federation publications, workshops, personal communication, and "exchange" of personnel greatly facilitated rapid introduction of modern technology into the production of abstracts, indexes, bibliographies, and tapes for sale or for online or network use, as well as for selective dissemination and retrieval.

NATIONAL AND INTERNATIONAL RELATIONS

The opportunity for the Federation to represent the U.S. abstracting and indexing community came about early on. In October–November 1959, a delegation of five persons from the United States, under the leadership of Miles Conrad, president of the Federation, visited VINITI to assess the quality, efficiency, status of automation, and effect of centralization on progress and growth in the USSR.

VINITI was and is the largest single A&I service in the world. It has achieved amazing results in the past 30 years under the able leadership of Professor A. I. Mikhailov, who has been long respected in the international documentation community as well as in the science information and information science communities (FID, International Council of Scientific Unions Abstracting Board [ISCU AB], and Unesco).

The delegation from the United States included Miles Conrad; John Green, from the Department of Commerce, Officer of Technical Services; Ray Jensen, Executive Secretary of NFSAIS; Dale Baker of CAS; and M. Hoseh of CAS as interpreter.

A second exchange took place in May 1961, when a delegation of four from NFAIS services held a dialogue with leaders of the Japanese information service and documentation community at the invitation of the Japanese Science Council. This meeting was represented by Dale Baker (CAS), Miles Conrad (BIOSIS), John Glennon (American Institute of Aeronautics and Astronautics), and Malcolm Rigby (American Meteorological Society); by members of the Japanese Science Council; and by Professors Miva and Piva of the Japan Information Center for Science and Technology (JICST).

A third exchange, also with Japan, was held two years later (June 1963) with Miles Conrad, John Green, Foster Mohrhardt, and Malcolm Rigby as U.S. delegates. All these exchanges were supported by the National Science Foundation, and the U.S. services reciprocated by hosting the Japanese as occasion warranted.

More recently, contacts have been maintained on a continuing and active basis through such international agencies as the ICSU AB, which has U.S. representatives from the major abstracting services; FID; and the International Standards Organization (ISO).

2. The History of NFAIS 1972–1982

LOIS GRANICK, *American Psychological Association, Washington, D.C.*

MARTHA CORNOG, *National Federation of Abstracting and Information Services, Philadelphia, Pennsylvania*

It is difficult to think of the more recent past as history. After all, the actions and activities begun in the recent past are not really finished yet. Today's path is a logical extension of decisions made and directions taken just yesterday, or last year—the reasons are still clear to us. No curtain has come down to divide NFAIS's 26th year from its 25th, so, naturally, the difficulty. Perhaps this article can be better thought of as a part of the next compilation—10 or 25 years in the future. Thus, we will write for those readers.

Rather than proceed through this history year by year, we will note certain activities and accomplishments, all of which either began or culminated (sometimes both) within the time span.

CENTRAL OFFICE LOCATION AND STAFF

When NFAIS was reorganized in 1968, the headquarters office was moved from Washington, D.C. to the BIOSIS building in Philadelphia. There the new staff was able to work rent-free, due to the generosity of BIOSIS. In 1972, this arrangement was no longer necessary, and the Federation relocated to 3401 Market Street in Philadelphia's University City.

Although a modest excess of income over expenditures was recorded during 1977, a larger preexisting deficit kept the celebration small. Proposals were advanced early in 1977 to move the NFAIS office to less-expensive quarters, since the current rental was increasing. Other suggestions, including combining efforts with a sister organization such as the American Society for Information Science (ASIS), were also advanced, but nothing emerged to offer sufficient incentive. The search for adequate space was continued, and NFAIS finally moved to 112 South Sixteenth Street in Philadelphia during mid-1978. In 1982, the office was relocated in larger quarters in the same building, allowing for a conference room and a microcomputer/word processor.

A large part of NFAIS's strength as an organization has been due to the outstanding qualifications of its executive directors. Stella Keenan, the executive director who successfully assisted with the renaissance of NFAIS in 1968, resigned in 1974 to return to her native England. A search committee of the board of directors was successful in locating and hiring Dr. Toni Carbo Bearman to continue in the position. Under Dr. Bearman's tenure, NFAIS's visibility and reputation were increased by involvement in a number of research efforts, publications, and liaison with other organizations. When Dr. Bearman resigned in 1979, another search committee was formed. M. Lynne Neufeld was selected; she assumed the position of executive director in September 1979. Ms. Neufeld's major thrusts have been to expand membership, to stabilize Federation finances and facilities, and to continue NFAIS visibility through research, seminars, and liaison.

DUES PLAN

Dues assessment and increases have been debated and continually revised since NFAIS's inception. At the annual meeting in 1977, a proposed increase in dues for 1978 sparked a lively debate. The graduated schedule for dues inevitably presented member organizations with a sudden leap to a new category of higher dues if they were in a growth situation. Some members argued strongly for a progressive schedule that would use percentages or other valuable bases, allowing for the same rate of increase in dues as in overall growth. This movement was successful in 1981, when a progressive dues scale was adopted for 1982 on. Associate member dues have also undergone scrutiny since 1975 and are currently under revision.

FUTURE PLANNING AND THE ROLE OF NFAIS

As early as 1971, plans were made to develop a position paper on the role of the Federation. This paper was published in 1973 as *NFAIS — History and Issues, 1958–1973*. At the same time, a decision was made to broaden the scope of the Federation membership and to drop the word *Science* from its name. Throughout 1973 and 1974, a Five-Year Plan for the Federation was developed and debated. In 1978 and 1979, an entire meeting of the NFAIS Board of Directors was reserved to discuss NFAIS's role, present and future. These particular meetings succeeded in articulating several roles for NFAIS in speaking for the A&I community, in sharing coverage of peripheral literature, in providing a national forum for members, and in developing standards. These ideas continued to grow and develop within the membership, and a 1980 task force on forward planning was successful in reaching unanimity on several mechanisms for implementation. These were brought to the full membership for vote in 1981 and were overwhelmingly approved. To prepare NFAIS for a more substantial role, it was voted to enlarge the membership and encourage increased representation by changing Affiliate Membership to Associate Membership, to add associate members to the board of directors, to include Canada and Mexico in the Full Membership category, and to include for-profit A&I organizations as associate members. (Inclusion of for-profit groups was originally suggested as far back as 1975.) In 1982, the name change to The National Federation of Abstracting and *Information Services* took place, further broadening the organizational scope.

EDUCATION

The Indexing in Perspective Seminar, now the staple of the educational program, began rather modestly in Philadelphia in 1969. Throughout the 1970s, it was held semiannually and in many locations. In 1972, the executive director was authorized by the board to request Unesco support for a European indexing seminar. This plan came to fruition in 1976, and the seminar was presented in Warsaw. Unesco also provided funds to develop the *Indexing in Perspective Education Kit*, which has since been used very successfully with the seminar and also sold as a separate Federation publication.

More recently, seminars on other topics have been held: "Information Sources in Social and Behavioral Sciences and the Humanities" (1980) and "Energy and Environment Information" (1981). A spin-off of the latter was the Federation publication *Energy and Environment Information Resource Guide*. In 1982, the User Education Committee, under the able leadership of Cathy Ferrere, put together a very successful "Trainers' Day" educational program for online trainers. Plans are being made for additional "Trainers' Days" in the near future.

CONSULTING SERVICE

As early as 1973, John Creps suggested beginning an NFAIS consulting service. When Lynne Neufeld took over as executive director, she revived the idea, and, with a steering committee headed by Ron Wigington, the NFAIS Advisory Service debuted in 1981. The service is designed to provide clients with short-term expert advice by high-level staff members of Federation organizations. Income is donated to the Federation.

RESEARCH PROJECTS

Four research projects of significance were completed by the Federation between 1972 and 1982.

In late 1973, a proposal was made to conduct a study of science literature indicators (SLIS). The proposal was subsequently funded by the National Science Foundation (NSF). Specifically, the study was designed to examine the publishing patterns of U.S. scientists in terms of percentage published under the auspices of various types of organizations, for different disciplines, over a period of time. In 1975, a report on the study was published, and, in 1977, an update (*Science Literature Indicators Study 1975: Update of NFAIS-75/1*) appeared.

The SLI study was hardly under way in 1974 when the Federation received additional funds from NSF to conduct a study to determine the degree of coverage overlap among its member A&I services. Fourteen services supplied coverage data. Project work was completed in 1976, and a report, entitled *A Study of Coverage Overlap Among Major Science and Technology Abstracting and Indexing Services*, was published the following year.

In 1981, the Solar Energy Research Institute (SERI) expressed interest in contributing funds to a study of options selected by database producers in making their databases available to the public. SERI was a new member of NFAIS and was just getting started in database publishing. A survey was taken of some 60 database producers (member and nonmember organizations), and the results were published in late 1981 (*A Study of Database Access Alternatives: Final Report*).

Most recently (June 1981–December 1982), the Federation has been a subcontractor to the Syracuse University School of Information Studies in examining the values added in information processing, specifically during abstracting and indexing procedures. The project, funded by NSF, has involved extensive interviews and data collection on all phases of abstracting and indexing at nearly a dozen organizations of different types. The final report is being issued early in 1983.

The reports from the three completed projects are still in print—a testimony of their significance to the information community.

INTERACTION AND COOPERATION WITH OTHER ORGANIZATIONS

NFAIS's cooperative activities have been numerous. As far back as 1972, the Federation undertook tentative planning with the Information Industry Association (IIA) for joint activities for mutual benefit. In 1982, the executive director joined IIA as an individual member, and the two organizations agreed to exchange mailing lists.

NFAIS has had an active Standards Committee, which works closely with Committee Z39 of the American National Standards Institute (ANSI). In addition, in the mid-1970s a project was undertaken by NFAIS, Association of Scientific Information Dissemination Centers (ASIDIC), European Association of Scientific Information Dissemination Centres (EUSIDIC), and International Council of Scientific Unions Abstracting Board (ICSU AB) to work out a standard format for the exchange of machine-readable bibliographic records. A grant from NSF enabled the groups to meet in 1975 to begin to identify a minimum set of data elements and their content descriptions needed for effective searches of machine-readable databases. The *UNISIST Reference Manual for Machine-Readable Bibliographic Descriptions*, published in 1974, represented the most comprehensive work in existence on the subject but had been developed in response to publishing and library concerns; thus, it did not focus on use in retrieval or exchange.

The Federation has worked closely with the American Society for Information Science (ASIS) and the Special Libraries Association (SLA) on several occasions. *Key Papers on the Use of Computer-Based Bibliographic Services* was published jointly with ASIS in 1973, and the 1980 seminar on social sciences information services was held prior to the annual ASIS conference as an ASIS continuing-education course. NFAIS sponsored a session at the 1978 Annual Conference of SLA, and held the Indexing Seminar at the SLA conference in 1981. In 1982, the Federation sponsored a session at each of three conferences: ASIS, International Federation for Documentation (FID), and International Online Meeting.

A small grant from NSF to NFAIS facilitated another cooperative effort, headed by Dick Lineback of the Philosophy Documentation Center, to convene representatives of social sciences and humanities database producers. These meetings were held twice in 1980 and allowed the producers to discuss new technologies, standards, and other areas of common interest.

PUBLICATIONS

Many NFAIS publications are the products of research projects. The *NFAIS Newsletter* dates back to the earliest days of the Federation and now incorporates the "Member Service Statistics" (February issue) and the Miles Conrad Memorial Lecture (March issue). (Before 1975, the Miles Conrad Lectures were generally published individually and were not as accessible to the general public.) During 1974, a special Member Services Supplement to the *Newsletter* was inaugurated, and, in recent years, the *Newsletter* has enjoyed wide circulation through purchase and exchange to the information community worldwide.

During 1973, a "Member Service Descriptions" was published. Five years later, this concept reappeared in the first edition of the *NFAIS Membership Directory*. In 1979, the *Directory* became a biennial publication and has emerged as a significant vehicle of outreach for member services.

The most recent Federation publication grew out of a real information need. Each year, the NFAIS office responds to many requests from the general public for information. When these requests began increasingly to focus on information about careers in abstracting and indexing, the Federation prepared and published the *Abstracting and Indexing Career Guide*. This *Guide* describes what abstractors and indexers do, what types of organizations employ abstractors and indexers (with typical salaries and benefits), and future trends for abstracting and indexing.

The Miles Conrad Memorial Lectures: Background and Significance

INEZ L. SPERR, *Executive Director, Migration Information & Abstracts Service, President, NFAIS, 1983-1984*

The National Federation of Abstracting and Information Services established the Miles Conrad Memorial Award in 1966 to recognize outstanding contributions to the field of abstracting and indexing. The recipient of the award presents the Miles Conrad Memorial Lecture at the annual conference of the Federation. Typically, the lecturer speaks on a suitable topic related to documentation but above the level of any specific abstracting and indexing service. The award was established to honor the late G. Miles Conrad, first president of NFAIS and one of its founders.

Miles Conrad (1911–1964) achieved wide recognition as a biological scientist, documentation specialist, and administrator. He was a prolific writer and gifted speaker in all three areas. As the Director of *Biological Abstracts*, he introduced electronic data processing in the preparation of its publications. As an expert in the field of communication of scientific information, he was appointed or elected to many national and international positions. In NFAIS (then NFSAIS—the National Federation of Science Abstracting and Indexing Services), he contributed to the efforts of the science information organizations of the United States to extend their services to meet the needs of the scientific community. Miles Conrad was the English-language service representative on the International Council of Scientific Unions Abstracting Board (ICSU AB). He was a member of the Advisory Committee for Scientific Publications of the U.S.

Public Health Service, National Library of Medicine; the American National Standards Institute Committee Z39 on Standardization in the Field of Library Work and Documentation; the Office of Critical Tables of the National Research Council; and various committees of the American Association for the Advancement of Science (AAAS), of which he was a fellow.

Miles Conrad, representing the abstracting and indexing services of the United States, was chairman of the U.S. delegation of science information specialists to Japan in June 1963. The delegation was part of President John F. Kennedy's program for the United States–Japan Joint Committee on Scientific Cooperation. In September 1963, Conrad served as chairman of the meeting of the first Working Party on Scientific Publications of the United Nations Educational, Scientific, and Cultural Organization (UNESCO), held in Philadelphia. He participated in NFSAIS missions to observe the science information programs of the Soviet Union in 1959 and Japan in 1961. His affiliations included the New York Academy of Sciences (fellow), the American Documentation Institute (now American Society for Information Science), the American Institute of Biological Sciences, the Conference of Biological Editors (now the Council of Biology Editors), the Special Libraries Association, the Explorers Club, the Cosmos Club, Phi Delta Kappa, and the Society of Sigma Xi.

For the record, his first name was George, and he was a graduate of Oberlin College (Bachelor of Arts, 1933) and Columbia University (Master of Arts, 1938). During 1936–1939, he participated in six scientific marine expeditions for the American Museum of Natural History. He served in the China-Burma-India Theatre during World War II and received the Bronze Star and Conspicuous Service Cross. Prior to his appointment as Director of *Biological Abstracts* (now BioSciences Information Service [BIOSIS]), he was the assistant curator of comparative and human anatomy at the American Museum of Natural History in New York (1934–1943); a technical editor and market research director at Hazard Advertising Company in New York (1943–1948); an editor with Graphic Science Associates, Inc. in New York (1948–1950); and a documentation specialist for the Library of Congress in Washington, D.C. (1950–1953). His numerous publications include scientific research reports in comparative anatomy and paleontology, fish life, and marine environments, as well as articles on popular biology and documentation. One bibliography of his works lists 234 items published between May 1934 and December 1965.

On September 9, 1964, Miles Conrad died suddenly and unexpectedly. The members of NFSAIS sought for some way to honor his memory. At its annual meeting in 1965, the Federation established a lecture series in his name. The proposal called for a "Miles Conrad Memorial Lecture to be presented every year at the annual meeting of the Federation by an outstanding person on a suitable topic in the field of abstracting and indexing but above the level of any individual service." The plan included the presentation of an award to the lecturer and the continuation of the lecture series indefinitely. The motion to accept the recommendation was passed unanimously.

We have little information on record about the content of the first lecture in the series. It was given as a banquet address in 1968 by Robert Cairns, Chairman of the Committee on Scientific and Technical Communication of the National Academy of Sciences–National Academy of Engineering (NAS-NAE SATCOM), and seems to have been a general, informative, after-dinner talk.

In 1969, one small change was made in the original plan that proved to be significant. The Program Planning Committee for the annual conference of NFAIS did not feel that a banquet address was an appropriate format for the kind of penetrating analysis and discussion of issues that had been envisioned when the lecture series was established. To highlight the presentation, the committee moved the lecture to the final session of the conference, organized a panel of seven people to respond to it, and obtained a copy of the text in advance for the panelists to use in preparing their comments. The lecture itself was expected to last 20–25 minutes. Thus began the collection of the written texts of the Miles Conrad Memorial Lectures that culminates in the publication of this volume.

There have been further developments over time. The panel of respondents has been dropped, and an entire session is now devoted to the lecture, with a brief period of time allowed for comments from the audience. The written text of the early lectures was distributed only to the panelists. Now the full text is published by NFAIS after each annual conference for general circulation. These developments have allowed for more thorough treatment of the subject matter and broader dissemination of these significant contributions to the literature of information science and documentation.

The lecture series proved to be an appropriate, fitting memorial. Taken together, the presentations reflect something of Miles Conrad:

1. His penchant for identifying and attending to important aspects of matters and for separating significant issues from ephemeral concerns.

2. His balanced appreciation for the scholarly nature of content, the technical requirements of information processing, and the sound principles of organization, administration, and management.

3. His developmental stance. This perspective encompasses Miles Conrad's focus on anticipating needs for information; his encouragement of the use and continuous updating of technical capabilities (such as new

machinery, new approaches to abstracting and indexing, and new modes of distribution); and his appreciation that change is the normal expected environment of the information and documentation community.

4. His emphasis on cooperation at all levels among specialists and among services in examining and exploring mutual problems and objectives.

Thus, our memorial to him embodies his legacy to us — the thoughtful action and spirit of cooperation that imbues NFAIS, benefits the community, and draws its strength from the generosity of the sharing.

I acknowledge, with gratitude, notes on the life of G. Miles Conrad by two of his former colleagues, Phyllis V. Parkins and Ann L. Farren. The meticulous minutes of meetings recorded by those historians of NFAIS, its director-secretaries, made the research and documentation for this paper an unalloyed pleasure.

PART II

Perspectives

In the Beginning

RAYMOND A. JENSEN, *Office of Water Research and Technology,*
U.S. Department of the Interior,
Washington, D.C.
Executive Director, NFAIS, 1959–1966

I was a delegate to the conference in Philadelphia when the idea for the National Federation of Science Abstracting and Indexing Services first came up in 1957. At that time, I was with the Armed Services Technical Information Agency (ASTIA). Shortly thereafter, I represented ASTIA at the Federation's first meeting. Sponsors included the National Science Foundation (NSF), the American Association for the Advancement of Science (AAAS), and professional societies. Initially, most of the delegates represented the professional societies.

Around 1959, enough money had been accumulated for the Federation to open an office. Miles Conrad was president and I was executive director, and we worked across from the Folger Library. *Meteorological and Geoastrophysical Abstracts* was in the same building. Several years later, we moved across the street to East Capitol because we needed larger quarters. We were doing a list of journals covered by members of the Federation (our first joint project). We also published a list of world abstracting services, with the help of the Science and Technology Division of the Library of Congress. All I had to handle was the printing, layout, and publication. The Library did all the rest of the work. I think the information field was more exciting then, although others may feel differently.

The Federation was given impetus by the surge of interest in U.S.

technology following Sputnik. Senator Hubert H. Humphrey, who was chairman of a Senate government operations subcommittee, was holding hearings on the management of scientific information and was prodding the abstracting and indexing (A&I) industry. Burt Adkinson, who was head of information services at NSF, told us that money was available and that all we had to do was build this cooperative activity. There was a considerable amount of excitement and motivation. It was a growth period for A&I services. The idea was to recapture the technological advantage from the Russians in all areas.

It was an exhilarating time at NFAIS. The membership was small; if it were not for NSF grants, a headquarters could not have been supported. But this modest membership conducted a considerable amount of activity. The idea for the *Heller Report* (the search for a national plan) came from NSF, and NSF money seemed limitless. Just after the study, though, the money dried up, but at least we got some ideas about how the A&I services could support themselves in a changing marketplace. As I read the *NFAIS Newsletter* today, it seems to me that more and more Heller-like collaboration is taking place in the Federation among member services—for example, the recent cooperation between Chemical Abstracts Service [CAS] and BioSciences Information Service [BIOSIS] in producing BIOSIS/CAS *Selects*. Everybody felt that Christmas was over when the money ran out and that NFAIS would have to get by on its own. I suspect that feeling still exists. The Federation wasn't the only group receiving federal money; most of the services were receiving money via grants, for example, BIOSIS and CAS. They all felt it wasn't going to last forever.

Things have changed since Miles Conrad's day. Some of the changes, I think, Miles would have liked. But some he wouldn't have wanted. He wanted the Federation to be only science and technology oriented and wouldn't have thought about including the nonscience A&I services. Also, he would have been extremely upset at the idea of for-profit organizations becoming members. I think he felt that for-profit groups ought to be in their own ball park and not-for-profit groups in theirs. Miles would probably adapt to change, but at that time he felt science and technology was the way for the Federation to go. When the Federation lost Miles Conrad, it lost much of its drive.

Later, NFAIS went through a period when survival was more important than anything else. It had to regroup. Stella Keenan came in as new executive director. "Science" was taken out of the name. The focus was redirected, and the membership was broadened. (I think NSF was also broadening its thinking at that time to areas beyond science, but now it seems some reversal is taking place.)

I believe considerable thought should still be given to overlap and duplication of effort in order to avoid costly redundancy. All the members are concerned about what the future looks like with the trend to online systems. The time may not be far off when A&I publications will cease to exist. It seems to me that the industry is moving a lot faster in that direction than it realizes. Personal computers are ubiquitous—people either already have them or are buying them. Only a few years ago, producers were talking about standardized profiles, 40 different versions of one journal, or many different predetermined SDI profiles. We don't want this; we want customized profiles, or, better still, a tailored subset of one or more of the large databases on floppy or hard disks. The technology is available now.

Nevertheless, the organizations that contribute to this type of file tend to fear losing control and are overly concerned with proprietary rights. These problems will be solved, and I believe the distributive custom database is the wave of the future.

Signposts of the Past and Future

STELLA KEENAN, *Loughborough University, Loughborough, England*
Executive Director, NFAIS, 1968–1974

It is with great pleasure that I write this contribution for the 25th anniversary of NFAIS. I have been asked to look forward, but I cannot resist first taking a glance over my shoulder. When I refer to the Federation in discussing my past life (professional, that is) and say "the Federation," I get strange looks from colleagues. "The Federation" sounds to them like a galactic mass born out of *Star Wars* (although in reality it was born out of Sputnik).

The signposts in Federation history are numerous, and many of them are people—far too many to name—but I have special memories of Dale Baker (with his feet on the desk); Ev Brenner and his argumentative style; Malcolm Rigby and his combination of enthusiasm and memory bank; Ben Weil with his open heart and home; and Bill Woods, who tried hard to turn me into a model executive director. I also particularly recall three lovely and gracious ladies: Carolyn Flanagan (NFSAIS President, 1965–1966), Marjorie Hyslop (NFSAIS Board member, 1968–1969), and Phyllis Parkins (NFSAIS President, 1966–1968).

When I returned to England in 1974, it took me about two years to eradicate my American accent, and it will take today and many tomorrows to assess the Federation's impact on my life. Since I have taken up full-time work in education, it has become clear to me that I am much more concerned with abstracting and indexing as services than with abstracting and indexing techniques. I believe that our students need to understand that these services are valuable information resources which can be used many different ways.

For the past year, I have been using a small cartoon character to summarize a discussion on future developments in information work. It is a signpost with three arms that point down roads labeled *micro*, *electronic*, and *videotex*. These three roads represent the exciting developments in information that are currently being explored in terms of their potential for the information profession. Microcomputers are becoming cheaper and more powerful and are being marketed aggressively. Computer literacy is being developed at the mass-media level, and a British government program aims to put a microcomputer in every high school by 1984. Electronic-publishing experiments are being funded nationally and build on the experience of earlier experiments in the United States. Although these developments may be many years away from full implementation, their impact on the published word cannot be denied or ignored.

Videotex (interactive viewdata and broadcast teletext) experiments are being conducted in different environments—the office, the home, and the library. Although these are signposted for different roads in my cartoon figure, they represent a convergence of technology that Isaac Auerbach discussed at length in his keynote address at the 1982 Federation Conference. He identified the three converging circles as computing technology, communication, and information. He spent some time elaborating the point that information is a unique resource with particular characteristics.

Technological developments have always caused changes in the abstracting and indexing service industry, and they will continue to do so. Repackaging of the product and its production on the basis of "single input, multiple output" were significant developments. Changes in the physical form of the product (printed page to card to magnetic tape to floppy disk) have already occurred and will continue to occur. There is a growing blur between bibliographic and subject descriptive information and hard factual data, with hybrid databases emerging as the result.

Of course, technological developments do not necessitate discarding traditional tools. The printed publication will be needed both for retrospective use and in those parts of the world not technologically sophisticated. I believe (along with Russell Rowlett) that we will need improved abstracts to cope with searching full text in electronic form. Chris Hansen, an elder statesman of the information profession in England, observed wisely at a meeting a few years ago that "the researcher still only has the same amount of time to spend on reading."

One problem that the abstracting and indexing industry has not yet resolved is that of bibliographic standardization. Although on the surface this is an obvious priority, many years of effort on this topic seem only to uncover additional layers of problems rather than agreement and increased compatibility between services.

Twenty-five years is a respectable and mature age, and there is the expectation of an active life ahead. I hope that the Federation and its members will continue to cope with the problems that arise and respond to changes in user requirements. On this silver anniversary of the Federation, may I wish it the ability to live up to the adjectives applied to silver: may it be "malleable, ductile, and lustrous."

Toward the Fourth Era of Information Services

TONI CARBO BEARMAN, *National Commission on Libraries and Information Science, Washington, D.C. Executive Director, NFAIS, 1974–1979*

It is a great pleasure to have the opportunity to contribute my personal perspective on the abstracting and indexing field on the occasion of the silver anniversary of the National Federation of Abstracting and Information Services.

I feel that my perspective is a somewhat different one from the others in this volume because I began my career more than 20 years ago, working for an abstracting and indexing (A&I) service. When I first started to work for *Mathematical Reviews* in February 1962, I had little idea what an A&I service was. But after a year and a half at the American Mathematical Society, I began to gain some understanding of the importance of secondary services. Going from there to work in university and special libraries, I developed a strong appreciation for the high-quality A&I services available. After working in research on the measurement and use of secondary services, I then had the honor of serving as executive director of NFAIS for more than five years. Returning directly to the A&I community, I had the pleasure of working for a London A&I service—INSPEC—which gave me a very different perspective, because I was able to look at the United States from "across the pond." Although my current job is primarily in the area of information policy, the secondary-service community continues to hold a special place in my heart, as well as a special role in information transfer.

41

In looking back at my 20 years of NFAIS's 25, I have seen several major changes and developments. In this brief perspective, I would like to look at just three of these major developments. These are a shift into the fourth era, a blurring of the lines among the elements of the information-transfer chain, and an increase in international activity.

Vincent Giuliano, in his *Into the Information Age* (1978), identified three major eras. The first era, of *discipline*-based service, incorporates the traditional service and spans the 19th century through the present. The second era, of *mission*-based service, began during World War II, reached its height in the 1960s, and continues today. Giuliano argues that we are now in the third era, of *problem*-based service, which began in the late 1960s and received growing attention during the 1970s. "Each era represents a value system, a context of activities and a set of corresponding goals and objectives (which may be more or less explicitly articulated)" (p. 10).

I believe that we are in the fourth era, of individualized, customized information services tailored to meet specific needs of individuals, such as the citizen in the home or the scientist in the workplace. Several A&I services have developed customized services, and many are looking at building new, total packages for their customers. Some of these packages may include specific subsets of databases, software, user manuals, document backup, numeric files, and even hardware.

Traditionally, the flow of information has been seen as a continuum from the producer to the publisher, to secondary services, to online vendors, to information-on-demand groups, to libraries, and ultimately to the end user. There have been some variations on descriptions of this continuum, but the basic elements have remained more or less the same.

Now that some secondary services have become retailers instead of wholesalers, we are seeing a shift in the role of secondary services as they become the primary means of providing access into their databases. Similarly, we are also seeing database producers bought by publishers, databases being brought together with other databases, and publishers themselves entering the business of creating databases. This blurring of the roles of the elements in the information-transfer chain has already led to important new implications for secondary services and is very likely to continue to expand the role of secondary services in providing more direct contact with their users.

Information has never stopped at national boundaries, and, especially since World War II, there has been increased international activity in the entire information field. Major secondary services have always tried to cover the world's literature by discipline or as part of their efforts to fulfill specific missions. The problems of the 1970s, such as pollution and the energy crisis, increase the need for expanded international coverage. The transborder data-flow issue and other international information policy questions of the late seventies and eighties will continue to increase the need for secondary services to participate actively in international activities and programs. Competition among services, and in many cases among countries, continues to increase. For example, the United States is now concerned that it is falling behind Japan and other countries in the information field. The European Economic Community is increasing its effort to market European products in the United States. Some countries have developed policies that treat information products as commodities subject to tax and regulation. In the United States, questions have been raised concerning whether information in computer-readable form is high technology and therefore subject to export restrictions. These are but a few of the many international issues that will continue to challenge us during the 1980s.

In looking back at my first 20 years in the information field and NFAIS's first 25, I cannot help but wonder what the next quarter century will be like. It is safe to assume that three areas—a shift into the "fourth era," a blurring of the lines among the elements of the information-transfer chain, and an increase in international activity—will continue to be of importance in the 1980s, as will the increased impact of technology on the production, delivery, and use of information products and services.

I am looking forward to continuing to work with NFAIS throughout its second 25 years in our efforts to improve the delivery of information.

REFERENCE

Giuliano, V., et al. *Into the Information Age.* A report prepared by Arthur D. Little Co. for the National Science Foundation. Chicago, American Library Assn., 1978.

Abstracting and Indexing Services — Past, Present, and Future

DALE B. BAKER, *Chemical Abstracts Service, Columbus, Ohio*
President, NFAIS, 1961–1963

NFAIS has operated for 25 years (1958–1982) to strengthen the nation's secondary information system by fostering cooperation among member services in order to better enable them to serve their communities of users. These years may well prove to be the "best years" long into the future. The abstracting and indexing community during this time has worked hard to overcome the "information crisis" in science and technology (particularly due to Sputnik). It has seen strong support and growth in all physical and social science research and development. Abstracting and indexing services are used by more people than ever before. In addition, powerful new graphic and electronic tools are at the disposal of these services to improve the efficiency and effectiveness of acquisition, processing, and dissemination operations.

Today, the international environment for information services is changing dramatically. It is expected that an "information war" will be raging throughout the eighties. The sources of conflict are economic, political, and social. The legal issues of copyright, fair trade, resource sharing, value-added tax, transborder data flow, technology outflow, classification and freedom of information, regulations, and security are current topics of much concern in the international information marketplace. Every nation is setting up its own system of control and protection mechanisms for the information flow within its borders or that which is exported.

The information world is a victim of its own successes. The modern computer and communication systems permit greater control of information dissemination than ever before. The eighties will be a decade of trial and error in determining how best to deal with the very complex challenges confronting secondary services. No individual or organization now possesses this knowledge, and the motivation for finding mutually satisfactory solutions to these problems may not always be for the "common good," but rather based on self-interest and even survival.

Among the consequences of the changes in technology that support information communication is the blurring of the distinctions among primary, secondary, and tertiary forms of information. Networks of large, centralized institutions for the control and management of information will shorten the information chain from author to users. These institutions may be joint ventures of multiple database producers. They will maintain much of their independent role and responsibility in collecting, reviewing, editing, processing, and marketing information in their fields of interest, but they will collaborate carefully to improve dissemination (standards, packaging, and the like), increase their revenue sources, and strengthen their political influence, both nationally and internationally. They will become gatekeepers of knowledge. Thus, continued viability of database producers in the coming decade will center around these "information centers" as national resource utilities.

NFAIS will change dramatically in the coming years. The "A" will be dropped from its name before the end of the decade. It will grow and diversify. It will continue to provide a forum for free and open discussion of common challenges. It will encourage joint studies of common interest in the field of information. And, it will help formulate and support common positions on information policy. Long live NFAIS!

From Isolation to a Community

CAROLYN M. FLANAGAN, *Engineering Index, New York, New York*
President, NFAIS, 1965–1966

Congratulations to NFAIS on its 25th anniversary. Some 26 years ago, we who ran the individual abstracting and indexing services were rather smug in our belief that we were providing useful information in our specialized fields and that our problems were unique. Many of us applied for grants to improve production procedures and, thanks to the National Science Foundation, discovered that no one service was an island. We met our counterparts in other fields of science and technology, learned that we all had similar problems, and joined in a common effort to improve the flow of information.

Thus, NFAIS was born of necessity and has been both the forum and collective agency for the dissemination of scientific and technical information for all United States member services, as well as those in related international fields.

Changes have occurred as the need for more up-to-date information has increased. With the advent of the computer and related equipment, products have taken on a new look. Online services now supply industry, government, societies, libraries, and universities with research findings that have aided progress at the national level.

NFAIS has an ongoing opportunity to serve its members through cooperative efforts in the fields of marketing and promotion. It also enjoys the possibility of combined research results from the products of individual services.

As we look at the current status of communications, it is not too difficult to imagine a database in the sky sometime during the next 25 years, bouncing back needed information.

These first 25 years have not been without problems, but it is appropriate to reflect on the past, evaluate the present, and plan for the future. NFAIS has weathered wars, economic crises, and changing social values, and—because its foundation is strong—it is vibrantly alive today.

A View of Things in Their True Relations

KENNETH C. SPENGLER, *American Meteorological Society,*
Boston, Massachusetts
President, NFAIS, 1970–1971

My dictionary gives several definitions of the word *perspective*. For my purpose here, I have chosen it to mean "a view of things in their true relations or according to their relative importance." I am adding to this a definition of the word *view* as "one giving a distinctive impression of distance." In this case, *distance* concerns time—both past and future. Although my view looks mainly to the future, I believe such a perspective can be sharpened by first looking at the past.

Earlier this year, NFAIS became the National Federation of Abstracting and *Information* Services. For the preceding 10 years, it was the National Federation of Abstracting and *Indexing* Services, and before that—from the time of its establishment in 1958—it was the National Federation of *Science* Abstracting and Indexing Services.

NFAIS originally had 14 members. We came from several fields of science and federated for the purposes of cooperating with and helping each other, studying and solving common problems, and communicating information useful to science abstracting and indexing services. Members got to know each other personally and much was accomplished on a one-to-one basis. The annual conferences became not only times for exchange of information but also provided opportunities for renewal of friendships. They were a lot like club meetings—very useful club meetings in which a great deal was accomplished.

Persons outside the sciences saw the value of such a federation; those of us within saw that we could help the others. Just as important, these individuals could help us, for they had been dealing with similar problems and devising many good solutions. Thus membership requirements were amended, and new organizations entered the Federation. *Science* was dropped from the name, and the acronym became NFAIS.

Things were changing in the abstracting and indexing services, both in terms of concept and technology—the conceptual changes often being driven by technology. New committees were formed and new studies started; the time frame for exchange of information became more urgent. Membership requirements were again amended, and more organizations joined. NFAIS changed to meet the new problems and the new opportunities. Abstracting and indexing services could no longer be easily distinguished from other types of information services; therefore, NFAIS changed the word *Indexing* in its name to *Information*. And now, as NFAIS completes its 25th year of service, it shifts its view toward the future.

Just as *Science* was dropped and *Indexing* gave way to *Information* in the Federation's name, can one expect *Abstracting* to be dropped or to give way to some new term in the future? What are the upcoming changes that new technologies will bring to abstracting and information enterprises? What new problems will these services face? What new opportunities? In his 1981 Miles Conrad Lecture, "Abstracts, Who Needs Them?", Russell Rowlett gave us clear, unequivocal answers, which I believe will stand up for a long time.

I am certain that the future holds many changes, as did the past. I am also certain that NFAIS is a strong, broad-based institution that will serve the information community well in the future, just as it has in the past. It will adjust as necessary to meet the changing needs of its members, to solve their problems, and to move into new areas of service. Just as it lost much of its club-like atmosphere in the interest of serving a broader constituency, it will likely change in many ways in the future, and, while the "A" in its acronym may never stand for "All," NFAIS will continue its devotion to communicating "all the information" its members need to operate their information businesses successfully.

The NFAIS perspective as seen from the past is reassuring. Its perspective for the future is even brighter.

The User — Once and for All

EVERETT H. BRENNER, *American Petroleum Institute, New York, New York*
President, NFAIS, 1972–1973

Each year seems to have produced a new "information science" catchword. The most commonly used is surely "the user." At every information science meeting, someone in the audience rises and most profoundly pronounces that "we really must take 'the user' into consideration." Below is my list of catchwords for the years 1958–1983. The dates bear little relationship to the catchwords; I am availing myself of prosaic license as a means of reviewing my historical perspective over 25 years of NFAIS existence.

Catchwords with Historical Scope Notes (SN)

1958 *Computer*
   SN: The computer age affords us an opportunity to be more creative than ever before in disseminating information.

1959 *The User*
   SN: We ought to take a look at him, but we're too busy stuffing the computer with garbage.

1960 *Keywords*
Used for Uniterms, Terms, Concepts, Descriptors, etc., etc., etc.
SN: Mortimer Taube is our most creative force, and we learn to live with freer input language.

1961 *The User*
SN: After all, why not use the user's language?

1962 *Thesaurus*
Related terms: Roles and Links
SN: We're not ready for natural text, so let's just clean up the input vocabulary a bit—but not too much, okay?

1963 *The User*
SN: You're getting to be a pain. It's difficult being concerned with you when you take so little interest in us.

1964 *Concept Coordination*
See also Boolean algebra, Optical coincidence
SN: Like Humpty Dumpty, after you break up the language you have to put it together again.

1965 *The User*
SN: Who is the user?

1966 *Search Strategy*
SN: The complexity of input vocabulary makes it complex to put Humpty Dumpty together again.

1967 *The User*
SN: Oh, you're an end user, not a user.

1968 *KWIC Indexes*
See also SDI (Selective Dissemination of Information)
SN: My God, maybe Mortimer Taube was right. H. P. Luhn and P. Baxendale never doubted it.

1969 *The End User*
SN: You're complaining about readability of computer printouts? Oh well, you'll get used to them.

1970 *Batch Systems*
SN: A grand failure except for SDI.

1971   *The End User*
       SN: His lack of interest in information systems is justified by the garbage produced by batch searching.

1972   *The Disk*
       SN: Our savior.

1973   *The End User*
       SN: Bring on the questions.

1974   *Online Searching*
       Related Term: Browsing
       SN: Mortimer Taube, you're a success!

1975   *The End User*
       SN: You need help.

1976   *The Intermediary*
       SN: I'm here to help.

1977   *The End User*
       SN: Thank you.

1978   *Time Sharing*
       See also Database producers, Database vendors
       SN: Online searching is too cheap. Printed products aren't.

1979   *The End User*
       SN: Teachers now bring "Apples" to students instead of the other way around.

1980   *Multiple Databases*
       SN: Life is more interdisciplinary and complex than ever.

1981   *The End User*
       SN: Let's be friends.

1982   *Friendly Systems*
       SN: To be friends, we need friendly systems.

1983   *Economics*
       Used for Money
       SN: Make this term retroactive from 1958 to 1982.

A Hexadecimal Dump Is Not a Greenwich Village Dive

JOEL J. LLOYD, *American Geological Institute, Falls Church, Virginia*
President, NFAIS, 1973–1974

The information community of the late 1960s and early 1970s was relatively small and uncomplicated. The for-profit sector was minuscule and hardly the force that it is today. IBM, still manufacturing sophisticated typewriters and adding machines, was years away from becoming "the Information Company." (There must be a Ph.D. dissertation lurking somewhere on the dynamics of capitalism as manifested by its incursion into the information business during the last decade.) We talked, in those days, like Old Testament prophets about the information and technology explosion that would leave the United States behind if it didn't shape up and do something, and like all the Jeremiahs of time gone by, we found few people willing to stand still and listen. Or so it seemed. Those of us who were involved with the nongovernment, not-for-profit (NFP) systems were banging on the doors of the National Science Foundation (NSF) for sums usually far less than half the price of a Sherman tank and finding only boredom in the higher science echelons. The world was divided between the pure and private NFP systems—the poor but honest and humble servitors of science, and a handful of government services—the fat cats (in our view) of the day. The Federation was still the National Federation of Science Abstracting and Indexing Services (NFSAIS). You can tell how innocent we were—we didn't even know we were dead on our feet without a pronounceable acronym. But it was our club, our forum, and our school. Many of us were newcomers, both as information professionals and as science services, and this is where we met the big boys — Chemical Abstracts Service (CAS), BioSciences Information Service (BIOSIS), and Engineering Index (*Ei*). In a world of buzzards and piranhas, it was an eye-opener for us little ones. We were accepted and welcomed sincerely and found not only a willingness to cooperate but a genuine eagerness to offer advice and share experience. Those "big boys" taught many of us our trade.

In my own shop, the American Geological Institute, we were merging and expanding an old service that had been issued from behind the stacks of the U.S. Geological Service library in a pretty, hot-type format and that treated as "current awareness" anything printed within the past 15 years. Many geologists throughout the country thought the computer was a flash in the pan and that it was perfectly okay for abstract journals to appear in the tempo of geological time. A few academics, when you spoke of an "alerting service," replied that they didn't really care when news of a scientific breakthrough reached them as long as it had no split infinitives, dangling participles, or improper hyphenation. They didn't hesitate to express their opinion of our enterprise either. I had been pulled out of the jungle for a learn-on-the-job experience, and I would probably have slipped back into the trees had it not been for the trust and confidence of the executive director of the Institute, Linn Hoover; for Burt Adkinson at NSF, who encouraged and supported the enterprise (as he did the Federation); and for my Federation connections.

Yes, we all did our best. We dropped that cumbersome "S" in our name, and brought in the large population outside of science. We recognized that the government services shared many of our problems and could help us find answers. We made our peace with the burgeoning commercial services and learned to live together. We discoverd the Old World and learned that the natives had left their caves and were not only good customers but actually knew some things that were useful to us.

So here we are now, in a bright, sparkling — albeit somewhat frightening — new world. We have yet to learn how to cope with international copyright disparities, transborder data snarls, freedom-of-access politics, satellite leasing, East-West rivalry and North-South misunderstandings, and a dozen other minor problems. But the solutions can be found with good will, patience, perseverance, and, above all, the absence of provincialism — the very qualities that NFAIS, which is nothing but the combined spirit of its individual members, has so ably demonstrated in the past and will continue to demonstrate in the future.

A Perspective on Fifteen Years in the Abstracting and Indexing Field

H. E. KENNEDY, *BioSciences Information Service, Philadelphia, Pennsylvania*
President, NFAIS, 1974–1975

When I entered the abstracting and indexing field in 1967, NFAIS was known as NFSAIS, an acronym for the National Federation of Science Abstracting and Indexing Services. The name was changed in 1972, not only to represent changes in the organization but also to acknowledge changes that were taking place in the community of abstracting and indexing services. In 1982, NFAIS once again changed its name, this time from the National Federation of Abstracting and Indexing Services to the National Federation of Abstracting and Information Services, a further modification in response to the changing community and constituency it serves.

To a greater extent than is immediately obvious, these changes in the organization's name reflect a very considerable evolution in the field of information transfer. In the mid to late sixties, information services designed for those segments of the community that were not oriented to science and technology were clamoring, with good reason, for acknowledgement of progress. Now, in 1983, the evolutionary process in the information-transfer community has reached the point that to identify our roles as only abstracting and indexing is not just archaic, restrictive, and unresponsive to advances with the times, but also misleading. Between the late sixties and early eighties, online tape spinners, information brokers, information centers, a largely expanded commercial sector, and many government agencies have become important components of the information-transfer community and are interrelated with the private, nonprofit abstracting and indexing services. The search to find the appropriate name for NFAIS in this decade is not unique. The same situation is occurring in the International Council of Scientific Unions Abstracting Board (ICSU AB): Is Abstracting Board in the title appropriate for the 1980s? That organization, too, is seeking a new name and direction to help keep both the institution and its name in perspective with the times.

In looking back over the titles of the Miles Conrad Memorial Lectures that have been presented since their inception in 1968, I found several that suggested change. For example, in 1970, Bob Hayes titled his lecture "The Changing Role of Information Services"; in 1973, Phyllis Parkins spoke on "Scientific Information Services in an Environment of Change"; and, in 1978, Ben Weil addressed the topic "Information Transfer in a Time of Transition." Even Russell Rowlett's 1981 lecture—"Abstracts, Who Needs Them?"—questions whether abstracts that were essential in the past are still considered so necessary. To question that abstracts may not be needed in today's scenario suggests that another change may be taking place.

The old adage, "The more things change, the more they stay the same," is tried and perhaps a bit tired. Nevertheless, in the case of abstracting and indexing (information) services, it speaks the truth. Let us try to bring into perspective the events of the past 15 years and see where we are. Since 1967, I have probably heard the word *change* more than any other single term, perhaps even more than *abstracts, indexes, tapes,* or *online*. We have talked about preparing for change, changing technology, impact of change on user habits, changing user habits, changing user needs, impact of changing technology on distribution and use, and so on. Indeed, many changes have occurred during this period, and many came about more rapidly than was predicted. For example, online service became a reality in a shorter period of time than was forecast. The ensuing shift from a 100-percent revenue base from printed services to revenue bases consisting of a significant percentage contribution from tape services has been realized quicker than many expected. Also, the acceptance by users of the concept that information is no longer a mysteriously free service of the library, but rather a service that has value and hence must be paid for, has occurred more rapidly than one might have thought (albeit somewhat slowly if use charges are to offset erosion of income from declining subscriptions).

Other predicted changes have been slower in materializing than originally expected. For example, the inclusion of hard data to supplement bibliographic databases has not materialized to the extent and with the speed projected a few years ago. Happily, the rapid demise of the printed page has not occurred and any predicted demise of the primary journal is premature.

Other changes, such as electronic publication on demand (which could have far-reaching impacts on the relative roles and relationships of primary, secondary, and tertiary services and on user behavior and use patterns) and expanded networking to facilitate transfer are anticipated. Some of these changes result from new generations of users that have been raised in an atmosphere of computer technology, electronics, rapid change, and "future shock." These changes are confidently predicted to have a far-reaching impact on services in the 1990s.

In spite of the many changes information services have undergone since NFAIS's conception in 1958, many aspects of abstracting and indexing are unchanged. We still capture bibliographic references, prepare and produce abstracts, and print copies of both. These procedures still constitute a major portion of our effort and the major source of our income. They still form the foundation of our organizations and services. While changes are many, and at times may seem rampant, they actually are changes in the way we do things, not in the basic purposes we serve. Those changes that are worthwhile will survive, for, in the long run, they will result in more effective and economical services for the user. Other changes will fade with time and will be looked back on as "flashes in the pan." Perhaps some were ahead of their time and others simply the results of misjudgments. Despite Don King's 1979 Miles Conrad Lecture entitled "The Information Community—Its Dilemma . . .," I maintain that these are fortuitous times for those of us who are established in the information-transfer field as our society moves from the industrial to the information age. I predict that the challenges and problems will make for a very exciting future.

Will Abstracts Survive Technological Developments? And Will "Cheaper Is Better" Win Out?

BEN H. WEIL, *Exxon Research and Engineering Company,*
Linden, New Jersey
President, NFAIS, 1975–1976

Good abstracts have long been valued by readers of journal articles and by literature searchers, including online searchers. That is why, in the past, more and more primary journals have included abstracts, and why most major access services have considered their publication a *sine qua non*. In the last few years, however, the unique value of abstracts and their cost-effectiveness have been challenged by some technological developments and — history seldom fails to repeat itself — by some newer access-services managers.

At first glance, it might seem unnecessary or repetitious for an NFAIS past-president to comment on this subject in the same volume with Russell Rowlett's dynamic Miles Conrad Lecture, "Abstracts, Who Needs Them?". But even in the brief interval since this lecture's preparation, there have been clear signs that some present students of communications and some present access-services managers do not understand the true value of abstracts. Also, to borrow from the old saying that "bad money drives out good," it seems possible that some bad-money technological developments and producer economics may drive out good-money use of abstracts. I would like to elaborate on this a little.

Admittedly, including abstracts in an alerting or access service — in any form — is more expensive than not including them, especially if the abstracts must be specifically written for that service. But it is sophistry to pretend that titles or titles plus descriptions are equally as useful as abstracts to information users trying to determine whether they need to obtain a given reference. Ask most journal or system users. Look at the literature. Cheaper *not to include* abstracts? Yes. Better for users *to include* abstracts? Also yes.

Full-text searching of complete digitalized papers also has its unique values, many of which we are still discovering. By their very nature, titles and abstracts must be too brief to include all the subjects covered and all the details included, even when the abstracts are backed by deep indexes. We already know the value of searching the full texts of titles and abstracts. We suspect that the present inelegant textual images and printouts of pertinent document portions can be backed up, on a volume basis, with quality images and printouts from digitalized versions of composed pages. But it is much too early to be at all certain that full-text searching will eliminate the need for abstracts, just as it is too early to feel confident that the majority of information users have access to full-text searching. The jury will not be in on this for quite some years.

Because of technological advances, some prophets for a future paperless age of information have recently gone on to assume that the merging and discriminating powers of the computer will eventually spell the end of the need for access services as such. In other words, abstracts from the original computerized documents can be computer accessed in their stead, and indexes will not be needed. I suppose that intricate computer-searching programs could eventually do what indexers presently do (when would that be possible or economically feasible in the sciences?), but I wonder whether author inclusion of good abstracts could really be mandated for unpublished "papers" (what will we call a paperless paper?), and, if not, whether abstracting services could later be resurrected.

Yes, I view the future of abstracts with some alarm and sincerely hope that future access-systems managers will think more than twice before they decide they can do without abstracts just because doing without them is cheaper. I also hope that future information-systems managers will think more than twice before they abolish access services in favor of the ubiquitous computer.

NFAIS: Some Thoughts

JOHN E. CREPS, JR., *Engineering Information, Inc., New York, New York,*
President, NFAIS, 1976–1977

Over the past 25 years, much in NFAIS has changed. I refer not just to names and faces but to the character of the organization. The annual meeting of today is a far cry from the first such meeting I attended. It differs not only in the number of persons attending, but also in the number of activities that occupy the attention of those present. Likewise, the daily involvement of staff and members has changed with the new demands of the businesses of "information dissemination," "housekeeping," "referrals," "study," "training," and so on. Yes, the change is very apparent and gratifying to those of us who have been involved in it.

In a less hurried mood, however, the most important aspect of NFAIS — at least from my point of view — is its *sameness*. That which may not always be so apparent and, if apparent, may not be considered good, are the less changing aspects of our association. I refer here to the steady concern and dedication of effort to the problems and opportunities of "information handling," "packaging," "analyzing," "transfer," "storage," and the like. The *sameness* of these concerns may not always be clear to those involved. In fact, I'm sure there are those who will disagree with me that these concerns are the same at all. Often the discussions in vogue, the present jargon, or the heat of a point of view, mask the underlying principles that were just yesterday discussed with different jargon and in a different context, but still with the same fervor and intent of purpose.

Those of us involved can never forget the early discussions between the so-called producers and spinners of tape. The concept of magnetic publishing and transferral of printed material in nonprinted format was so important to both parties involved that often more heat than light resulted from the meetings. Contracts were waved in the air with verbal challenge to respond or lose the business. These discussions were concerned with property rights, reuse, distribution control, and economic viability. I doubt very much if such subjects are worn out. (Doubt? I know!) These discussions have moved from the quiet of the association meetings to public television. The producers of entertainment are seemingly the leaders of the present discussions, but the subject is the same and continues to be an area of concern to those in NFAIS. New players and new fields of battle, but the *sameness* of real concern.

Who can forget the early responses to the new technologies that moved their way into the field. Committees were appointed, studies were undertaken, and cooperative efforts were investigated as the impact of technologies became clear. New individuals with new expertise were invited to join and participate. I recall, among many subjects, discussions regarding data elements (quantity, batch mode usage, online usage, and so on). Meetings were held to discuss the various implications involved. Manuals were written to give guidance. More meetings were convened to evaluate the manuals, to appoint new writing groups, and to consider the newest developments. Have any of these concerns changed? No, but none are static, either. The technologies continue to develop, and new manuals are written, discussed, discarded, and rewritten. The *sameness* again remains.

This *sameness*, I feel, is one of the healthiest aspects of NFAIS. Our organization began in one small area of that complex sleeping giant "information handling" and as such could concern itself only with the specific financial problems of its organizers. Like the railroads who forgot—or never knew—they were in the transportation business, NFAIS could have busied itself in a sameness of a confining nature. Its proper concern with standards, indexing procedures, and abstracts could have been a sameness to no end. But the *sameness* that has kept the organization in the forefront of the information business is the new and renewing concern of those involved.

Now, lest you think one year on the sidelines has turned my view of the major involvement in my life into rose-colored memories and a tourist's view of what once, in daily involvement, demanded realistic appraisal, let me say that not all sameness is healthy. There is some sameness to be seen in NFAIS that should be of concern to the organization and dealt with in new and creative ways. Institutions must keep changing so that the *sameness* continues to provide strength and vigor. For example—

1. *The same "old boys" club.* Have you heard this phrase used to describe NFAIS? I doubt I've been the only one to hear it. The responsibility for leadership is carefully guarded and offered only to the "old boys." In fact, responsibility and honor are passed down as turns on a merry-go-round are awarded to play-yard children. NFAIS has been open to the world with ideas, but to the industry it has been a closed shop. Stone-throwing is easy to do and thus easy to ignore. But it really isn't a matter of deciding if we are such a group or if we aren't. It is a matter of being aware of the strength of change in people and in institutions. If NFAIS can pursue its purpose with vigor and remain open to change, the "old boys" club will no longer be a matter of concern.

2. There has been and may still be a sameness of financial uncertainty. Note the use of the word *uncertainty*. My concern here is not so much the amount of the budget, or, for that matter, the budget deficit. Rather, I refer to the endless amount of time that might be spent dealing with the idea of the budget or budget deficit. Such activity can be, has been, and will be the weakening force of any institution. Of course, it's important to have a sound financial situation. I could not have been so involved as a treasurer and not believe that statement beyond any doubt. But a sound financial situation is possible without endless statements and discussions about "the budget." Let sound thinking and realism prevail, but very little sameness of preoccupation with the budget.

3. One may suggest a sameness of structure in NFAIS. By *structure*, I mean the method used to undertake endeavors. Mostly this refers to *committee* meetings. Committees can become institutions within institutions! Who served last year? Who hasn't been chairman? How many committees is he on? How much funding should this or that committee have? When should the committees meet?

Now I won't deny the power of the committee structure. But I might suggest that the energy expended on the structure could be better expended on the subject at hand. Remember, long committee reports seldom do more than bring praise to those who prepare them. When a committee does not report, the demand is made that the committee be expanded and extended. Let us look at the sameness of committee structure and question it rather than accept it.

These thoughts may not be added to the canon of writings for NFAIS, but perhaps they will have a place as notes to the text. For me, it has been a pleasure to serve the organization. It is now an honor to reflect on its history and its present and to ponder its future.

Information Dissemination: Evolution or Creationism?

RUSSELL J. ROWLETT, JR., *Chemical Abstracts Service,*
Columbus, Ohio
President, NFAIS, 1977-1978

In the midst of the current discussion of evolution versus creationism, I read a fascinating collection of 33 essays by Stephen Jay Gould (1977) entitled *Ever Since Darwin, Reflections in Natural History.* Dr. Gould's writing stimulated many thoughts, a few which I can relate to the future of information dissemination.

Is the future information system going to arise by evolution or by the creative efforts of one or two entrepreneurs? I have been involved in countless discussions on design for this system for the 1990s and beyond. For the most part, such long-range speculation has little permanent value. After assimilating Dr. Gould's thoughts, I am convinced that information dissemination in the future will arrive via evolution. It is not going to be created by a committee of the 1980s or any number of individuals.

Now, what do I mean by *evolution*? I use the word as it has been expropriated from the vernacular as a description of Darwin's "descent with modification." Darwin and the 19th-century evolutionists did not use the word in the original editions of their books. In their day, the *Oxford English Dictionary* defined evolution, in part, as "the process of developing from a rudimentary to a mature or complete state." "Thus," Dr. Gould states, "evolution in the vernacular was firmly tied to a concept of progress."

The central concept of Darwin's theory is natural selection of a species for the environment in which it is to live. But environments change, and so do selected species. The crucial idea of natural selection implies nothing more than the "survival of those who survive." Some have tried to read into this the survival of the fittest. Fittest for what? Only for living and doing the necessary jobs in the environment in which they find themselves.

If we look at the whole of information dissemination as analogous to a biological genus, we can see many species—among them, printed publications, microforms, computer-readable services, online services, depositories of all types, and videodisks. We also see many environments into which these species may be selected for use: academic institutions, government agencies, industrial organizations, individual researchers, and a host of others. Such information environments change just as natural environments change. Thus, both environments demand different, changed species for ultimate survival.

We do not have natural selection of an information species, but we do have user selection of a species to fulfill a need in the user's environment. When the need changes, the selection of the information species changes to fit the new or modified environment. The process parallels Darwin's theory of "descent with modification." It may not be survival of the fittest, but survival of the information-dissemination technique that best serves the users in a particular environment. As in nature, several species may survive in one environment. A selection of information species that fulfills the needs of one user environment may have to be entirely different when selected for another environment.

Dr. Gould emphasizes that "independent criterion of fitness is indeed, 'improved design,' but not 'improved' in the cosmic sense. To Darwin, *improved* meant only 'better designed for an immediate local environment.'" Indeed it is the goal for improved information dissemination to offer a catalog of improved species of services from which user selection will provide better services to fit specific needs.

An animal breeder artificially selects favored traits in his species. He knows what he wants. For example, he may select for a race horse that, as a three year old, will be able to circle a mile track in the shortest possible time. He is creating a preordained species. Nature is not an animal breeder, and no preordained purpose regulates the history of life. Similarly, in a complex development such as information dissemination, there can be no preordained right way to develop the species for the 1990s. There is no animal breeder to pick only the traits best suited for all purposes. The information species that survive will be those best suited to serve the user environments. User selection will parallel natural selection. There will be "descent with modification." The processes will continue just as natural selection continues.

Surviving information producers and vendors will be those who provide the users with sufficient species from which to make choices to fit the needs of their environments. The publisher, database producer, or vendor who spends time trying to "breed" the system of the future will end up serving only a single environment. Like nature, the information-dissemination markets of the future will include many environments. User selection will determine those species which best suit each environment and can adapt to that environment as it also changes.

The principle of natural selection has been compared to a composer by Dobzhansky; to a poet by Simpson; to a sculptor by Mayr; and to Shakespeare by Huxley. I am presumptuous enough to compare it to the developing information-dissemination systems of the future.

REFERENCE

Gould, S. J. *Ever Since Darwin, Reflections in Natural History.* New York, W. W. Norton & Co., 1977.

The Key Role of NFAIS to Information Services: Past and Future

H. WILLIAM KOCH, *American Institute of Physics,*
New York, New York
President, NFAIS, 1978–1979

This publication to commemorate the first 25 years of NFAIS provides an excellent opportunity to project the key role of NFAIS in the future of the information industry.

NFAIS was formed in 1958 at a time when abstracting and indexing (A&I) services were not yet recognized nationally or internationally for their seminal contributions to accessing the world's journal and report literature. Since then, NFAIS has gained significant recognition for A&I services. We have done so by helping to communicate and coordinate the important application of computers to A&I operations. Now, after 25 years of NFAIS efforts, A&I services are largely computerized and are recognized as leaders in the information field.

Over the next 25 years, NFAIS will certainly be able to work toward increased recognition of A&I services, not only due to computerization, but also to the coupling of A&I services to the primary body of journal and report literature. That literature is moving in the direction of full computerization as well, guided in part by the experiences of the A&I services that were there first. After all, it is more economical and much simpler to computerize excerpts, such as abstracts, than it is to computerize the full content of that literature.

That A&I services were computerized before primary literature is not the only reason why these services and NFAIS will play critical roles in the future of the information industry. Each A&I service acts as a focus for the literature in a given discipline, mission, or institution. Therefore, these services have an opportunity through NFAIS to continue to provide the coordination and leadership that is critical as the total literature becomes computerized, if we will but recognize the appropriate roles and the copyrights of all individual components of the total body of literature. If we do so, then I am certain that NFAIS can serve its membership in the future, as it has in the past, by providing a forum and a communication mechanism, not only for A&I services, but for the whole information industry involved in production, accessing, communicating, and utilization of information on the national and international scene. As members supportive of NFAIS, let us dedicate ourselves toward that kind of future.

Perspective of a Humanist

RICHARD H. LINEBACK, *Philosophy Documentation Center,*
Bowling Green, Ohio
President, NFAIS, 1979–1980

During the last 25 years, NFAIS has kept up with the changing times and has served its members and the whole information community with distinction.

When the Federation was founded in 1958, its membership was limited to abstracting and indexing (A&I) services in the sciences. It was originally called the National Federation of Science Abstracting and Indexing Services. Fifteen years later the reference to science was deleted and the name was changed to the National Federation of Abstracting and Indexing Services. At the same time, organizations from the humanities were invited to join. The *Index to Religious Periodical Literature,* now the *Religion Index,* was our first representative of the humanities. The Philosophy Documentation Center joined one year later.

When I attended my first business meeting as the official voting representative of the Philosophy Documentation Center, I expected little. After all, most members were in the sciences and the center was in the humanities; most were large organizations and the center was small; and most were members for many years, whereas the center was new. Contrary to my expectations, the members were friendly, open, and willing to share and help new members, regardless of their size or discipline. This same openness permitted me to take an active part in committee work, to be elected to the Board of Directors, and soon thereafter to be elected president of the Federation. As a member of NFAIS, I can honestly say that I have received far more than I have given, and, from a financial point of view, membership in the Federation has been money well spent.

Turning from the Federation's fruitful past to the future, I would like to offer the following expectations.

First, I expect that new members from the for-profit organizations will be warmly welcomed into NFAIS and will be regularly invited to participate in the Federation's activities, just as the humanities were a few years ago. I also believe that the exchange between the for-profit and the not-for-profit organizations will be mutually beneficial.

Second, the rapid growth of technology presents all information services with an uncertain future. I assume and expect continued technological progress and greater use of online and other computer services. Whether scholarly journals continue to be distributed in paper format or whether there is a major move to microform or electronic journals, the existence of indexes and abstracts will become more important. (I think it would probably be difficult to thumb through a journal stored on videodisk.) Thus, I see a continued need for A&I services.

The change in the name of NFAIS from the National Federation of Abstracting and Indexing Services to the National Federation of Abstracting and Information Services also reflects recent developments in the information community. Although I anticipate continued growth of numeric and other nonbibliographic databases, I do not expect this growth to be uniform across all disciplines. The recent change in the name of *Engineering Index* to *Engineering Information* reflects the fact that scientific information tends to be more numeric and to lend itself to efficient storage and retrieval. In contrast, the most important information in the humanities is not easily reduced to numbers and cannot be compacted for storage in computer memory. For example, the most important information in philosophy is the arguments presented in support of a given thesis. Hence, I believe that emphasis on the dissemination of nonbibliographic rather than bibliographic information will be more successful in the sciences and business than in the humanities.

Proposed: A Code of Ethics for the Information Community

LOIS GRANICK, *American Psychological Association, Washington, D.C.*
President, NFAIS, 1980–1981

There are many issues and problems of concern to the organizations that form NFAIS. Each group will solve the problems and confront the issues by making decisions that seem to best suit the current and future needs of that organization. They may act unilaterally or in concert with others, whatever seems most appropriate. An issue that should be the subject of concerted consideration and action by all NFAIS (as well as other) organizations is that of ethical practices and standards for the whole information community.

WHY WON'T BUSINESS ETHICS SUFFICE?

When I first raised this issue in the late 1970s, and when I appointed an NFAIS Committee on Ethics during 1980, the most frequent argument I heard was "normal business ethics will take care of the problems." It has been difficult to obtain a statement of what is meant by "normal business ethics," but it appears that this is an unwritten code, made up of reliance on federal legislation, legal contract provisions, and *caveat emptor*. In the information community, there is little or no relevant federal legislation. Contracts exist between producer and vendor, vendor and user, vendor and broker, and broker and user, but not between producer and user, producer and broker, and (frequently) vendor and ultimate user. *Caveat emptor* is a concept totally alien to most persons and organizations now involved in information generation or dissemination activities. Where does all this leave our ethical standards? Nowhere, unless something is done to describe a set of practices that are agreed on as ethical and to which organizations pledge to adhere.

WHAT MAKES INFORMATION UNIQUE?

There have been attempts to liken information to a commodity — a thing bought and sold, such as a manufactured product. Other comparisons have been made: a natural resource, like grain or minerals, or the output of a public utility, such as electricity. These models all fail because information is unique. No other product, resource, or utility is capable of infinite reuse and has as an integral part of itself a quality that can only be described as "truth."

WHAT SHOULD A CODE OF ETHICS COVER?

This quality of "truth" or "fact" or "validity" is the most difficult with which to deal. No database producer, distributor, or broker believes that he or anyone else willfully produces, distributes, or brokers untruths, nonfacts, or invalid data. Yet we all misinterpret information, record incorrectly, load files incorrectly, delay in making known corrections, edit inappropriately, fail to track down obscure references, or promote the use of one information source over another for a variety of reasons that may have no relation to the user's needs. Should the hypothetical code of ethics simply say that "Everyone is going to try hard to do the right thing"? Of course not. Rather, I think the interests of the user will best be served by a set of statements describing the ideal practices of each of the participants in the information chain. Such statements should cover not only practices regarding data or information activities, but also practices relating to interactions with all other participants, regardless of whether they are linked by contractual obligations.

If such a code of ethics could be constructed and adopted by the information community, it is my conviction that many of the other issues and problems confronting us would be more quickly, easily, and equitably solved. It is my hope that NFAIS will continue to provide leadership in this important area.

Change and Renewal

E. K. GANNETT, *Institute of Electrical and Electronics Engineers, Inc., New York, New York*
President, NFAIS, 1981–1982

An unusual number of major organizational changes within NFAIS during 1981–1982 made it evident that NFAIS had entered an important period of transition that might greatly affect its future. These changes also reflected significant trends in the information community at large.

The most important of these changes were the change in NFAIS membership, the change in the composition of the Board of Directors, and the change in the organization's name. Together, these events reveal an interesting modification in the perceptions of traditional abstracting and indexing services, regarding how they see themselves and what they do.

The change in NFAIS membership during 1981–1982 took the form of admitting, for the first time, organizations from the for-profit sector. This possibility had been discussed periodically over the prior decade. The fact that the for-profit barrier walls had at last come tumbling down was highly significant. It meant that the not-for-profit community recognized that its similarities with the for-profit sector were substantially greater than its differences. In fact, one could ask whether there were any real differences at all.

Broadening the composition of the NFAIS Board of Directors to add representatives from beyond the not-for-profit services in North America, and thus also to include representatives from for-profit, overseas, and U.S. Government services, permitted, for the first time, the total community to have a direct voice in the governance of NFAIS. And, also for the first time, there was a full appreciation of what constituted the "total community." The distinctions that once seemed so important had now become distinctions without differences.

Amending the name of the Federation had great symbolism. NFAIS had changed its name only once before—by dropping the word *Science* so as to broaden its scope. Finally, more than a decade later and after two years of intense debate, NFAIS voted to substitute the word *Information* for *Indexing*, therefore becoming the National Federation of Abstracting and Information Services.

The term *Indexing* did not die easily, for it described an activity that was even more universal to the current NFAIS membership than "abstracting." It was becoming clear, however, that a growing number of organizations were—or soon would be—getting into new types of services, for example, document delivery, numeric databases, or full-text online files. Although the particulars of these future services might still be unclear, there was no mistaking the growing indication that the future lay less in exclusively providing information about information and more in directly providing that information. The shift from the word *indexing*, with its secondary-service connotation, to the word *information*, with its broad primary-service implication, is more than a hint of the future. It is a promise.

In looking back at the aforementioned changes, one can see a strong indication that the community is broadening, both as to the organizations involved and the products and services they provide. One is struck, however, not only by the implications of these changes for the community at large, but also by their significance to NFAIS. For above all, they demonstrate that NFAIS possesses the most important ingredient that any organization can have: the ability to change with the times and thereby to renew itself.

Influences for the Future

RONALD L. WIGINGTON, *Chemical Abstracts Service,
Columbus, Ohio
President, NFAIS, 1982-1983*

The organizations that are members of NFAIS must learn to cope with a new environment. This sounds trite, but it is true. The underlying role of abstracting and indexing is now extended to more general information services. The changes in NFAIS, from its founding days with a hard science and technology scope to the present, have been signaled by the changes in its name: first, dropping *Science* from the name and, in 1982, substituting *Information* for *Indexing*.

The role of the member organizations requires continuing the collection, analysis, and organization of information to help users find knowledge of interest. Boundaries, however, are merging, with publishers on the one hand and libraries on the other. All these segments of the information community are expanding their functions and roles because of, and to take advantage of, the new environment brought on by computer and communication technologies. The old technology — print on paper — had nice, neat boundaries enforced by the physical embodiment of the information transfer and location medium.

WHERE DOES THIS ALL LEAD?

As I reflect on, and try to understand, the forces that will shape the future of the industry that NFAIS represents and, thus, NFAIS itself, three general influences stand out: technology, economics, and sociology. The rapid advances in technology and what it is making possible, especially in information acquisition, organization, and use, are well known and perhaps overemphasized. For those who have been involved in the development of information technology over the last 20 to 30 years, what is happening is no surprise. We have known for some time what could be done, based on physical phenomena, and the limits of real accomplishment have depended on other factors that govern the transformation of basic knowledge into useful applications.

The influences of economics and sociology are more complex. They are, of course, interrelated with technology. The economics of making what is possible, from the point of view of science and engineering, to become reality depends on the cost of creation of facilities and services and the price that people are willing to pay to use them. The cost of creation of information technology has been dropping due to advances in the production methods for electronic devices, in contrast to all other products and services for modern society. But, the price that people and organizations are willing to pay for information services remains low relative to the value that can be derived from them. Information services, of concern to NFAIS, still are not in the mass-marketing domain that can finance extensive services and get the unit cost and consequent price down to low levels affordable to a wide audience. Unfortunately, society seems to value entertainment more highly than information services to support intellectual accomplishment. Sometimes it is frustrating to see—even in our own homes—that soap operas, rock music recordings, and Pac-Man are more important to society than information to support science and technology, intellectual pursuits, cultural enrichment, and civic responsibilities.

Another factor in economics is the establishment of ownership of resources and capabilities that are the basis of economic viability. The vexing problems of establishing and protecting copyrights and other ownership mechanisms are an illustration that the economic base for information services still does not rest on a firm foundation of definition of property rights and of the separation of public and private interests.

The dominant factor, however, is sociology—the reactions of populations to their environment and the group relationships that determine how people behave. Relating to the interests of NFAIS, we are more dependent on how people will want to acquire and use information in their intellectual pursuits than we are on the means we can develop to assemble and provide that information. Technology and economics certainly will have their impacts on what people can use for information purposes and what they can accomplish with it. But suppose any conceivable information service were possible in a time less than the tolerance limits of a person and that it were free. How would a person interact with that information source to arrive at decisions or to produce new information? At least, since the days of Memex in the mid-1940s, there has been a vision of information support systems that would augment human intellect and eliminate the constraints of finding and communicating information relevant to productive intellectual work. Yet we still know little about how large groups of people would actually behave if such capabilities were readily available.

NFAIS members, as organizations whose missions relate to making it possible for people to find the information they need, must understand more fully how their services must change to respond to a sociological environment that is only partially influenced by technology and economics. Individual and group behavior will be the final determinant of what is used. In contemplating the future, the NFAIS organizations must understand those needs in the context of a new sociological environment and not just work to improve their ability to provide old services with new tools.

I believe that the future environment—in the office and in the home—will rapidly turn to online, on-demand delivery of information. Our present abstracting and indexing activities will have little influence on establishing that environment. For our survival and vigor, however, we must anticipate and understand it and be prepared to exploit it. The consequent behavioral changes in the way people acquire and use information will more drastically alter the way we operate in the future than have the technological changes of the past altered the way we produce today's services.

PART III

The Miles Conrad Memorial Lectures

MARCH 20, 1969

Merging Operations Internationally

J. R. SMITH, INSPEC, *Institution of Electrical Engineers, London, England*

In discussing the need for and the likelihood of achieving international cooperation, it is necessary to make some assumptions:

1. The scientific community needs and desires wider and more speedy dissemination of information (perhaps thought of as a natural extension of the verbal interchange of scientific knowledge, although there may now be other motives).
2. Service to the community is not a sufficient basis for persuading existing services to become involved in any necessary changes.
3. There must be no disadvantage to the services involved, either as to their effectiveness or their financial situation. It would not be unreasonable to say that there must be some direct advantage.

It must be recognized that existing services face very serious difficulties if they are to be expected to make widespread changes in procedure. It also must be recognized that these services, in some cases, represent very large vested interests and operate on large budgets. Although they may be nonprofit organizations, they have a considerable outlay of money that must be matched by an equal income if they are to survive.

For this reason, we should perhaps consider that such goals as standardization of formats and input/output compatibility have been achieved when all or nearly all major interested services make little or no change. (The inferior alternative would be basing these achievements on some unattainable definition of an idealistic approach probably devised by some committee.) I doubt whether anything can be achieved if tremendous upheaval will be caused to existing services, even if these services are in a position to undertake such changes. I suppose what I have in mind is that cooperation of the kind we are talking about will not come from the establishment of international committees but from active cooperation based on a real desire to cooperate by those involved. In fact, I believe that any cooperative moves can come only from the development of good personal relationships. For the same reason, small steps that can easily be implemented and that are in the right general direction relative to the overall plan are the only ways of making real progress (although I believe that some overall plan should be developed). One of the biggest problems we face is the way in which services have developed independently. Although they have generally grown in the same direction, existing services have taken many different courses to achieve very similar ends. Hopefully, they have not progressed too far for the modest changes of direction that may be suggested.

A number of approaches to international cooperation have been and are being discussed. I would like to devote the rest of this talk to reviewing some of the work that is being done.

The first approach (Figure 1) is a manifestation of some of the work of the International Council of Scientific Unions Abstracting Board (ICSU AB) and is largely based on bilateral agreements that follow discussions by all member services in a particular discipline. This type of international cooperation is already being actively pursued. An example of this concerns an interaction that has developed in an experimental way among three abstracting journals in the area of physics: the English-language journal *Physics Abstracts (PA)*, the French-language journal *Bulletin Signalétique (BS)*, and the German-language journal *Physikalische Berichte (PB)*. ICSU AB conducted a survey of the journal literature of physics as covered by these three abstracting services. A comparison identified that there were three areas of productivity in the journals that were scanned by the various services. Quite arbitrarily, distinctions were drawn between journals of so-called high productivity (producing more than 100 titles per year), medium productivity (11–99 titles per year), and low productivity (10 or fewer titles per year). In the high-productivity group, there were approximately 80 common periodicals; these were thought of as no more than a useful list and perhaps yet another definition of core journals.

In the area of low productivity, the situation was much more interesting. *PA* and *PB* scanned some 1,600 periodicals, and each of their

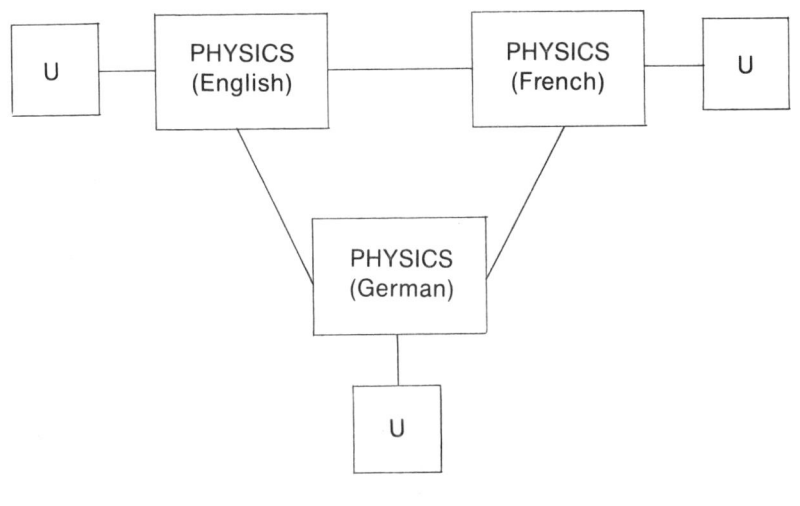

Figure 1 A diagrammatic representation of the work of ICSU AB on international cooperation among three abstracting journals. U represents "user."

lists contained more than 350 periodicals that fell into the low-productivity category. The acquisition of and selection from these periodicals may be expensive and difficult to justify in terms of return, but nevertheless may be essential if the coverage is to be satisfactory. *BS* (which covers all fields of science and technology), on the other hand, acquires and wholly abstracts around 9,000 periodicals per year. So it can be seen that if *BS* is prepared to send to *PA* and *PB* copies of articles that it allocates to physics and that appear in any of the periodicals not taken by *PA* and *PB* and in the 350 low-productivity journals of *PA* and *PB*, *PA* and *PB* would then be able to ensure at least the same coverage that they presently have — probably better — without having to concern themselves with the 350 periodicals of low productivity. A pilot project is in progress to determine the feasibility of following this practice and whether — and this is of prime importance — there are economic advantages to the participants, with no drop in the effectiveness of their services (e.g., time delays in publication).

In the medium-productivity class, a further experiment is being conducted in which *PB* is providing *PA* with abstracts in the English language of material appearing in selected German-language periodicals. The command of foreign languages in continental Europe is much greater than it is in the United Kingdom, and it is possible, both on the scores of cost and time, that it would be advantageous to the United Kingdom to follow this course. In return for this service, *PA* would provide *PB* with a record, in machine-readable form, of all the bibliographic data of articles selected for inclusion in *PA* (other than those coming from German-language periodicals) that would help *PB* (particularly with regard to English-language material) to ensure that their coverage is more complete.

I am sorry to have discussed at such length these small experiments, but I think they deserve the time, because they are examples of active cooperative international experimentation. They represent something that is already happening which may prove to be advantageous to all participants.

The second approach to international cooperation is being undertaken by the ICSU/Unesco (International Council of Scientific Unions/United Nations Educational, Scientific and Cultural Organization) Committee (UNISIST), which is studying the feasibility of the proposed World Science Information System (Figure 2). The study is based on the concept that this World Science Information System should be a flexible network based on the voluntary cooperation of existing and future information services. It is headed by a central committee chaired by Professor Harrison Brown and is supported by a number of working groups and an advisory panel that comprises some of the large existing operating systems. One working group is concerned with questions of standardization of bibliographic descriptions that may expand into classification, indexing, and abstracting; a second working group is concerned with the identification of research problems that must be studied to achieve an efficient worldwide system; a third group is studying the problems of natural and machine languages, especially from the point of view of transferability and mechanized processing; and a fourth group is working on the problems of

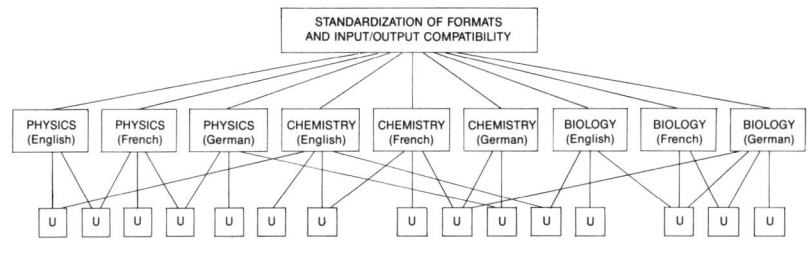

Figure 2 Representation of a World Science Information System as envisaged by UNISIST. U represents "user."

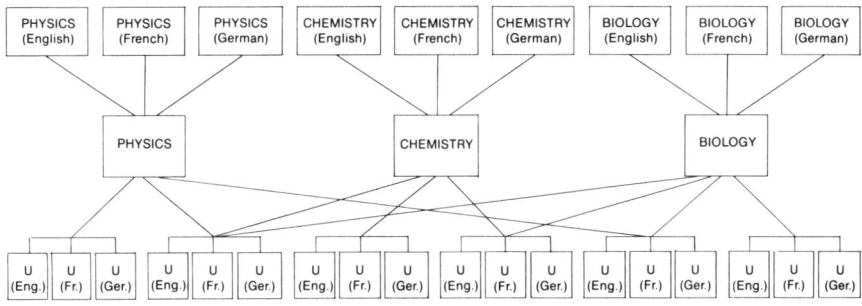

Figure 3 Diagram depicting a third approach to international cooperation, whereby each discipline would have one major information service into which all existing services would feed. U represents "user."

developing countries and their contribution, and access, to the worldwide system. The position of the advisory panel is an important one, since it is here that the views of operating services can be heard. It is only by their active cooperation that a voluntary network of the kind envisaged could succeed. It has been suggested that an international conference be held, where, in formal terms, the establishment of the proposed system could be discussed.

The third approach to international cooperation, which is not attributable to any one organization but which has been fairly widely discussed in Europe, is that of establishing one information service in each of the disciplines into which the existing services would all feed (Figure 3).

For the purpose of discussion, it has been assumed that the information services established will be in English and that services in other languages will agree to feed material into the system. It is then proposed that instead of having the same information processed a number of times in different languages, it will be processed only once, in one language, and subsequently made available by translation, if necessary. Some of the thinking of this nature is based on the concept that if cooperation of the kind referred to in the ICSU AB activities develops, we may end up with a number of different services dealing with identical material, each in its own language. There may be much merit in the proposal of a one-language system, but there are obvious difficulties, too.

The fourth approach — the mission-oriented concept — is already well known (Figure 4), particularly in the United States and to a lesser extent in Europe, except that one international system of this kind is already operating and a second is under active consideration. International systems such as this would rely on an input of national material from each of

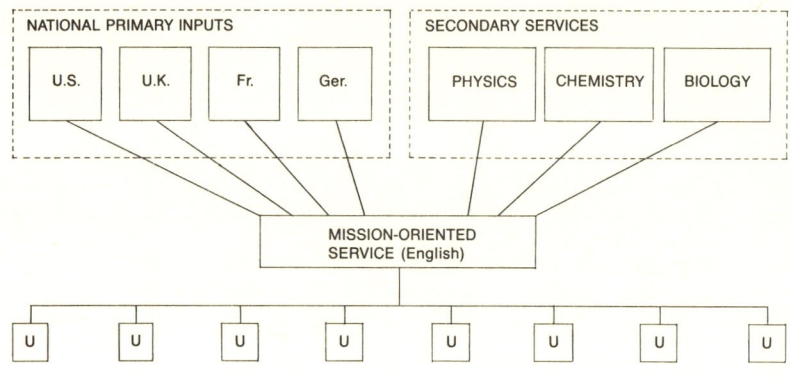

Figure 4 The mission-oriented approach to international cooperation among information services. U represents "user."

the countries producing work of interest to the system and would receive, in return, outputs covering all the material that had been included.

The last approach I wish to mention is that concerned with the establishment of a formal World Information System, the inputs to which are essentially controlled by government and the outputs of which are made available to users in all languages. This presupposes government control of the existing services, who would be directed to comply with the requirements of the system (Figure 5). Such an approach seems to be wholly unrealistic, since I cannot imagine, for instance, that in the United States the major existing services could see themselves directed in such a way by the government.

In illustrating the various approaches, I have been forced to choose some subjects, some languages, and some countries, but this does not indicate that those referred to are are the only ones involved in the work that is going on. For example, the USSR and Japan are very much involved in many of the discussions and, indeed, the USSR will actively be taking part in the ICSU AB experiment I described.

A wish to cooperate internationally is not sufficient, nor are bilateral arrangements aimed at no particular end. A haphazard approach will produce a situation similar to that existing among individual services today in their lack of standardization and compatibility. I believe that if it is possible to agree on the broad concepts required of an international network of the type envisaged by UNISIST, it may be possible to move, in small steps, toward a much more orderly worldwide system of storage and retrieval of scientific information.

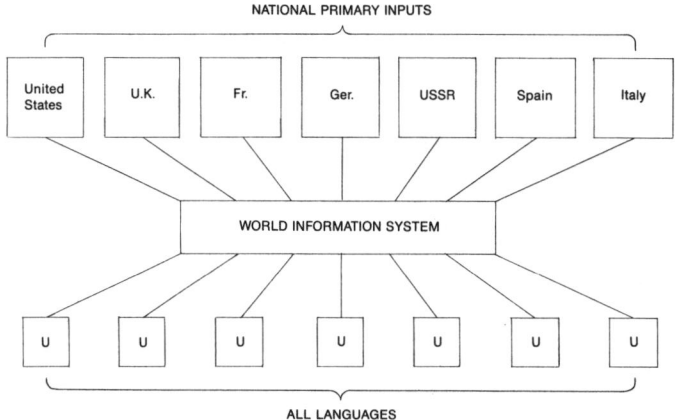

Figure 5 The World Information System: inputs are controlled by government. U represents "user."

MARCH 12, 1970

The Changing Roles
Of Information Services

ROBERT M. HAYES, *University of California,*
Los Angeles, California

It is indeed an honor to participate in the program today, especially in the framework of the Miles Conrad Memorial Lecture and as keynoter for further discussions. Unfortunately, my role as keynoter is complicated. The issues seem to be well covered by the program. At most, therefore, I can set a stage within which the interrelationships can be seen.

The general context is, of course, familiar to us all — increasing concern by both government agencies and professional societies for the need to develop and maintain adequate means for access to scientific and technical information. The Crawford report, the Weinburg report, the activities of the Committee on Scientific and Technical Information (COSATI), the research and development supported by the National Science Foundation (NSF) through the Office of Science Information Service (OSIS), the services provided by the mission-oriented agencies, and the progress at the three national libraries all attest to the importance with which the Federal Government has viewed this problem. The recent study by the Committee on Scientific and Technical Communication (SATCOM) for the National Academy of Sciences shows the concern of the professional societies.

As a result of all this, there has been a continuing clarification of the essential roles of the principal information services: the primary literature as the basic source, the secondary literature as the means of intellectual access to it, the research library as the means of assuring its availability, the information analysis center as the means of bringing substantive expertise to bear on its analysis. Repeated efforts have been made to improve the effectiveness of each alone and in combination. Mechanization, networks, and the systems approach have been invoked as essential answers, and there have been many attempts to apply them.

Still, there are problems: the principal publications, both primary and secondary, steadily increase in number, size, and publication cost. The capital investment in creating the database—whether in the indexing and abstracting services, in libraries, or in information analysis centers—has become so huge that few institutions can afford it for their own needs. Above all, despite our belief that there is a need for these services, there continues to be a lack of any real market. The resources are just not used as they could, and should, be.

Much effort has been made to solve these problems. We have turned to mechanization in the hope of reducing or at least restraining costs. Every one of us has looked to the computer: the indexing and abstracting services for publication, the libraries for acquisitions and catalog production, and the information analysis centers for retrieval services. But in each case, the reality has repeatedly been that mechanization almost never reduces costs. It increases them, and we must justify the increased costs on the basis of new services. So we turn to new services and new products in the hope that new sources of income will arise from the same capital investment. But again we find ourselves in a dilemma: more than half the costs of new services turn out to be directly related to the costs of producing and distributing them and not to the database. Therefore, we make efforts to cooperate, hoping to share the costs across institutions and kinds of services. Cooperation, however, is most exhibited in the talks of those with an ax to grind, and the efforts to create networks have faced almost insurmountable organizational and political barriers.

The basic problem remains: the market is presumably there, but as a group, we seem unable to tap more than 5–10 percent of it. It is this dilemma to which I now direct my attention, discussing changing roles in the context of marketing.

THE MARKETING PROBLEM

For years, I have thought about the pattern of marketing in the book business, with its dependence on a series of middlemen, from the distributor to the retailer. Now, viewing the problem we face in "information service" as a marketing problem, this pattern becomes very meaningful. We must create the market by creating the marketers.

The analogy I would like to draw is this: we have a number of wholesalers—the primary and secondary services, including in particular the members of the National Federation of Science Abstracting and Indexing Services. We are starting to create a set of distributors—points at which the products from several wholesalers can be focused for repackaging and distribution—in the form of dissemination centers, some based on computer facilities, some on libraries, and some on both. Finally, we can view the information analysis centers as retailers, providing direct information service to the ultimate consumers. The point of this analogy is that the publishing business discovered many years ago that books could not be sold directly from producer to reader. The market may be there, but without the middlemen—the distributors and the retailers—to stimulate it, only a small percentage of it will be tapped. This means that cooperation among wholesalers, distributors, and retailers is crucial. We are all mutually interdependent—almost symbiotic—to the extent that we must support each other in our aim toward generating the market.

THE PATTERNS OF COOPERATION

There are, of course, efforts to establish cooperation among the wholesalers: the attempts to transfer machine-readable data from primary to secondary publisher; the sharing of abstracts among secondary publishers; and the establishment of the Information Industry Association (IIA) and the National Federation of Science Abstracting and Indexing Services to represent common wholesaler interests. There have been comparable efforts to establish cooperative arrangements among the distributors: the formation of networks among libraries; the introduction of union catalogs and interlibrary loan standards; and the establishment of the Association of Scientific Information Dissemination Centers (ASIDIC) to represent common interests of information processing centers. There have also been several networks among information analysis centers.

But there is now the need to establish patterns of cooperation between wholesalers and distributors, between distributors and retailers, and even between retailers and wholesalers. Many of the indexing and abstracting agencies are already establishing formal working relations with dissemination centers—"franchising" them to provide specified services to their customers. This is most evident with respect to magnetic tape database services, but comparable franchising may also arise with respect to printed publications and microforms. There are real needs to be met and problems to be solved, however, if these relationships are to be smooth. There are needs for union catalogs of magnetic tape databases, for standards for access to resources, and for procedures for sharing them. There are problems in pricing policies: lease versus sale, SDI versus retrospective searching, and batch versus online processing. Solutions will require the recognition of the mutual interdependence between wholesalers and distributors.

There is the need to establish patterns of cooperation between retailers and distributors. For too long, information analysis centers have been established without recognition of their need for access to adequate libraries and dissemination services. Repeatedly, they have tried to develop independent collections and retrieval programs. The continued growth of information analysis centers will, I feel, depend on establishing cooperative arrangements between information analysis centers and the indexing and abstracting services—the wholesalers. The former are aware of what kind of information packages the market needs; the latter have the capability of producing them.

SUMMARY

My story is simple. There are no changing roles, merely changing views of the problems. For years we have preached that user needs must be understood while we have devoted our energies to the solution of problems essentially unrelated to the user. I have suggested today that if we view the roles of information services in the framework of a marketing problem, they will be better understood, their interrelationships will be clarified, and our attention can be focused on the basic problem. Marketing, and only marketing, is the means by which user needs will be recognized, understood, and met. And that is why we are here, is it not?

FEBRUARY 24, 1971

After Organization X — What Next?

BURTON W. ADKINSON, *American Geographical Society, New York, New York*

I wish to recall to this audience that one of the ground rules for this lecture is that the subject must be a broadly based discussion on secondary services. The consideration of such a topic led me to the conclusion that it might prove useful to review, in present-day context, the principal conclusions and recommendations of a national plan issued by the National Federation of Science Abstracting and Indexing Services (NFSAIS) in 1963. In 1962, the Federation commissioned Robert Heller and Associates of Cleveland, Ohio to make a study of science abstracting and indexing services in the United States and to suggest actions that could improve the effectiveness of U.S. activities in science abstracting and indexing. The ensuing report, which was based largely on 1961 data and other information, was entitled, *A National Plan for Abstracting and Indexing Services*. It eventually became known as the *Heller Report*.

CONCLUSIONS AND RECOMMENDATIONS OF THE HELLER REPORT

The recommendation that received the most attention was the establishment of an organization that was identified by the letter "X." This organization was to be a focal point for repackaging and marketing the products from the professional abstracting and indexing services. (One can now see the basis for the title of this presentation.)

The main conclusions drawn from the *Heller Report* are

1. The scientific community needs better secondary publications of both professional and project types. Professional-type publications have little market-growth potential because their market is restricted largely to institutional customers. Such publications vary widely in format, coverage, and timeliness, and many are below acceptable standards. Professional-type publications need to eliminate duplication of effort and coverage and develop common procedures for repackaging material for project use.

2. Project-type publications are needed to meet the growing demand for interdisciplinary and more specialized intradisciplinary secondary services. Project-type publications have a large market-growth potential if they are designed for small, coherent group or individual subscriptions.

3. In general, there will be a continued growth of literature; a rising trend in costs that will cause serious economic problems; a need for increased cooperative planning leading to compatibility for an interchange of products; and a need for greater attention to many industry-wide problems, such as public and government relations, industry standards and statistics, and cooperation with other segments of the scientific community.

On the basis of these conclusions, the *Heller Report* made the following recommendations:

1. Upgrade 18 professional-type publications so that worldwide scientific and technical literature is comprehensively covered.

2. Establish an operating unit to provide project-type products. (This was to be a joint venture of the 18 professional groups identified as Organization X.)

3. Coordinate activities of profession-oriented services. (Heller estimated that such an action would reduce costs of these 18 services by $5 million.)

4. Use Organization X to reduce costs of project-oriented services.

5. Increase the production and use of author abstracts.

6. Expand the Federation so that it includes related activities of libraries, journal publishers, scientific societies, and foreign organizations to allow more effective joint efforts in market research, system and equipment development, industry standards, user education, and industry statistics.

7. Broaden Federation membership to include all sections of society

directly related to the production, organization, distribution, and use of abstracts and indexes.

Heller and Associates estimated sales but would not hazard a detailed estimate of cost. The report said that sales of Organization X should be $15 million by 1971 and that it would require more than $60 million to upgrade professional services and to initiate Organization X. It predicted that three years after the development program was accomplished, the abstracting and indexing (A&I) services and Organization X would be self-supporting. Also, it suggested that the National Science Foundation (NSF) should be the major funding source of this development effort.

REACTION TO THE HELLER REPORT

The Federation did respond to some suggestions in the *Heller Report*. It took steps to broaden its membership, but in a very selective manner. It also asked NSF to support an experimental Organization X. NSF took a dim view of the experimental Organization X, because there was no effective way to repackage the wide diversity of products being produced by the A&I services. Also, NSF was convinced that most professional A&I services still believed they could serve the individual scientist, engineer, or educator. Because these services did not seem willing to deal through organizational retail mechanisms, NSF suggested that Organization X would be considered as a potential competitor. In addition, A&I services were not convinced that it was possible or profitable to attempt to get the cooperation of primary publishers, research libraries, or government information services. More importantly, these services were not willing to initiate realistic programs to develop common technical procedures nor to investigate the possibility of sharing through agreed-on allocations for comprehensive coverage of the world's scientific and technical literature.

In light of the *Heller Report* and the reactions to it, what are some considerations that should influence planning and programming for the future development of a national abstracting and indexing service?

CONSIDERATIONS FOR FUTURE PLANNING

Information and the services that make it readily available are national resources in which all sections of society have an important stake, whether recognized or not! Scholars and especially research scientists and engineers depend on the distribution and acceptance of their intellectual products to gain stature within their fields. Research and development organizations in both the public and private sectors must depend on new ideas that are generated both inside and outside their own organizations. Technical and economic advancement of any nation relies on the effective exploitation of these resources, as well as the abilities of individuals and organizations to develop effective production, distribution, and marketing mechanisms. Therefore, it is suggested that information and all activities related to its production, organization, and effective distribution are just as much public services as telecommunications and other transportation systems, education, and library services. All these are either supported by government funds or are under close government control.

Many persons have equated information systems with telecommunications systems and have insisted that an effective information system should be patterned after a telecommunications system. This may be partly true, but telecommunications systems are only responsible for transmitting (including switching) and temporarily storing and reproducing the information products to be communicated. Information systems, on the other hand, must have the additional capability of short- and long-term storage of billions of bits of information and the repackaging of these stores into different forms and different combinations for distribution to a myriad of groups and individuals with varied information requirements. In addition, information systems must be able to select items according to specific criteria and often analyze, evaluate, reduce, and then reformat the information for a specific purpose. Finally, information activities are not an end in themselves. They support other activities, such as education, research, development, management, planning, or production.

What are some of the factors that must be considered to improve the present scientific and technical information activities in the United States? To begin with, one has to consider what are called the economic and human engineering problems, for lack of better terms. Let me elucidate on these through the use of some illustrations.

First, there is the economic factor. Who is to pay for the revamping, upgrading, and operation of a U.S. scientific and technical information network of systems? Today, as in the past, large research, developmental, data-gathering, educational, and other projects are planned, funded, and implemented without serious consideration being given to the information requirements necessary to launch such endeavors or to the need for the orderly organization, evaluation, or distribution of the information products of such activities. An example is the International Geophysical Year (IGY). World Data Centers for gathering, organizing, and distributing information products were created, but far too late in the game: before these centers could gather the resulting data, the IGY was officially over. Many of these centers have now been curtailed to the point of ineffectiveness.

As another example of economic problems, the National Aeronautics and Space Administration (NASA) began to develop plans for the collection, dissemination, and use of information obtained in space after planning operations were well under way and information had become a nuisance. The technical information activities and the technology utilization program came too late to be effective.

An entirely different economic situation is where government agencies, scientific societies, and industrial, commercial, and educational organizations derive information products from primary publications and other sources and charge for the secondary products they produce, but yet pay no royalty or license fee to the primary producers. Only in some elements of the arts, humanities, and business are information products viewed as valuable resources for which large prices are paid.

It is my belief that information is an integral part of scientific and technical research, development, planning, and management. Adequate information resources should be part of the cost of such activities and should not be viewed as a separate or unrelated activity. Therefore, primary publication, information analysis, abstracting and indexing, data handling and publication, and libraries should be supported by a realistic percentage of the funds allocated to the research, development, planning, and management of a project. This should be done on an organizational basis, so that individual R&D program managers, administrators, or planners need not allocate funds piecemeal. Yet, one seldom finds such a condition. Information activities are usually supported on an ad hoc basis or are completely separate from the activity for which they are a service. Frequently, users not directly connected with the scientific or technical organization are required to pay a disproportionately large share of the cost.

SUGGESTIONS FOR FUTURE ACTION

I have had the urge to develop and present my own national plan for information activities in the United States—certainly this forum would be an appropriate occasion. But I have resisted this urge and instead will attempt to suggest some ideas and possibilities for action.

1. There needs to be increased, realistic cooperation among primary publishers, secondary services, and research libraries. Until the primary producers of scientific and technical information can develop common technical procedures and effective working relationships with secondary services and libraries, they cannot fulfill their role as effective disseminators of information.

The programs initiated by the American Chemical Society and the American Institute of Physics, whereby their primary publications are being coordinated with secondary services, are examples of necessary technical and marketing programs. The programs of the Department of Defense and NASA to issue a condensed version of a primary report with the full presentation available on request should be given serious consideration by other governmental and private organizations.

Both primary and secondary scientific and technical producers of information should work closely with research libraries and information centers in academic, industrial, and commercial organizations to see that libraries and information centers have the necessary information products in a form that enables them to serve their clientele with a minimum of effort. We can no longer afford the luxury of primary and secondary producers and library and information centers all having different technical specifications for identifying a primary source. Nor can we afford to have the material organized by numerous technical standards and formats. The *Heller Report* recommendations addressed these problems, albeit somewhat ineffectively.

2. A realistic system for determining both topical area and informational-type responsibilities among the myriad of scientific and technical information organizations in the United States must be developed.

The scientific and technical information activities in the United States will never gain the recognition they deserve nor develop the necessary services they need as long as the participants view this area as an arena of competition instead of a platform for hard-headed, realistic cooperation and coordination. Most participants will have to accept the fact that a laissez-faire attitude can no longer be afforded or tolerated.

Primary producers of information will have to organize so that their products can be issued under common technical standards. This means that small primary journals must develop stables or groupings that can produce at reasonable cost technically acceptable products for secondary services and library and information centers. The quality of the content can remain in the hands of the individual professional group, but individual biases in technical presentation and organization can be tolerated from neither the technical presentation nor the marketing aspects.

3. The abstracting and indexing services must develop a planned program to identify and adopt realistic technical standards and delineate topical areas of responsibility. Comprehensive coverage of the world scientific literature could continue to be the responsibility of the professionally oriented services such as chemistry, physics, mathematics, biology and medicine, and earth sciences, but only if these services developed compatible technical standards, realistic apportionment of topical areas, and

translation programs to allow for the combination of the intellectual organization of their products.

4. Project- or problem-oriented services such as university information centers and libraries or specialized commercial or government secondary services should be able to derive most of their raw material from the professional services at less cost than when each covers the primary sources.

5. The last two areas that need to be considered are the economic and organizational aspects of scientific and technical information services. It is strongly suggested that the costs of organizing primary scientific and technical information to the point that it can be readily distributed should be the financial responsibility of the organizations underwriting the research and development. Since federal and state governments and a few large industries and private universities underwrite most research and development in the United States, their organizations should be the prime sources of financial support. No realistic mechanism now exists for distributing this support because most primary scientific technical information is issued through scientific and technical societies, commercial information services, and a few government agencies and large industrial or commercial organizations. Page charges have been one means, but this technique has many faults, although it has served a useful purpose over the past 35 years.

As the distribution of primary results of research and development over the next quarter century changes from a heavy dependence on the printed page to electronic transmission and new types of display, copying, and storage, new support mechanisms must be devised. Also, the organization of the primary results of research and development will increasingly include the basic identification elements, as well as a concise summary of findings, and the focal point for initial distribution may well change from present journals and comprehensive data compilations.

Therefore, a challenge is issued to you, the members of the Association of Scientific Information Dissemination Centers (ASIDIC) and the Federation, to begin to rethink your role in the dissemination and use of scientific and technical information. Instead of being collectors, organizers, and distributors of scientific and technical information, you may very likely find yourselves more like the investment and insurance brokers of today. Your major responsibility may be to identify sources of scientific and technical information and to be the mechanism whereby that needed information is delivered to the user. You may not handle the corpus of the scientific data any more than the investment or insurance brokers handle stocks and bonds or insurance policies.

Finally, all these changes will require new organizational structures with a great increase in cooperative programs among the various participants and a great increase in federal and state government regulations, just as in the financial and communications fields. This will necessitate carefully planned joint programs and procedures among ASIDIC and Federation members, a well-planned federal support program, an intelligent and reasonable regulatory mechanism, and, last but not least, aggressive and intelligent participation in the development of international scientific and technical information programs and projects so that the resources of other countries will be readily available to the United States 25 years from now.

MARCH 8, 1972

The Canadian National Scientific and Technical Information System: A Progress Report

JACK E. BROWN, *National Research Council of Canada, Ottawa, Ontario, Canada*

I understand that in this series of Miles Conrad Memorial Lectures the speaker should emphasize a topic related to the field of abstracting and indexing. It was further indicated that, in my case, I should relate this topic to the ongoing evolution of a national scientific and technological information (STI) system in Canada. To meet these two requirements, I shall review the steps that led to the present policy of developing a decentralized national STI system and outline the elements of this system as it now exists. I also shall discuss in some detail our national Selective Dissemination of Information Service, CAN/SDI, which is an essential element of the national system and whose operation is, of course, based on abstracting and indexing services, most of which are produced in the United States.

Because of the spirit of nationalism that now pervades all aspects of Canadian life, I must state, probably unnecessarily, that in the development of a national STI system we are not attempting "to go it alone." To make such an attempt would be quite unrealistic and probably impossible, particularly when it is realized that Canada is primarily a consumer rather than a producer of information.

From both an economic and cultural point of view, Canada has benefited greatly by having a rich, powerful, and generous neighbor on its southern border. This proximity, however, has unfortunately tended to stifle and discourage innovative and imaginative thinking on the part of

Canadians. Our prime minister, Pierre Elliott Trudeau, graphically illustrated this predicament when he said our relationship was like sleeping with an elephant— when the elephant turns, the bedmate has no alternative than to turn in the same direction.

This stifling effect has been particularly evident in the information field. In the past, Canadian librarians and others have been too content to rely on the information resources and services so abundant in the United States and made so readily available by our neighbor. Let me give you an example of this state of affairs. Traditionally, Canadian publications have been well covered by abstracting and indexing services produced in the United States. These services have served us so well that Canada has no national abstracting services of any consequence. We have even failed to produce adequate keys to those parts of Canadian literature that are not included in international abstracting services. It is too late and quite pointless to reverse this procedure by producing, let us say, a "Canadian Chemical Abstracts" or a "Canadian Biological Abstracts." We can, however, help both ourselves and the international scientific community by taking aggressive action to ensure that relevant Canadian literature is fully covered by these existing services. If the information needs of the Canadian scientific and engineering communities are to be met, we also must produce indexes covering topics of specific interest to Canadians, strengthen our own information resources, and develop new techniques or adapt existing ones that will expedite the flow of information in Canada. This is the direction in which we are now hopefully headed.

Canadians are often accused of being too introspective and too concerned with detailed self-examinations. This is certainly exemplified in the field of science information, for during the past four years, Canada has carried out six major studies dealing solely or partly with the establishment of science information policies. These reports have been widely distributed and, therefore, I assume that some of their contents must be known to this audience. Thus, I need only draw to your attention those reports that have had the greatest impact on our current activities. The most extensive of these studies is Special Study No. 8, *Scientific and Technical Information in Canada*, published in 1969 by the Science Council of Canada (1969b). This and related studies were used by the Science Council in preparing the recommendations contained in its Report No. 6 (1969a), *A Policy for Scientific and Technical Information Dissemination*, released in September 1969 (the so-called *Katz Report*). A third report, *A Science Policy for Canada*, based on a two-year study by the Canada Senate's Special Committee on Science Policy (1970–1972), must also be mentioned, for, despite its primary concern with science policy, it has much to say about science information policy. Volume 2 of this study has just been published [1972], and, although not yet complete, its findings and recommendations have already created a furor among the scientific community.

We have even been examined by agencies outside Canada. For example, there is the Organization for Economic Cooperation and Development's *Review of Science Policy in Canada* (1969) and *Review of National Scientific and Technical Information Policy — Canada* (1971). If Canada does not develop within the next few years a truly effective system for disseminating scientific and technical information, it certainly will not be for a lack of studying the problem.

Needless to say, these studies, taken as a whole, have aroused tremendous interest in and an awareness of the vital role that scientific and technical information plays in the social and economic development of a nation. They agree on one point: immediate and vigorous action must be taken to ensure that all scientific and technical information now available in the public domain is fully exploited by scientists, engineers, industrialists, policymakers, and anyone else having a need for such information. These reports show less unanimity, however, when it comes to proposing how this goal might be achieved.

Despite this lack of unanimity, positive action has been taken, and the Canadian government, in keeping with the recommendations contained in the *Katz Report*, has assigned to the National Research Council of Canada (NRC) the responsibility for developing a national scientific and technical information system. When this responsibility was announced in January 1970, a major misconception occurred. It was assumed by many, both in Canada and abroad, that this concept of a national decentralized STI system that, as outlined by Katz, used information resources and services wherever they existed, was something quite new. Of course, this was not the case, for Canada has long had the foundations of a national STI system and, as far as I can determine, is the only country where such a system exists.

As early as 1924, Dr. H. M. Tory, first president of NRC, envisaged the NRC Library as a national resource center that would supplement the resources of other scientific libraries in Canada. Tory's plan was adopted, and the NRC Library's resources and services were developed in close cooperation with other scholarly libraries throughout Canada for the specific purpose of reinforcing local services. As a result of these and international cooperative measures, the NRC Library was soon performing the functions of a national science library and serving as the focal point of a national STI network. In 1966, through a revision of the NRC Act, this *de facto* position was formally recognized. Clearly, the changes brought about through this long series of government decisions and directives have been evolutionary, not revolutionary.

The network, as it now exists, is basically an informal and frequently inadequate system leaving much to be desired. It is these deficiencies we are now endeavoring to correct. But before speaking of plans for the future, and to provide a better appreciation of these plans, I shall outline the major elements of our present national STI system.

The National Science Library (NSL), a division of NRC, is not a library in the conventional sense of the word, but rather an information transferral agency. Its resources and services, as already mentioned, are developed in close cooperation with all major libraries in Canada and are designed to supplement and complement local information services. Tangible evidence of this cooperation is the *Union List of Scientific Serials in Canadian Libraries* (1971), a database that stores on magnetic tape, for rapid retrieval or printout, the titles and holdings of 48,000 scientific and technical journals received by 225 libraries in Canada. Each of these libraries has agreed to make the contents of these journals available by means of loans or photocopies. Since journals account for at least 80 percent of scientific and technical literature, Canadian scientists, through NSL or their local library, have access to the major portion of the world's scientific and technical literature. This form of cooperation for transferring information accounted for approximately 500,000 transactions in 1971, of which one-third were provided by NSL.

Since this is a decentralized system, seekers of information are encouraged to first use their local information resources, that is, their public, university, company, or provincial research council library. When these sources fail to provide an answer, NSL serves as a referral and backstopping agency. Through a combination of literature resources, human skills, and inventories of special subject resources throughout Canada, NSL is providing a wide variety of information services. These are described in detail in a brochure published by NSL, so I need mention only the most important ones.

1. A question and answer service is provided by a reference and research staff trained in scientific and technical subjects, having competency in foreign languages, and skilled in using the keys to the world's scientific and technical literature. This staff also is trained to carry out literature searches, compile bibliographies, and identify and locate obscure references and publications.

2. Loans and photocopies of material not readily available in other parts of Canada are available via NSL. These requests are now being processed at the rate of approximately 300–400 per day.

3. The Clearinghouse for Technical Reports and Government Publications issued by national and international agencies has been established. Publications are normally produced as microfiche copies and are received at the rate of 40,000 per year. NSL has appropriate equipment to provide

either copies of the microfiche or enlargements of each page on the microfiche.

4. Many directories, indexes, and other tools designed to facilitate the use of Canada's scientific and technical literature resources are published.

5. The Translations Index and Information Centre identifies and locates translations of foreign-language scientific and technical papers prepared in all parts of the world.

6. As I mentioned earlier, there exists a national Selective Dissemination of Information Service, the CAN/SDI Program.

The CAN/SDI Program is a computer-based current-awareness service that alerts individual scientists, engineers, and others to the existence of recently published papers in their specific fields of interest. Under the system, nine databases, containing bibliographic data on papers published in approximately 15,000 journals and covering all fields of science and technology, are processed weekly or biweekly and matched against individual interest profiles.

The system, which became operational on a national scale in April 1969 after three years of testing and experimentation, now provides service to 936 individuals working in universities, industry, and government. Regarding databases used, subscriptions number 1,565. Since each subscription is used by an average of three persons, this means we are providing personalized bibliographies to approximately 4,700 users in Canada. Carrying these calculations a bit further, CAN/SDI is disseminating 225,000 citations per month or 2.7 million citations per year. NSL endeavors to subscribe to all the journals covered by these databases and provides photocopies of cited papers not available through local sources.

It is estimated that presently more than 80 databases covering numerous subjects are commercially available. The tapes we are now using are Chemical Titles, Chemical Abstracts (CA) Condensates, INSPEC, Science Citation Index (SCI), Biological Abstracts Previews, Geological Reference File, Medical Literature Analysis and Retrieval System (MEDLARS), and Pollution Information Project (PIP).

The PIP database has been developed by NSL in cooperation with NRC's Biology Division and its Environmental Secretariat and with other federal departments concerned with pollution and environmental quality. It is an interactive online system with both current-awareness and retrospective searching capabilities. PIP, although still an experimental project, now includes 36,000 citations dating back to September 1968. Selection of citations is achieved by matching CA Condensates, SCI, and Biological Abstracts (BA) tapes against standard profiles covering broad disciplines such as actions related to pollution, standards and criteria, specific pollutants, and biological targets. Relevant documents not covered by existing databases are being incorporated into the system through manual methods.

I have mentioned the MEDLARS database as being an integral part of the CAN/SDI Program. There is no need to enlarge on this except to explain why the Canadian MEDLARS Centre forms a unit of NSL. In November 1966, the Canadian government directed NSL to establish a Health Sciences Resource Centre. This action came about following yet another survey (Simon [1964]), this one concerned with library support of medical education and research in Canada. The survey concluded that Canada did not require a national medical library but rather that existing bibliographic resources and information services should be coordinated and strengthened. A committee representing Canadian medical colleges, medical libraries, and the Medical Research Council further recommended that this Health Sciences Resource Centre should be established as a unit of NSL. A full account of the activities of this center can be found in a paper by its former head and now chief of STI services at NSL (Ember [1970]).

New databases are added to the CAN/SDI system in keeping with a recognized national need and the ability of the NSL staff to cope with an ever-increasing work load. Thus, by April of this year [1972], Computerized Engineering Index (COMPENDEX) tapes will be operational and will be followed by Metal Abstracts Index (METADEX) and the National Technical Information Service (NTIS) tapes. These additions recognize an increasing demand for an SDI service that gives greater emphasis to the fields of engineering and technology.

During the early stages of the development of CAN/SDI, it was found that normally the construction of effective interest profiles required direct contact between the user and someone familiar with the user's subject interest and trained in SDI techniques. Accordingly, CAN/SDI functions as both a centralized and decentralized system. The programming, systems design, reformatting, and processing of the magnetic tapes is centralized at NSL. On the other hand, the construction of interest profiles, user contact, and, in some cases, the distribution of the computer printout, is decentralized and carried out by 250 search editors trained by NSL and located in universities, provincial research councils, government departments, and industrial firms located throughout Canada. The bulk of this training is carried out in two-day seminars held at NSL in Ottawa. Training teams, however, do go into the field whenever groups of potential users are identified, as, for example, at industrial parks and large universities.

To assist them in utilizing CAN/SDI, users and search editors are provided with the *Profile Design Manual* (1972). This manual, now in its third edition, is continually being reworked and updated to incorporate descriptions of new databases and refinements in the system and to clarify instructions that have proved inadequate.

Finally, I'd like to say a word about costs of the CAN/SDI service. The price of subscriptions to the service is based primarily on the databases used and the computer time required to carry out a search. Thus, annual subscriptions range from $45.50 to $117.00 and average approximately $100.00. These rates enable NSL to recover all operating expenses except for research and development and the leasing of databases and the associated royalty payments.

I apologize for this perhaps undue emphasis on the activities of NSL. I have been trying to stress, however, that Canada has a system whereby any request for scientific and technical information or publications can be met, providing the need is made known and directed to NSL or to another library and/or information center. We have not yet discovered how to meet the requirements of those who do not make their needs known, but we are working on it. For example, CAN/SDI does, in some respects, anticipate and meet information needs. NRC's Technical Information Service (TIS), through its field officers, has also developed some rather effective ways of dealing with this problem.

One of the most discouraging and frustrating aspects of the information business arises from the popular belief that the term *information system* or *information network* implies a fully mechanized and computerized system wherein the world's total information on any given subject is stored in computers awaiting only the touch of a button for almost instantaneous retrieval, that requests for information are electronically transferred without human intervention to the most appropriate information center, and that retrieval is obtained through an interactive system via a miniature video screen located in each person's home or office. NSL has already used and tested the necessary electronic techniques that make it possible to retrieve bibliographic information from computer-generated databases and transmit this information, or copies of cited papers, to all points in Canada within minutes after a request is placed. The majority of information seekers do not require this type of service, however, and the use of such techniques will be feasible only when the benefits derived are in keeping with the charges the individual is willing to pay directly or indirectly (through government subsidization).

If Canada has all these national services, what more needs to be done? A great deal. In many cases, the dissemination of information is incomplete and slow; special subject skills and resources in various parts of Canada are either not known or are not being used to the maximum; and the total scientific and technical information requirements of Canadians are not being met effectively and efficiently. The ways and means of overcoming these constraints is the task that has been assigned to NRC.

To assist in the further development of the existing system, and in keeping with the cabinet directive, NRC has appointed an Advisory Board for

Scientific and Technological Information (ABSTI). The membership of the board consists of 20 leaders in the fields of science, industry, and education and represents the users, producers, and processors of information. As its name implies, ABSTI has the responsibility for formulating general policies, establishing priorities, and making recommendations regarding the implementation of these policies. Since the rapid retrieval and dissemination of information is dependent on the use of rather sophisticated and expensive techniques and equipment, many of the ABSTI plans are, of necessity, long term in nature. Action is now being taken in the following areas:

1. Improving existing STI services. For example, with the modest increase in funds and staff made available during the past year, NSL now provides a 36-hour response time to all requests for information, photocopies, and loans.
2. Publicizing the availability of existing services. It is evident that one of the major constraints to the flow of information is the fact that many potential users of STI are completely unfamiliar with the services available to them.
3. Providing training in the use of new information retrieval techniques, e.g., CAN/SDI and the use of online terminals.
4. More fully identifying and exploiting local and regional information resources.
5. Developing information analysis centers at points where specialized skills and information resources already exist.
6. Seeking, through testing, experimentation, and evaluation, ways and means of placing on a sound economic basis electronic techniques for processing information. This includes facsimile transmission devices, dedicated lines, online terminals, and computer/communication networks.

It must not be concluded from my remarks that the information policy now in effect in Canada has the unqualified support of all users of information services. It would actually be quite amazing if this were the case. Some people claim that an effective national STI system cannot be developed by a single agency, in our case NRC, that is responsible for both policy and services. Only time will prove or disprove the validity of this belief, but it should be noted that ABSTI, which represents the opinions of the nation as a whole and which is primarily responsible for advising on policy, will act as a deterrent to misguided action.

A closely related criticism is based on the belief that NSL, because of its origins and administrative ties with NRC, cannot devote its full attention to providing national services. Any deficiencies in service are all too often blamed on preferential treatment to NRC personnel. Accordingly, it is frequently argued that NSL should be separated from NRC, removed from Ottawa, and that information services should be separated from bibliographic resources.

In responding to these criticisms, it must be pointed out that no matter where NSL is located, people having direct access to it will inevitably receive speedier and more personal service than those who must use indirect means (mail, telephone, Telex, and so on) to make their needs known. Also, the provision of information services to NRC is the responsibility of divisional libraries, which are administered by NSL under contract to NRC.

Based on my experience at NSL, I am convinced that information services and the tools and resources on which these services are based must form an integrated unit. Furthermore, the close association of NSL with an organization such as NRC — where the information specialists have direct access to the combined knowledge of 2,500–3,000 scientists representing most fields of science and technology — engenders an unusually high quality of information service.

I cannot conclude this talk without saying a few words about the relationship of NSL and the National Library and their relative responsibilities for developing a national information system. The directive given by the Canadian government to NRC says, in effect, that NRC shall develop a national STI system under the general direction of the National Librarian. This clause is intended to ensure that a national system for STI, which is the responsibility of NRC, and a national system for information in the humanities, social sciences, and the arts, which is the responsibility of the National Library, are completely compatible and developed in parallel. It further recognizes that both systems must be governed by common policies and standards, which, in turn, must be the responsibility of one agency — in this case the National Library.

To further facilitate this essential liaison between the two national libraries, the National Librarian and the National Science Librarian are ex officio members of ABSTI. Even more important are the practical steps now being taken to integrate the information systems of the two national libraries. For example,

1. NSL is collaborating with the National Library in developing an SDI service covering the humanities and social sciences. This service, which beginning next month will use the MARC (Machine-Readable Cataloging) II and ERIC (Educational Resources Information Center) tapes, will operate as an extension of CAN/SDI, with the National Library taking responsibility for construction of interest profiles and other user contacts and NSL taking responsibility for processing these databases.

2. NSL expertise and its computer programs are being used to convert the National Library's manual files for the production of a union list of

serials in the humanities and social sciences that will be compatible with NSL's computerized Union List of Scientific Serials in Canadian Libraries.

3. The two national libraries have collaborated in submitting a brief to the Canadian government outlining the requirements for a major computer installation specifically designed for handling bibliographic data and dedicated to the needs of the two national libraries and other federal libraries in the Ottawa area.

Looking to the future, what are the chances of establishing a truly effective national STI network? Until recently, the prospects were rather bleak, what with austerity measures, staff shortages, and inadequate working quarters. But now that NRC has been given responsibility for STI and the necessary funds and staff are gradually being made available, the outlook is much brighter. NSL's space difficulties will soon be alleviated: last September [1971], construction was begun on an ultramodern building to house NSL. This structure, scheduled for completion in December 1973, will hold two million volumes and is designed to use the latest mechanized techniques for processing and disseminating information.

All these activities represent a crucial point in the development of a Canadian information policy. The speed and success with which the elements of this policy are implemented, however, will depend in large measure on the degree of imagination and energy with which ABSTI, NSL, and the National Library tackle their respective responsibilities.

REFERENCES

Canada. Senate. *A Science Policy for Canada*. Report of the Special Committee on Science Policy. Vol. 1: *A Critical Review: Past and Present*. Vol. 2: *Targets and Strategies for the Seventies*. Ottawa, Information Canada. 1970–1972.

CAN/SDI. *Profile Design Manual*. 3rd Edition. Ottawa, National Science Library, 1972.

Ember, G. "The Health Sciences Resource Centre: A New Information Service of the National Science Library of Canada." In: *Proceedings of the Third International Congress of Medical Librarianship*. Amsterdam, Excerpta Medica, 1970, pp. 383–389.

Organization for Economic Cooperation and Development. *Review of National Scientific and Technical Information Policy – Canada*. Paris, 1971.

_____. *Review of Science Policy in Canada*. Paris, 1969.

Science Council of Canada. *A Policy for Scientific and Technical Information Dissemination*. Report No. 6. Ottawa, Queen's Printer, September 1969a.

———. *Scientific and Technical Information in Canada.* Special Study No. 8. Ottawa, Queen's Printer, 1969b. Parts I and II.

Simon, B. V. *Library Support of Medical Education and Research in Canada.* Ottawa, Association of Canadian Medical Colleges, 1964.

Union List of Scientific Serials in Canadian Libraries. 4th Edition. Ottawa, National Research Council, National Science Library, 1971. 2 Vols. NRC No. 12135.

MARCH 7, 1973

Science Information Services in an Environment of Change

PHYLLIS V. PARKINS, *BioSciences Information Service, Philadelphia, Pennsylvania*

"Science Information Services in an Environment of Change" stands as a shining example of a title so broad that it was obviously chosen in an indecisive moment. To do it justice, one could undoubtedly fill at least a small book. It is my intention, however, to highlight only a few of the more significant environmental changes that have occurred over the past 15 years, to consider with you several of the alterations taking place in today's environment, and to question what we can do to deal with them effectively. Finally, let us try to gain perspective on certain changes in the making and consider resources we may have for managing such change.

In the late 1950s, science was still riding on the wave of popular opinion and support, which, in large part, derived from public recognition of the invaluable contributions scientific research had made to the military effort in World War II. There naturally followed a general willingness, even an eagerness, to promote science. This involved increased emphasis on the education and training of scientists, which, in turn, led to increased prestige and affluence for the established scientific training facilities in colleges, universities, and research institutes. All in all, the climate for science teaching and research appeared to be a sustained "fair and warmer." At about this same time, the purveyors of scientific and technical information began to feel pressure from the increased output of scientific research. The ever-continuing healthy growth of science and the consequent proliferation of scientific publications seemed assured.

Then came the launching of the first Soviet Sputnik, creating a worldwide shock wave, which, among other effects, created within our Federal Government, as well as in the scientific and engineering communities, an even greater awareness of the value of scientific and technological research and its published record — scientific and technical information. It became widely known that in the available scientific literature, clues had existed, which, had they been uncovered, would have at the very least reduced the surprise factor involved in that first Soviet space shot. Thus, renewed impetus was given to scientific and technological research, while the abstracting and indexing (A&I) services redoubled their efforts to provide accurate and timely coverage of the world's research literature.

In the late 1950s, computer technology was already available for application to problems of information handling. But only a few of the more affluent federal agencies, each largely independent of any other, could afford to pioneer in the development of mechanized information support for their respective missions. By 1958, the year in which NFAIS was founded, none of the present member services was mechanized to any remarkable extent. For many of them, the most sophisticated piece of data-processing equipment on their premises was a Flexowriter.

Virtually all the original member services were not only lacking electronic devices, but they were also under-housed and under-equipped. Many of the services were also seriously understaffed for the tasks at hand. Too many were actually subsidizing their user groups by pricing their services unrealistically low. Each of the A&I services had been working in virtual isolation: the staff of one service had little or no opportunity to meet their functional counterparts in other organizations. There was seldom, if ever, an opportunity to exchange common experience or to recognize common problems except, perhaps, at the highest level of management, where the lack of communication between the A&I services was first acknowledged to be a matter of serious concern.

Another situation, basically economic but with political overtones, concerned the existing A&I services. Although they realized the need for major expansion of coverage to keep pace with the extraordinary growth of the scientific literature, they were grossly underprepared to finance this expansion and to acquire and adapt for their purposes the new technological tools that would make growth possible. Abstracting and indexing services in the private sector were supported financially and guided in policy matters by scientists. There was scarcity of investment capital necessary for retooling. Their sponsors, the scientific societies, could not realistically bear the costs. It appeared that only subvention (some considered it "intervention") by the Federal Government could provide the sizable sums involved. But it was feared that this kind of funding would mean eventual federal control, with concomitant loss of control by the scientific community. (The apprehension was not at all allayed by occasional proposals, usually congressional in origin, for creating a centralized monolithic information system with federal funding, jurisdiction, and control.)

What was becoming painfully obvious to the Federal Government, as well as to the A&I services of this country, was the absence of a coherent national system for the transfer of scientific and technical information. There was the equally obvious and urgent need for voluntary cooperation among the services and for coordination of certain activities. It was recognized also that the functions of the different services were basically similar, that the fundamental problems of one (acquisition, editing, indexing, and management) were to one degree or another the problems of all, and that the work of seeking solutions to these problems could probably be approached jointly.

It was in this environment—a mixture of apprehension, a grudging but growing sense of inadequacy to meet the needs of scientists and the nation, and a recognition of the strength to meet problems that would come from concerted planning and action—that just 15 years ago a conference (held in Philadelphia at the Sheraton Hotel) agreed to form the National Federation of Science Abstracting and Indexing Services. A new era was launched with 14 charter member A&I services prepared to face the uncertain future together.

Science in February 1958 ("National Federation of Abstracting Services" [1958]) carried news of the infant Federation, including the following paragraph:

The objective of the newly formed federation is to improve the documentation (abstracting, indexing, and analyzing) of the scientific and technological literature of the world in such a manner as to make it readily available to all scientists and technologists: (i) by encouraging the development of abstracting and indexing for those specialized subject fields not at present covered by such services, and the further development of existing services; (ii) by seeking greater uniformity in such matters as journal citations and abbreviations, and transliteration of foreign language titles; (iii) by cooperation, education, research, and the pursuit of mutually useful enterprises, to strive for the best possible research information services for science and technology in the United States and abroad.

My apologies for riding roughshod over the Federation's early history and for now assuming that what has transpired between then and now is fairly well known. In any case, for those who are interested, a more detailed account of the first 15 years exists in the Federation "Position Paper" (National Federation of Abstracting and Indexing Services [1973]), which was prepared for presentation before The National Commission on Library and Information Science. Copies are available from the NFAIS Secretariat, 3401 Market St., Philadelphia, PA 19104.

Today, in the early 1970s, a quite different situation exists. Another era has begun or, perhaps to put it more accurately, has become recognized. Its origin was implicit early in the 1960s. One needs no great insight or depth of perception to recognize the deterioration in prestige that science and technology has suffered over the past several years. It should come as no surprise, for we were amply forewarned by sociologists of science that the exponential growth of science and scientists could not be sustained indefinitely without reaching ridiculous proportions in terms of its share of the total economy, its overall manpower requirements, and its competition with other important nonscientific concerns of every kind.

The downgraded position of science today did not develop overnight. Perhaps one of the first signs of its decline, at least in the United States, was the trend that became noticeable around a decade ago on our college and university campuses: a turning away from the sciences toward the humanities and social sciences. In choice of careers, we have seen many of our ablest students reject scientific endeavor in favor of law, political science, economics, or sociology. Of the various scientific disciplines that have attracted recruits, it is also significant that what we call the "soft" science of psychology ranked highest in students' choice of career.

Moreover, in recent months we have seen an anti-intellectual attitude surfacing even among the much younger student population. The secondary school graduate — it was recently documented by an able staff writer on one of our Philadelphia newspapers — seriously questions the wisdom of attending a four-year college or university. If he or she considers college at all, the two-year junior or community colleges are favored as being less expensive (expense is a critical factor to parents today who have unemployment and inflation to reckon with). Many young people are vocationally oriented, the reasoning goes, and perhaps two years are more than sufficient to allow for deciding on and preparing for a career that will satisfy the individual's lifetime goals and requirements. Among the students shunning further academic training are many who have reached the highest achievement levels in their high school programs of study.

The disenchantment with science and technology, not only among our young people but in the minds of the public and among many professions, is accompanied by a greatly elevated respect for "opinion" or "feeling" as opposed to "fact." Harvey Brooks (1971), in a recent *Science* article, questions whether science can survive. He points out that "the national investment in astrology is between ten and twenty times that in astronomy. Eastern religions are enjoying a great vogue, and everywhere there is rising preoccupation with the emotion, the sensual, the affective aspects of human experience at the expense of the cognitive, systematic, and analytical aspects. Emotion-centered personality types are emerging as heroes to be emulated, again especially among the younger generation." Strange cults, mystics, and psychic experiences have strong appeal for the young and for some of the not-so-young. It is conceivable that a well-known guru could attract a larger audience than a Nobel prize winner.

Brooks comments further on this trend: "It is possible that all this represents simply a pendulum's swing away from what may have been an overemphasis on the cognitive aspects of human personality, and an undue status for personalities which excelled in cognitive, verbal, and analytical skills. Some such reaction is probably healthy and was overdue. But to the extent that it implies that feeling and sympathy can substitute for reason and evidence in the management of human affairs, it is retrogressive and threatening."

As though we needed further evidence of the decline in favor of science within the Federal Government, the president has now severed any direct personal contact with science or communication with scientists by failing to appoint a new science advisor and by abolishing the President's Science Advisory Committee and the Office of Science and Technology (OST). Consequently, OST's Committee on Scientific and Technical Information (COSATI) was also a victim. All these bodies had provided the president, at least nominally, direct access to the thinking and the position of the country's scientists. With the functions of OST transferred to the director of the National Science Foundation (who also carries the additional post of science advisor), scientists no longer speak over a direct line to the president. *Business News* reports details of the new advisory system under the title, "It's Austerity Time for BASIC Science" (1973) and the subtitle, "The academicians are out and so is the emphasis on backing basic research." Instead, the ideas of Dr. Horton Guyford Stever, Director of the National Science Foundation (1972-1976), must pass to the president filtered through the Office of Management and Budget. Research budgets have been drastically reduced, and training grants have been virtually eliminated. The universities are suffering from withdrawal symptoms because their funds for support of staff and facilities have been severely cut. Library budgets are being slashed. All these events ultimately impact on the budgets of information services, for our users—certainly in biology—are predominantly academically oriented.

Let's look briefly at the reasons for the decline of science, especially basic science, in political and in academic circles, as well as in the minds of the public who, after all, must pay the bills for science. What are the explanations most frequently advanced?

1. *Lack of communications.* We have failed to explain to the layman the meaning and value of basic scientific research. In contrast, the case of goal-oriented research is ably presented, especially that which is geared

toward socially acceptable ends, such as the cure of societal or medical ills.

2. *Changing Social Values*. Science is often confused with technology in the minds of the public. A certain mistrust and fear of technology exists among the citizenry. We have used technology's products to destroy humanity. We suffer from a superabundance of nondegradable consumer goods that, discarded, fill our lands with rubbish. Our technology has pointed us toward eventual exhaustion of our fossil fuels, the resulting end products polluting our limited environment.

Changes on every front during the past two decades have brought us to the present situation — one which changes with the passing hours. On the economic front, the information services face, at best, uncertainty. Institutional subscribers are hard pressed for funds: university science continues to attract fewer students, undergraduate and graduate. Research has declined in volume. Basic research lacks the support it once had; problem-oriented research is favored. Industrial research and development appear to be in better shape, except (temporarily perhaps) in a few sectors related primarily to defense. The chief source of support for innovation among the NFAIS member services has been the National Science Foundation's Office of Science Information Service (OSIS), but drastic cuts in OSIS's budget have recently been announced. Secondary services face severe shortages — a critical one is paper. Inflation appears to be in full swing; increased costs of electronic equipment, materials, postage, and especially personnel are evident. Indeed, the economic picture is less than bright.

On the technological front, heightened opportunities for new approaches and media abound. Technological developments and applications in the last two decades have brought revolutionary changes in the way information services operate and have enormously broadened their choice of product ideas and opportunities. More powerful computers, much larger memory stores, terminals for direct access to computer stores, and sophisticated programs are all available. Photocopy devices are being improved. Cable television is coming of age. We have only begun to use communication satellites and video cassettes for display and recording. Time-sharing is becoming available on such a scale as to make it uneconomical for some organizations to maintain their own central processing units. Microform will undoubtedly increase in use as readers are perfected and production volume brings its price within reach of individuals. Also, optical scanning will soon prove an efficient cost-effective input to the computer. Which devices or combination of devices any given service uses is becoming a difficult choice, requiring extensive study and experimentation.

On the scientific front, what are the current factors having important implications for science information services? One aspect of the increased support for targeted research, as opposed to basic research, is the interdisciplinary character of the problems being investigated. Today, very few research projects fall within the boundaries of a single discipline. This emphasizes the need for effective coordination of output of information services in two or more disciplines.

Specialization in research has become a necessity, since more and more the necessary depth of knowledge can be acquired and pursued only in a relatively minute field. In one form or another, then, the information services must find ways to sift their data stores and respond to the individual researcher who needs access to the relatively few documents that closely match his specialty. This means developing a storage and retrieval system that will deliver small, highly specific packages at prices the individual can afford. The ultimate goal of each service must be to develop an online search and display system that permits the scientist-user ready access to the store at all times. He must be able to browse, choose the information he needs, and instantly copy what he wants and retain items for his personal information files. His own files could be made searchable in an online mode.

We must also be concerned with the relative decline in the influence of the scientific subculture among other subcultures. Even though NFAIS now embraces information services outside the realm of science, the majority of NFAIS member services are directly affected by the scientific environment. If the science information services survive the next decade reasonably well, it is my belief that NFAIS must not only remain keenly aware of and deeply concerned about changes on the scientific front, but must learn how to have an impact on events.

Politically, there is not only a national movement, but also a strong international movement, toward coordination of information services. Call it what you will, "networking," by one definition or another, in some form or another, must eventually come into being on a worldwide scale. It has, in fact, already begun. Whatever we as individual services (or as NFAIS) put into our long-range planning hoppers, we should keep this in mind. No longer can we think in provincial terms of our own small segments (disciplines) of the body of knowledge. I include here all new knowledge—the so-called nonscientific, as well as the scientific. We must be prepared if our services are to participate in a global information system.

Finally, for the user, perhaps the most critical factors we must take into account are the psychological. In seeking information through our services, users are often faced with abandoning old attitudes and establishing new ones. For instance, the familiar pages of an index, when machine produced, can appear strangely complex. Many of us have built mental barriers against new formats and new media; microfilm image is no substitute for the journal or book with leaves that we are accustomed to handling and to turning as we mark progress in reading. An online display has an ephemeral quality that may disturb some individuals. On the plus side, however, if our user is something of a gadgeteer or a seeker of novelty, he may be eager to experiment with new methods of approach and equipment. So we find diversity among the scientists we aim to serve. But, in general, human attitudes and habits are not easily changed. Thus, the incentive to change must be very great, and the rewards for doing so must be extremely attractive. (Many of you who have been inveterate smokers and have finally kicked the habit may testify to the difficulties involved. Furthermore, vigilance is a keyword, for the old habit patterns keep demanding to be reinstated.) This means, then, that innovation in information services must always take into account the degree of adaptability demanded of the user.

Another psychological problem associated with innovation, more vital to resolve than those that impinge on the user, concerns our own attitudes and those of our staffs. Deep-seated or drastic changes in an organization's overall system make demands on every person involved in producing information services. At every level, from the lowest to the highest, the attitude and willingness of the people involved to adapt to new situations can either slow to a halt or greatly accelerate the acceptance of new equipment and methods, new routines, and new activities demanded by the new system. Managing change of almost any kind involving people places a premium on understanding the difficulties involved and in carefully preparing the way for innovation.

It appears that our separate information services, as well as our umbrella organizations, have a task of enormous proportions to perform. I believe we must launch a massive educational campaign and wage it on a broad front. It is already late. We may need first to reeducate ourselves. We must look for opportunities within our own services to ease the problems of change. Our greatest effort needs to be focused on the user, actual and potential. We are making some progress as individual services and as umbrella organizations, but the effort is feeble when compared to the need. Our services are producing invaluable teaching tools that far too many of the college professors in our disciplines do not yet know exist. The same may be said for investigators engaged in industrial, academic, and federal research. We must find new approaches to reaching the user, for many of the traditional avenues we have followed have led us nowhere.

As individuals involved in the rapidly changing communications field and as contributing members of organizations that are working for the overall interest of our services, we must ask ourselves several hard questions. Are we ourselves comfortable with change, or are we too struggling with outworn patterns of thinking, hampered by obsolescent attitudes or unrealistic aspirations? Can we look to the future without flinching and take steps to meet it without bias, but with intelligence and enthusiasm? Without a doubt, we also must convince the federal sources of support that scientific information makes a vital contribution to the overall welfare of our country and to the world at large. We witness with some envy the current success of our counterparts in several other countries (particularly the Soviet Union, Sweden, and Japan; West Germany has also sharply stepped up support for scientific information in recent months) in gaining for scientific information the priority in support and recognition that it merits. We in the United States, with federal assistance chiefly from OSIS, have, over the past decade, become world leaders in the development of modern information systems. This leadership in the information field has paid off in terms of scientific and technological achievement in our own country and abroad, a fact that has not been lost on our colleagues in other countries. In this country, however, we seem to have forgotten, temporarily at least, that the research cycle starts and ends with information. It is the proper application of that information which stimulates the next phase of research. To quote Harvey Brooks (1971) once more, "A culture which accepts the primacy of the scientific method as a means of knowing, and provides political, economic, and psychological support for basic scientific activity, will also in the long run be prepared to accept and apply the knowledge gained. Conversely a society that fails to apply what it knows, will ultimately not want to know, and will repudiate the generation of knowledge, on the ostrich theory that what it doesn't know won't hurt it."

Inside the far-flung borders vaguely delimited by the title of this address, I realize I have ranged far and wide—possibly too far and wide. But this rapid and not overly organized flight into the past, over the present, and to a limited extent into the future has yielded, at least for me, clues as to where our science information services can allocate most profitably their human resources—creativity, wisdom, and experience—to make the best use of our advanced technological know-how and equipment. During the remainder of this decade and into the 1980s, we need to make new and concerted attacks on two fronts, both of which are vital to progress and perhaps to survival:

1. The information services must plan increased cooperation among their organizations, not merely a hit-or-miss, done-for-show variety, but formalized, systematized cooperation leading to the coordination of activities wherever this can be shown to result in more effective use of resources for the benefit of the participants and for the user community.

2. The information services must rediscover "total marketing" and how

this concept can be applied to serve their interests now and in the future. Here is an area in which cooperation can be extremely rewarding. For instance, do you think we have really begun to present our organizations, our products, and our services to the world of science, education, and government in an understandable and rational way? Are we planning or executing any joint studies of the community we want to reach? NFAIS has a marketing committee. What concerns that committee? What is its charge? What are its concerns?

It seems unfair to end this talk on a question, but it is not inappropriate. In considering uncertainty and change, there is no convenient place to stop. Let me conclude with a few words from a recent issue of the *Wall Street Journal*. E. Bradley Jones, Vice President of Republic Steel, in addressing a panel on "Marketing in the Not-So-Distant Future: Some Predictions" at a meeting of the Conference Board, said,

Ten years from now you will have hundreds of new competitors who do not even speak the same language you speak. It is even possible that in some future year the man who runs your company might not be an American citizen.

I also believe you will see companies in different industries from yours invading your markets with products altogether different from anything you ever dreamed of.

And as technology rushes onward, you will see many of the new products you develop in the years ahead becoming obsolescent before you are able to get them on the market.

REFERENCES

Brooks, H. "Can Science Survive the Modern Age?" *Science, 1974* (4004):21–30, October 1, 1971.

"It's Austerity Time for BASIC Science." *Business News*, February 3, 1973.

National Federation of Abstracting and Indexing Services. *National Federation of Abstracting and Indexing Services, History and Issues 1958–73.* Philadelphia, 1973.

"National Federation of Abstracting Services." *Science, 127*(3295):393, February 21, 1958.

ADDITIONAL READINGS

Bevan, W. "Science in the Universities in the Decade Ahead." *American Scientist,* 59(6):680–685, November–December 1971.

Boulding, K. "The Diminishing Returns of Science." *New Scientist and Science Journal*, 49(744):682–684, March 25, 1971.

Bush, V. "As We May Think." *Atlantic Monthly*, 176(1):101–108, July 1945.

Carroll, J. D. "Participatory Technology." *Science*, 171(3972): 647–653, February 1971.

Committee on Scientific and Technical Information. "Progress in Scientific and Technical Communications." *COSATI Annual Report 1971*. Springfield, Va., National Technical Information Service, 1972. PB 212-500.

Kidd, C. V. "Shifts in Doctorate Output: History and Outlook." *Science*, 179(4073): 538–543, February 1973.

Martin, D. "The Plight of the Academic Presses." *Change*, 5(2):44–49, March 1973.

Menard, H. W. "Science: Growth & Change." Cambridge, Mass., Harvard University Press, 1971.

National Academy of Sciences. *Libraries and Information Technology*. Washington, D.C., 1972.

National Science Board. *Science Indicators 1972*. Washington, D.C., U.S. Government Printing Office, 1973.

Pitzer, S. "Science and Society: Some Policy Changes Are Needed." *Science*, 172(3980):223–226, April 1971.

Somerville, F. "Abstract Journal Concept Being Examined." *Chemical & Engineering News*, 50(24):16–17, June 12, 1972.

Turoff, M. "Human Communication Via Data Networks." *Computer Decisions*, 5(1):25–29, January 1973.

Weizenbaum, J. "On the Impact of the Computer on Society." *Science*, 176(4035):609–614, May 1972.

MARCH 12, 1974

USSR/USA Scientific and Technical Information in Perspective

DALE B. BAKER, *Chemical Abstracts Service, Columbus, Ohio*

There is no other field of endeavor where the "payoff" is greater than the use of information by scientists and engineers.
—N. B. Arutiunov

The honor bestowed on me by this opportunity to present the Miles Conrad Memorial Lecture is deeply and humbly appreciated. I admired and respected Miles Conrad and indeed learned much from him through our many years of association and working relationships in abstracting and indexing activities. Miles was not only an outstanding scholar and fine gentleman, but he was also, in my judgment, one of the greatest leaders in our field. His dreams and concepts for the Federation, even before Sputnik, led to the founding of the National Federation of Science Abstracting and Indexing Services (now NFAIS), and that is precisely why we are here today and what this conference on "Information as an International Resource" is all about.

Soon after the "founding" meeting of the Federation on January 31, 1958, many articles appeared in the news media, as well as in the scientific journals, about the rapid advances in Soviet science. Some of these advances were attributed to the establishment of the All-Union Institute of Scientific and Technical Information (VINITI) in Moscow. VINITI was then and still is the largest single secondary information organization in the world. Because of the glowing reports of VINITI by visitors returning from Moscow during that period, the Federation decided to send a delegation of experts to visit the information organizations in the Soviet Union, particularly VINITI, to study the following points:

1. The quality of VINITI's work
2. The effect of centralization on its rapid growth
3. The status of mechanization of its information services
4. The efficiency of its operations

Miles Conrad, then NFAIS President, was leader of the five-man delegation that visited Moscow from October 20 through November 5, 1959. John Green, Mordecai Hoseh, Raymond A. Jensen, and I were the other members of that team. A report entitled *Some Counterparts in Perspective* was published by the Federation in 1960 as a result of those visits (Baker et al. [1960]).

As many of you know, there was an exchange of visits between Soviet and American information specialists in 1973 under the auspices of the U.S./USSR Agreement on Cooperation in Fields of Science and Technology. The eight-member U.S. delegation attended a symposium on scientific and technical information in Moscow on June 18 and 19 and then visited more than 20 leading information institutions in the Soviet Union. A report entitled "The USSR Scientific and Technical Information System: A U.S. View" was published by the National Science Foundation (NSF) in October 1973 (1973a). Subsequently, a 12-member Soviet team visited the United States in October, when a symposium was held in Washington, D.C. This was followed by Soviet visits to more than 20 U.S. institutions. The signing of a formal protocol, listing three areas of further cooperation, resulted from the 1973 exchange of visits. No report has appeared to date, either in the Soviet Union or the United States, as a result of the October discussions and agreements, but three U.S. task groups of experts are in the process of appointment for continuation of these exchanges in 1974.

So it is with this background that I wish to speak to you today on "USSR/U.S. Scientific and Technical Information in Perspective," just 15 years after the first NFSAIS visit to Moscow in 1959 and only 6 months after the Russian visit here. For the record, I also visited VINITI in 1963 and 1967, so I had a chance to observe, firsthand, developments in their operations in the intervening years.

First, I will talk about the status of the Soviet scientific/technical information system at the end of 1973, identifying the progress made in the past 15 years and highlighting some USSR plans for the future. Then, I will comment briefly on the U.S. system, followed by a discussion of some of the similarities and differences between the Soviet and American systems. I will end with some conclusions.

I take full responsibility for the ideas and statements contained in this paper (except those identified as quotations of others). These are one man's views and opinions and should be taken as such. It should also be clear that no matter how many sites are visited or how many questions a visitor asks, the limitations of time and language make it impossible to learn everything—to fully describe the *actual* processing steps and the status of *actual* procedures of a given operation. What is said to be done at a given time is often experimental or in transition toward what is planned or hoped. Thus, there can be an error in any evaluation.

STATUS OF THE USSR SCIENTIFIC/TECHNICAL INFORMATION SYSTEM

For more than two decades, the Soviet system for communicating scientific and technical information has been the largest, most highly controlled national system in the world. The Soviet system serves more users — scientists, engineers, technicians, administrators, and the public — than any other nation's system, first because there are more scientists and engineers in the USSR (National Science Foundation [1973]), and second because the system is geared to provide technical information to all Soviet citizens.

The Soviets are stressing extensive use of the popular news media (television, radio, and newspapers), films, and exhibits to announce and promote new science and technology. They call this "propaganda." But, according to Eng. Nikolai B. Arutiunov, "propaganda has a different interpretation in the USSR than in the U.S.; ours [the Soviet's] has a positive connotation or is simply to bring information home to the workers." We were told that there were 33,000 information agencies and 130,000–150,000 information workers presently in the Soviet Union. The Soviets readily and openly discuss the problems and the inadequacies of their information systems.

The concern of the Council of Ministers of the USSR with the provision of information to Soviet scientists and engineers has been reflected in a series of decrees issued from the 1950s to 1971, in increased allocations of resources for information, and in the council's endorsement of the programs developed by its State Committee for Science and Technology in collaboration with the Academy of Sciences and the branch ministries, such as agriculture, health, education, and defense.

The Information Directorate of the State Committee coordinates all Soviet information processing and disseminating activities by providing centralized policies, planning, and control. Arutiunov has been the dynamic director of this committee since the early 1960s. The State Committee has been dedicated to the development and operation of a Soviet national information system, embracing a multiplicity of specialized information networks servicing all Soviet science and industry. The State Committee approves all budgets; monitors expenditures and results; provides capital for building programs; approves establishment of all new journals and services and sets their prices; and even exercises control of all acquisitions of foreign journals, books, and references used in the USSR.

Time does not permit full description of the Soviet information system; this can be found in some detail in the Soviet literature, as well as in the October 1973 NSF report mentioned earlier. Suffice it to say, there are nine large Moscow-based All-Union institutes and agencies that provide centralized resources in support of the national system. There are 82 branch, or industrial, information networks, 15 information institutes serving the Union Republics, and 72 territorial "interbranch" institutes. In addition, there are said to be 10,000 departments of scientific/technical information in research institutes and enterprises and 23,000 scientific and technical libraries.

Rather than continue to recite statistics, I want to focus on the progress made by the Soviets since 1959 and then try to evaluate their plans for the future, especially from the point of view of the accessing or secondary services.

It must be remembered that in 1959, the large VINITI activities had been in operation for just seven years and were in an early state of development as well as rapid growth. The NFSAIS team in 1959 felt the work of VINITI to be on a par with work in the United States from the standpoints of quality and timeliness of the abstracts. But, the indexes of the *Referativnyi Zhurnal* series were very late in appearance, had a low density of entries per abstract, or were even nonexistent for some of the series. Research on mechanization at VINITI was just getting under way in 1959, and mechanization had no impact on operations. One experiment that received a great deal of publicity involved recording data on a card stock containing metallized spots acting as condensers. The efficiency of the VINITI operations at the time was considered to be less than average, based on production data. Although centralization seemed to demonstrate advantages in administration, acquisition, bibliographic control, and printing, the editorial offices of the various *Referat. Zhurnal* series enjoyed autonomy much the same as the decentralized secondary services in America. Different abstracts were being prepared for the different abstract publications. The inefficiencies in the vast amount of paperwork in VINITI's centralized operations were at the time obvious to the Soviets as well as to us.

VINITI has matured and made considerable progress in the past 15 years under the continuous leadership of its director, Professor Aleksandr I. Mikhailov. It has developed into one of the leading institutions of the world in abstracting and indexing work. Abundant credit should be given to Professor Mikhailov, who has achieved recognition and support for VINITI programs and operations not only from the scientific community through the USSR Academy of Science, but also—and perhaps more important—from the governmental bureaucracies through the State

Committee for Science and Technology. Eng. Arutiunov complements Professor Mikhailov and provides the political, business, and financial support for VINITI's activities. VINITI is now recognized as *the* leading USSR institution in the scientific and technical information system and has been cast in a key role for future developments.

Around mid-1973, mechanization at VINITI was well under way, Italian Optima paper-tape typewriters and Duramach units were being used for input, minicomputers were being used for processing support, four Minsk computers were working in parallel, and the Germal Hell Digeset photocomposers were used for output. Copyflow, Rank-Xerox, and Japanese microfilming equipment were also being used for duplication purposes. In June 1973, only one *Referat. Zhurnal*, the *Automation, Telemechanics, and Computer Technology Series*, was being produced by computer, but most of the indexes were computer produced. A quantum jump is expected this year (1974), when a new Ryad series computer and new model Digeset photocomposer are to be installed.

VINITI has increased its efficiency considerably. Publication of abstracts in *Referat. Zhurnal* is up from approximately 500,000 in 1959 to a little more than one million in 1973. Staff in the main offices of VINITI has increased 15 percent, from 2,200 to 2,560; overall VINITI staff totals 4,540, which includes 1,700 workers engaged in an off-site printing and publishing plant. VINITI now uses 24,000 abstractors, which is a 9-percent increase over the 22,000 used in 1959. Most important, greater efficiency has resulted in more timely publication of abstracts, now said to average about four months from the date of receipt of the document. There are also notable increases in timeliness and quality of indexes to the *Referat. Zhurnal* series. VINITI's budget appears to have tripled in these 15 years—from 5 million to 15 million rubles—but this may be due more to accounting changes, since the Soviet economy is said to be stable, with little inflation from year to year. Research and Development (R&D) at VINITI has changed dramatically in the past five years; all the former emphasis on hardware R&D has been dropped, and all efforts are now being devoted to software and systems development. VINITI's Vice Director of Research, Dr. A. I. Chernyi, claims VINITI's "main problems are not technical but intellectual." Distribution of the *Referat. Zhurnal* series has been increased to 400,000 editions or subscriptions (15 percent are shipped outside the Soviet Union). The 70 Express Information series have a total distribution of 140,000; distribution in the natural sciences is low, whereas in the applied sciences, it is high. VINITI is in the final stages of constructing a new, modern office building at a cost of 14 million rubles, which will nearly double its space for its growing operations. So much for the present status of VINITI; it is healthy and growing, and it is being strongly supported.

Probably the most significant factor regarding the future of abstracting and indexing in the USSR is VINITI's plans for a major, new automated Integrated Information System, named ASSISTENT, which in English means Automated Reference Information System for Science and Technology. One design criterion for ASSISTENT is that it must have a capacity for processing up to 2.5–3.0 million items a year, or about threefold what VINITI is now covering. According to Eng. Arutiunov, the system is to be implemented "in the next two or three years." In this first stage, all the bibliographic information involved in compiling VINITI's database will be converted to machine-readable form and will serve as the base for multiple services to be provided directly by VINITI and by all the many information institutes and agencies in the USSR and CMEA (Council for Mutual Economic Assistance) countries using VINITI's services. VINITI's abstract journals will be continued for the major fields of science, while, according to Chernyi (1972), "new, specialized problem-oriented abstract journals and services will be provided in magnetic tape and/or microforms." This system will also be capable of supporting a retrospective search for documents and patents. Requests for hard copies of the references retrieved will be met by VINITI or the State Library for Science and Technology in microcopies, which, in turn, will be automatically retrieved.

Chernyi states that, "ASSISTENT would be compatible and on a par with similar automated information systems in Western Europe, U.S. and Japan." One can only be impressed by the magnitude of the commitment that the State Committee for Science and Technology and the Soviet Academy of Sciences have made to ASSISTENT.

Another important factor affecting the future of abstracting and indexing (A&I) in the USSR is the establishment in 1972 at VINITI of a national depository system for handling unpublished manuscripts. In this connection, VINITI publishes a separate abstract publication, the *Catalog of Deposited Manuscripts*, as an alerting or current-awareness service for accessing the depository. The Soviets view primary publications as the weakest link in the present information chain and are taking steps now to change their system for the future. I understand that the British Library Lending Division and the Library of the Technical University in Hannover, Germany have become depositories for this film, but there are no U.S. depositories to our knowledge to date.

STATUS OF THE SCIENTIFIC AND TECHNICAL INFORMATION SYSTEM IN THE UNITED STATES

To aid in comparing the Soviet system with the U.S. system for handling scientific and technical information, especially in the field of abstracting and indexing, I would like to comment briefly on the U.S. system.

More than a dozen major studies and reports have appeared on the U.S. information system since the 1958 Baker Committee report for the U.S. Office of Science and Technology (Baker [1958]). The Weinberg report on *Science, Government and Information* in 1963 is still the most frequently quoted of these reports (President's Science Advisory Committee [1963]). The System Development Corporation's 1965 study on abstracting and indexing was certainly the most comprehensive of the U.S. field so far. The SATCOM Report of the National Academy of Sciences in 1969 was the latest and perhaps most comprehensive examination on the overall U.S. information system. The National Academy of Sciences report in 1972, *Libraries and Information Technology – A National System Challenge*, is the latest on the applications of computers to libraries and information systems in the United States.

First, it is apparent that we do not have in the United States a formal, fully coordinated information system for science and technology. In fact, the SATCOM report termed the U.S. information system a "pluralistic and decentralized scientific and technical communication complex." The information activities of the federal agencies are not coordinated to any degree, in spite of past federal legislation designed to promote such coordination, nor are the nongovernmental information activities significantly coordinated. Meaningful cooperation among information activities in the past has been the exception rather than the rule. There are organizations, however, such as NFAIS, the Association of Research Libraries (ARL), the Information Industry Association (IIA), the American Society for Information Science (ASIS), and the Association of Scientific Information Dissemination Centers (ASIDIC), which have recently been attempting to stimulate cooperation and to play a coordinating role.

In spite of numerous recommendations over the years, it is apparent that we have not established any national plans, policies, or priorities for information systems or information systems development in the United States. The Office of Science Information Service (OSIS) of NSF has, since 1952, played a major role in support of nonfederal information systems planning, research, and development. Also in recent years, OSIS has taken on additional leadership responsibilities in effecting cooperation and coordination among goverment services, as well as in developing adequate relationships between federal and nonfederal scientific information activities.

I like to look at the information-transfer chain in the United States as being classified into three main functions or organizational components: primary publications, secondary services, and libraries and information centers. The scientific/technical publishers in the United States, both of primary and secondary services, have traditionally been independent and controlled only in the competitive sense in the marketplace of supplying information to users in the most efficient and economical manner possible. It is interesting to note here that, together, the 14 original Federation member services have increased coverage of original documents from 540,000 in 1959 to 1.25 million in 1973, a 127-percent increase.

Libraries and information centers have also traditionally been independent and uncoordinated, although cooperative programs of interlibrary loan have long been established. In more recent years, however, there have been distinct trends among the libraries and information centers in sharing resources and amalgamating into consortium types of network operations. Examples include the State University of New York (SUNY), the Ohio College Library Association, Associated Libraries in Chicago, and the library systems of California.

Finally, governmental expenditures in the United States in support of both federal and public information systems for the past five years have plateaued or even declined, which, in terms of depreciated dollars, has resulted in serious reductions in public support for primary and secondary information systems development or for dissemination by library and information centers.

EVALUATIONS: SIMILARITIES AND DIFFERENCES

Arutiunov (1973) has written, "There are many fundamental differences in regard to the conditions under which information systems operate in capitalist and in socialist countries. They arise in the main from the fact that in capitalist countries access to scientific and technical information is determined on a commercial basis whereas in socialist countries access to such information is open to all." He made that statement when addressing the issue of requirements to be met by national scientific and technical information systems.

Clearly, we could all agree that there are fundamental differences in the conditions under which the information systems in the USSR and United States operate, and certainly "who pays" affects distribution and dissemination. But it is my position that published information is open to all as much in the capitalist countries as in the socialist countries and that the "commercialization" aspects in the United States have more strengths than weaknesses. Information of potential value is pursued, analyzed, packaged, and disseminated more vigorously in the United States than in the USSR. Arutiunov knows full well that there is a vast store of scientific/technical information of a proprietary nature in the industrial segment of the United States, whereas theoretically there cannot be any of a proprietary nature in the Soviet state. (The Soviets, of course, have a vast store and system of classified or security information, much the same as the United States.) Furthermore, there is much greater emphasis on and output of the patent system in the United States than in the USSR, but patents are growing and taking on new meaning as the Soviets increase their world trade. For example, Soviet patents in the field of chemistry in 1973 comprised 5 percent of the world total versus 20 percent for the United States.

I wish also to compare the Smithsonian Science Information Exchange (SSIE) program and the National Technical Information Service (NTIS) with the All-Union Scientific and Technical Information Center in Moscow. All ongoing research projects in the USSR are required by law to be registered, and the interim, or "unpublished," reports are disseminated and made available to all. Here, the SSIE program is purely voluntary, but the Soviet program is compulsory. The other major factor at work in the USSR, which is a fundamental difference from the United States, is the strong centralized planning, design, management, and control of the Soviet system compared with the uncoordinated, pluralistic approach in the United States. Along with the centralized planning and management of the Soviet information system, that government is fully committed to the needed financial and political support at all levels for the completion of a national system. It is my position that greatly increased financial and political support is highly desirable for the United States but that centralized management and control are not. The centrally controlled Soviet system is neither more comprehensive nor more efficient than the U.S. system. Strong controls place unnecessary limiting conditions on the Soviet system, whereas the competitive nature in the United States hastens progress and increases effectiveness.

In spite of these major differences, the development of information systems—input, processing, output, and dissemination—seems to be quite similar in both countries. Conceptually, the USSR is on about the same level as the United States, but the Soviets are just now entering into major phases of implementation of large-scale automated information systems, which is the most difficult aspect of development.

In the area of primary scientific and technical information, the Soviets tend to emphasize, according to Arutiunov, that "all available information must find its way into the system and must be transmitted." Undoubtedly, this is one reason why the primary literature of the Soviet Union has been growing at a more rapid rate than that of the United States. But, on the other hand, this is most likely one reason for what Garfield (1973) sees as the "low quality of so many papers appearing in the leading Soviet journals." In the United States and western world, it is clear that we have more restrictive policies of refereeing and reviewing for primary papers.

Although the collection and analysis functions of the secondary services for input, as well as for processing and output, appear to be very similar in both countries, there are significant differences in qualitative measures, such as depth of indexing, techniques and capabilities in processing, and forms and format of output. These are still quite limited in the USSR. But Professor Mikhailov, in his 1973 report entitled "Status of the Systems of Scientific Information," presented to the Presidium of the USSR Academy of Sciences, points out that VINITI's system is "without precedence in worldwide information practices, because of its methodological and organizational complexities" and because "integral information systems in foreign countries are largely sector or discipline-oriented and significantly different from the one being developed at the Institute." In studying the information and flowchart of the Integrated Information System, it can be argued that it is neither new nor unique in design. It appears to be more nearly a replica of what we have been designing and implementing in the United States for the past decade. The Soviets view scientific and technical information as a whole, but they do not plan to have all the data for the different sciences in one place, and they say they will implement their new system on a discipline-by-discipline basis. Chernyi (1972) states, "One system is proposed for all the basic fields of exact natural and technical sciences." Mikhailov strongly argues that "abstracts will be absolutely indispensable" and that "scientists will not do without abstracts and they will be published." It is interesting to note here that the President of the USSR Academy of Sciences, M. V. Keldysh, believes that the abstracting services "should not be burdened with abstracting of reports and this should become the task of other services" (Mikhailov [1973]), which is the approach taken by most abstracting services in the western world.

Regarding the library and information-center functions of transferring scientific and technical information to the user, probably the single observable difference between the USSR and the United States is the development, functioning, and use of the information dissemination centers. Although the USSR has many such centers in the branch networks or the industrial information networks, the centers presently operate primarily by manual methods of collating and dissemination. Few Soviet centers to date have developed any capability of computer processing of single or multiple databases for Selective Dissemination of Information (SDI) purposes. Centers in the United States have concentrated on mechanized searching for nearly a decade; this is now a fast growing segment of the American scene. No experimental work on online, interactive searching of the scientific and technical databases has so far been started in the USSR, although the Soviets have indicated very great interest in this field. Nevertheless, they have developed the necessary framework for building these automated information dissemination centers in the future.

CONCLUSIONS

Following is a brief summary of the major points in this lecture:

1. The Soviet interest in, dedication to, and support of development of information systems for science and technology at the highest levels of the government and scientific communities completely overshadows anything in the United States. This is the most important single factor favoring the Soviet Union in the long-term development and progress of an information system. The Soviets view scientific/technical information as a national resource and give it high priority in the present (1971) five-year plan. Furthermore, they believe that there is no other field of endeavor where the payoff is greater than the use of information by its scientists and engineers. As Arutiunov stated, "Each ruble spent for information work yields three rubles the following year!" Immediate coordination of the interests of government, industry, academia, and scientific societies in the United States is strongly recommended if we are to maintain leadership in the development and operation of information systems on a long-range basis.

2. Centralized planning, management, and control in the USSR have not produced a more efficient or effective information system for handling scientific and technical information. In fact, it appears that rigidly centralized planning controlled by bureaucrats has created managerial inflexibilities, which, in turn, have caused inefficiencies and have impeded introduction and implementation of certain new technology in the Soviet information processing system. Also, the Soviet lack of modern management techniques as we know them in America is likely another major limiting factor in the USSR.

3. The Soviets are experimenting with information systems with much ingenuity, although their research tends to be more on the theoretical than the developmental or applied aspects of the information problems. In spite of the lack of high technology, such as modern computer hardware, some excellent work is under way in the USSR in the development and use of their own and foreign equipment.

4. The Soviets have focused more on compatibility, standardization, and coordination in regard to all aspects of information systems and requirements than we have in the United States. The USSR is moving toward a single series of computer software packages for all national, regional, and local information systems — an uncomplicated and attainable goal. But they are at least a decade away from implementing this large-scale information system nationwide.

5. Training of systems analysts and computer experts is now being given high priority in the USSR and is considered to be the key to progress in development and implementation of more advanced systems. The In-

stitute for Advanced Training of Information Officers was established in 1972 in Moscow by the State Committee. The qualitative aspects of training of computer and information specialists in the United States are much more advanced than those in the USSR.

6. Overall, the Soviet progress in recent years in scientific and technical information activities (with the exception of computer-based systems) has been gaining momentum and has been more rapid than in the United States. But this should be so, considering the near "zero point" from which the Soviets basically started some 20 years ago.

7. The Soviets have more fully recognized than Americans the value and importance of abstracting and indexing as the principal means available for providing scientists and engineers with current awareness and retrospective searching of the world's literature.

8. Exchange visits between our two countries facilitate communication, increase understanding, and encourage dissemination of scientific/technical information. Scientific/technical information must be considered a major national and international resource that should be accessible to the largest possible number of users, for the social and economic benefits of mankind.

The Soviets have stated that their system might indeed be taken as a prototype of the "world science information system." A worldwide system would be less expensive than the present-day highly duplicative systems. Pursuing cooperative projects between our nations should hasten the day of full cooperation and development of compatible systems, a highly desirable goal for us all.

REFERENCES

Arutiunov, N. B. "The Requirements to Be Met by National Scientific and Technical Information Systems." *UNESCO Bulletin for Libraries*, 27(5):246–249, 1973.

Baker, D., et al. *Some Counterparts in Perspective: A Detailed Report on Visits to the Soviet All-Union Institute of Scientific and Technical Information, the Polish Central Institute for Documentation in Science and Technology, the Excerpta Medica Foundation, and Danish Technical Information Service, October 20–November 5, 1959.* Washington, D.C., National Federation of Abstracting and Information Services, 1960.

Baker, W. O. *Improving the Availability of Scientific and Technical Information in the United States.* Panel Report of the President's

Science Advisory Committee. Washington, D.C., LEASCO Information Products, Inc., 1958. ED 048 893.

Chernyi, A. I. "Integrated Information Systems." In: *Problems of Information Science.* Edited by A. I. Chernyi, Moscow, International Federation for Documentation (FID), 1972, pp. 167–207. FID #478.

Garfield, E. "Does the Quality of Soviet Science Justify Double Coverage in *CC*?" *Current Contents,* (52):5–8, December 26, 1973.

Mikhailov, A. I. "Review of the USSR Academy of Sciences." Presented at the Presidium of the USSR Academy of Sciences. *Vestnik Akad. Nauk:* 3–7, March 1973.

National Academy of Sciences. *Libraries and Information Technology: A National System Challenge.* A Report to the Council on Library Resources, Inc. Washington, D.C., Information Systems Panel Computer Science and Engineering Board, 1972.

National Academy of Sciences–National Academy of Engineering. *Scientific and Technical Communication: A Pressing National Problem and Recommendations for Its Solution.* A Report by the Committee on Scientific and Technical Communication of the National Academy of Sciences–National Academy of Engineering. Washington, D.C., 1969. NAS Publication 1707.

National Science Foundation. *Science Indicators — 1973.* Report of the National Science Board. Washington, D.C., 1973a.

———. *The USSR Scientific and Technical Information System: A U.S. View.* Report of the U.S. participants in the U.S./USSR Symposium on Scientific and Technical Information, held in Moscow, June 18–30, 1973. Prepared for the U.S./USSR Joint Commission on Scientific and Technical Cooperation. Washington, D.C., National Technical Information Service, October 1973b. NTIS-SR-73-01.

President's Science Advisory Committee. *Science, Government and Information.* Washington, D.C., U.S. Government Printing Office, 1963.

System Development Corporation. *A System Study of Abstracting and Indexing in the United States.* Springfield, Va., Clearinghouse for Federal Scientific and Technical Information, 1966. PB 174 249.

MARCH 5, 1975

Sharing — The Hope of the Seventies

MELVIN S. DAY, *National Library of Medicine, Bethesda, Maryland*

I am honored and privileged to present the Miles Conrad Memorial Lecture at this 17th Annual Conference. I knew Miles well, and this privilege has special meaning for me.

Miles Conrad was the epitome of help and cooperation, and, as one of the founding fathers of the Federation and its first president, he championed the principle of sharing. Miles was a pragmatist and a philosopher. He recognized clearly the vicissitudes of the human element and the timing element, and he dedicated himself in his capacity as president of the Federation to taking the first steps toward cooperation and sharing. The Federation today is a mature and sound organization. It is the best living organizational example of successful cooperation and sharing among the world's most important information services. I say this with full realization that in a literal sense only a few (but very important) steps in sharing have been taken to date. There still remains exciting potential for additional sharing, and many of you here today are the dynamic leaders in that movement.

As you know, the theme of the 17th Annual Meeting is "Information Interfaces," and, although the program does not carry the label "sharing," the spirit of sharing pervades the entire program. This spirit even carried through to the four preconference workshop sessions on writing abstracts, computer composition, marketing, and user education. The purpose of these workshops was to share experience for the benefit of all participating services.

The act of sharing is as old as man himself, and, in the information field, one might say that it goes back to Eve sharing with Adam the apple she picked from the tree of knowledge. The Bible states

And when the woman saw that the tree was good for food, and that it was a delight to the eyes, and that the tree was to be desired to make one wise, she took of the fruit thereof, and did eat; and she gave also unto her husband with her, and he did eat.

—Genesis, Chapter 3, Verse 6

Now, according to the Bible, this is where sharing started—in the Garden of Eden with Adam and Eve. You will recall that the fruit that was eaten was from the tree of knowledge. The knowledge evidently took effect because the next verse states "And the eyes of them both were opened." I will not quote further from the scripture because I believe it talks about nakedness and sowing together and the like. The only point I wish to make is that the sharing of knowledge and information goes back a long, long way.

SHARING AMONG LIBRARIES

As a social organization, the library is probably the oldest in the information field. In moving from the Garden of Eden through the ages to modern times, it would appear wise to begin with a brief word about libraries and their sharing activities.

Sharing of resources in the form of interlibrary loans has been a practice among libraries ever since library materials were in a form in which physically they could be transported and exchanged.

History reports that the first libraries established in the Near East around 3000 B.C. were repositories of clay tablets or papyrus scrolls that recorded such information as vital statistics, boundaries of land, political and historical events, and meteorological phenomena. The first recorded sharing of library materials occurred in the second century B.C., when the great Library of Alexandria loaned some of its manuscript materials to the Library of Pergamum.

Gutenberg's invention of cast movable type in 1450 A.D. had an explosive impact on western culture and certainly on the library as an institution. Printing overwhelmingly reshaped the world and to this day is still a basic essential medium of communication. There have been some 30 million unique titles published since Gutenberg.

Derek de Solla Price, in his book *Science Since Babylon*, has charted the growth in the number of scientific journals. He points out that there were about 10 scientific journals being produced in the late 1600s. This number increased to approximately 100 in the early 1800s and to 10,000 by 1900. His evaluation of the world list of scientific publications is that we are well on the way to the 100,000 mark. The impact of this literature growth on the library certainly requires no explanation for this expert group.

In the historical development of libraries, there can be observed an ongoing adaptation to their environment toward the sophisticated personalities that they have today. The kind and amount of material and the kind and number of users have changed radically over the centuries.

The characteristics of information storage and retrieval in our times, together with the heavy, often unpredictable, demands of users, indicate that sharing on a very much broadened basis is the only way for libraries to survive and continue to provide effective service. Libraries are not merely a conglomeration of books and the procedures for handling them, but a complex set of concepts and people that deal with the past and recorded aspirations of man and that relate man's present needs to the past. As people-oriented activities, libraries develop "personalities" of their own. In the past, such diverse personalities all too often mitigated against the extension of sharing to the processing part of library activities.

Sharply rising costs coupled with tight budgets are compelling forces that can no longer be ignored. Today the concept of sharing in libraries is spreading to the processing activities and information retrieval activities. Fortunately, the development of electronic logic, coupled to the new effective telecommunication systems, now provides to the library community an incredibly effective tool for facilitating the sharing of library processing activities. (Today's computers can perform process manipulation with logical content, as well as accept human logic manipulation.)

A basic requirement for effective sharing is the development and acceptance of necessary standards. Here the American National Standards Institute (ANSI) Z39 committee has a key role.

At the April 1974 meeting on National Bibliographic Control, sponsored by the National Science Foundation and the Council on Library Resources, several recommendations were proposed for standards for machine-readable indexing. One recommendation called for the formation of a working group "to establish the content designators for materials covered by abstracting and indexing services which are not now described in existing Library of Congress, Machine-Readable Cataloging (MARC) formats." The ground swell for standardized formats continues to gain strength.

The Council on Library Resources is working closely with the Library of Congress, National Library of Medicine, National Agricultural Library, and other major library organizations to develop a national bibliographic processing capability for library materials to be shared by the total library community. Here I am referring to the cataloging of monographs and serial publications.

Many of you have heard about the cost-effective online shared cataloging system developed by the Ohio College Library Center (OCLC). It is used by many libraries around the country. In the metropolitan Washington area, all the large federal libraries are participants, including the National Library of Medicine and the National Agricultural Library. In very simple terms, the system permits the user to determine whether a record for the item to be cataloged is already stored within the system. If the record is in the system, it can be used as is or the user can elect to modify the record for his own use. If, on the other hand, the record is not in the system, then the user can produce a record and add it to the basic database. The system can then be instructed to produce catalog cards or magnetic tape records for mailing to the user. This program is sharing at its best, and it is setting a new trend for shared cataloging in the United States.

In December, the Council on Library Resources and OCLC entered into a cooperative arrangement that heralds the initiation of a cooperative serials database building project called CONSER (CONversion of SERials). The basic file will use the Library of Congress MARC-serials file and the University of Minnesota Union List of Serials as its starting point. Large libraries like the Library of Congress and the National Library of Medicine will keyboard their new serials cataloging directly online into CONSER on the OCLC system for the general use of the library community.

Aside from the valuable service this program will provide, it is an excellent example of consolidating several separate collaborative efforts to eliminate expensive duplicative processing.

NFAIS AND SHARING

The library community is starting to make substantial progress in its shared processing programs, but I submit that the real "sharing" pro is the community represented by the National Federation of Abstracting and Indexing Services.

The Federation was born in 1958 out of a desire of its founders for cooperation in sharing their common problems and, hopefully, their solutions. Down through the years, the record is replete with sharing-related activities by the Federation and its members. You will recall that way back in 1962, the Federation commissioned Robert Heller and Associates of Cleveland to make a study of abstracting and indexing services in the United States and to recommend ways to improve the effectiveness of these abstracting and indexing (A&I) activities. The Federation issued the *Heller Report* in 1963, and for those of you who may wish to refer to the report, it is included in total as an appendix to the *Proceedings of the National Federation of Science Abstracting and Indexing Services 1963 Annual Meeting.*

My good friend, Burt Adkinson, discussed the *Heller Report* in his Miles Conrad Memorial Lecture delivered at the NFSAIS-ASIDIC (Association of Scientific and Information Dissemination Centers) luncheon on February 24, 1971. You will recall that the recommendation that received the most attention was the establishment of an Organization X that would be the focal point for repackaging and marketing the products from the professional abstracting and indexing services. Needless to say, no Organization X has been created, and by and large, the recommendations in the *Heller Report* have not been accepted by the A&I community. On the other hand, the paper itself did serve a useful purpose in stimulating a great deal of soul-searching on the part of the A&I community and in generating frank and revealing discussions among the Federation members. It is not my intention to praise or pan the *Heller Report* but rather to put it into historical perspective.

In the mid-1960s, the Federation explored the availability of literature from the Peoples Republic of China (PRC) and, with the support of the National Science Foundation, operated a program for several years to improve the availability of PRC scientific literature in the United States. Such a service facilitated the sharing of these information materials among the Federation members. In the fall of 1972, the board recommended that prime attention be given to the "development of standards that will help provide links between operating systems and will help facilitate the use of more than one system to serve the information requirements of the ultimate users as well as information centers and libraries." The importance of successfully implementing this recommendation cannot be overstated. The establishment and acceptance of common standards and protocols is absolutely essential to cost-effective sharing in the production of services and products and is equally important in maximizing their effective use. The Federation recognizes this, and even more important, its members are doing something about it. Last year Dale Baker presented an excellent report on the Soviet national information system. He reported briefly on the Soviet method for establishing and implementing standards. Here in the United States, standards are in reality developed and implemented from bottom up, whereas in the Soviet Union, they are developed and implemented from the top down.

The standards being developed here are the results of the cooperative efforts of experts at the working level, pooling and sharing their combined expertise and judgment. There is a give-and-take to reconcile differences and minimize negative displacement by or on any of the member A&I services. Compared with the Soviet system for establishing standards by proclamation, our system is slow, but I submit that it is much better and is the only workable system in our free society.

To me, what is so admirable and important in the efforts of the Federation members to reduce unnecessary overlap in processing is the dedication to this concept of cooperation and sharing by the staffs, as well as by directors and boards of member services. I say this as a result of having observed firsthand on a number of occasions the deliberations and performance of some of the working groups.

I would like to tip my hat to BioSciences Information Service (BIOSIS), Chemical Abstracts Service (CAS), and *Engineering Index* (*Ei*) for their constructive spadework in moving toward the reduction of unnecessary duplicate processing. This effort has been ongoing for some time. In April 1970, these organizations began a five-part study to determine the relationships between and the overlap in coverage in their printed publications and computer-readable services. The study itself was designed to provide to the three services the information needed for planning cooperative programs and for reconciling differences in their policies and practices to make their respective publications and services more useful to their user communities. The first results of the study were published in an article entitled "Overlap in the Lists of Journals Monitored by BIOSIS, CAS and Ei" in the *Journal of the American Society for Information Science* (23[1]:36–38, January–February 1972). The second phase of the study was to determine the extent to which these services covered the same articles within the journals. The results of this study were published one year later in an article entitled "Overlap Among Journal Articles Selected for Coverge in BIOSIS, CAS, and Ei" in the *Journal of the American Society for Information Science* (24[1]:25–28, January–February 1973).

The overlap between the journal articles selected for coverage by the three services is substantial enough to warrant further investigation, which is continuing. These studies are very significant and should eventually lead to shared bibliographic descriptions of articles, thus reducing duplication in processing effort and at the same time providing more efficient and economical service both to the producing services and the user community. I hasten to point out for the record that redundancy in the publication of the three services does not mean unnecessary duplication, since the services may analyze the article content in quite different ways to serve the needs of their own user communities.

The National Science Foundation is to be commended for supporting a study announced in November 1974. The purpose is to examine journal article overlap among 13 major science abstracting and indexing services in the United States. Hopefully, as with the BIOSIS, CAS, and *Ei* effort, this also will lead to shared bibliographic descriptions. CAS and BIOSIS are moving toward compatible computerized processing systems and this, too, should facilitate sharing.

Most of us represent substantial operating activities. Although our day-to-day operating problems differ in many ways, reflecting the differences in our organizations and programs, we have three serious problems in common. First, there are spiraling unit costs. Second, there is an ever-increasing volume of scientific literature to be processed, placed under bibliographic and subject control, and announced. Third, there exists the struggle to maintain a level of subscription income sufficient to offset operating costs.

During the last 30 years, we have seen the metamorphosis of many abstracting and indexing journals. We have seen them change from personal desk tools to institutional tools. I even remember when, as a fledgling chemist, I bought my own personal copy of *Chemical Abstracts* for $25 (now I know that was about 100 years ago). I should also point out that during this same period, the production processes in the A&I organizations have likewise undergone equally startling changes. The reasons for the changes in the nature, size, and costs of our A&I journals is understandable and justifiable. Our user communities have grumbled but have adapted, largely by reducing the number of subscriptions and then sharing the reduced number of copies. The resultant vicious circle of spiraling costs and reduced subscriptions has been a nightmare for all of you. As in the past, you have been constantly on the lookout for ways to lower costs and improve the quality of your services. You have enhanced and upgraded your processing capability through the application and use of modern computer technology. Your publications and services are now of higher quality and are more timely. This same computer technology and its machine-readable output also provide you with a new potential for sharing processed output among your member services. As responsible operating officials and as "pros" in the information business, you are moving ahead to capitalize on this potential. I am an operating official myself, and I recognize only too well the myriad of complexities and difficulties to be overcome—some technical, some human, and some legal. You are moving ahead deliberately and carefully, and this is commendable.

The ever-increasing speed of the "vicious circle" problem is beginning, unfortunately, to take on some of the characteristics of a whirling dervish, with each turn compounding the critical problem. Inside of me a little devil keeps pleading for a more rapid implementation of sharing as a survival remedy. You have accepted the need and the remedy for this change, and I am confident that you will not tolerate any unnecessary delay.

Our dear friend, Miles Conrad, recognized so clearly that one of the most beguiling perceptions men have pondered is the constancy of change. He was an apostle of cooperation and sharing. As a pragmatist, he accepted change as part and parcel of cooperation and sharing. History has shown that whatever man decides and commands will indeed be a driving force of the future. This is our hope for the 1970s.

MARCH 10, 1976

Comparative Development of Abstracting and Indexing, and Monograph Cataloging

FREDERICK G. KILGOUR, *Ohio College Library Center, Columbus, Ohio*

This lecture will be an essentially historical analysis of the relation between the activities and products of abstracting and indexing and those of library book cataloging; in particular, it will examine such aspects of the relationship as economic viability, cooperation, utilization of standards, and the impact of various technologies.

Abstracting and indexing and book cataloging are logically the same activity, and they are convergent. Each describes or lists a bibliographic item using primarily the information at the head of an article, on the cover sheet of a report, or on the title page of a book. Book cataloging has always emphasized the description of a book by author, title, and location so that the user can find the book. The abstracting and indexing industry, on the other hand, has always emphasized the subject approach to information in an item.

From a user's point of view, an abstract and index "catalog" is never as large as many of the huge library book catalogs. Therefore, the structure of the abstract and index tool does not have to be as precise and detailed as that of the large library catalog, and there can be no doubt that the simpler the structure of an index, the easier it is to use.

It seems certain that book catalogs existed in antiquity, but the earliest book catalogs extant are two prepared in the eighth century. Medieval catalogs rarely contain more than a few dozen titles whose entries were

151

presented chronologically, by shelf location, or by author's forename. Interestingly enough, cooperative library book cataloging began in the last half of the 13th century, when the Franciscans in England compiled a union catalog of books by 94 authors located in 183 monastic book collections. More than a century later, John Boston of Bury enlarged the Franciscan work to books by 673 authors in 191 British monastic libraries.

Conrad Gesner (1516–1565) published his celebrated *Bibliotheca Universalis* in 1545. Actually, *Bibliotheca Universalis* is not a catalog of a specific library, but rather a bibliography of books of Greek, Latin, and Hebrew authors. Gesner, however, arranged the listings in a proposed library arrangement, and suggested that librarians use his bibliography by writing the shelf locations of their books in the margins—another cooperative cataloging scheme. Subsequently, Gesner published a series of subject indexes to *Bibliotheca*, the first of their kind.

The 17th century opened with the appearance of the first printed general catalog of a library, namely that of the Bodleian Library at Oxford. Later in that century, the first abstracts appeared in the *Journal des Sçavans* in 1665. It was not until the last half of the 18th century that abstract journals began to appear, particularly with J. G. Hager's *Geographischer Büchersaal* in 1764 and L. F. F. von Crell's *Chemisches Journal* in 1778.

Until the beginning of the 19th century, individuals were largely responsible for publication of abstracts and indexes. But early in the 19th century, it began to be recognized that it was important for the continuance of the publication of abstract journals to have an organization responsible for them. During the second quarter of the 19th century, important abstract journals began to be published in Germany, some of which were to continue publication for more than a century. Still, the major abstracting publications in existence today were born in the 20th century.

The French Revolutionary Government initiated a grand scheme for a national union catalog in 1791 when it issued rules for cataloging books on the blank backs of playing cards. Each library in France was to catalog its collection and then send the cards to Paris where they would be assembled for printing in a huge union catalog. Actually, the catalog never appeared, but there are playing-card collections extant with examples of catalog entries on the backs of the cards.

At mid-19th century, C. C. Jewett proposed another type of cooperative union catalog. Jewett's plan provided for American libraries to send catalog entries to the Smithsonian, where they could be converted into inexpensive clay stereotype plates, each marked with the code of the library holding the item described. If an individual library wished to have a new edition of its printed catalog, plates holding that library's code would be selected and printed, thereby making it unnecessary for type to be set each time a library wished to print a catalog. Jewett realized that cataloging standards would be necessary to his plan. His guide, *On the Construction of Catalogs of Libraries and Their Publication by Means of Separate Stereotyped Titles, with Rules and Examples*, which appeared in 1853, served as the basic code for cataloging for nearly a quarter of a century, when it was superseded by C. A. Cutter's *Rules for a Printed Dictionary Catalogue*. The stereotype catalog, which W. F. Poole ungraciously called a "mud catalogue," was a failure, largely because of distortion of the clay plates.

Five years before the appearance of Jewett's *Rules*, Poole had published the first edition of his pioneering index to articles in general periodicals. He published the second edition in 1853. At the first meeting in 1876 of the group of librarians that were to become the American Library Association, it was decided to undertake the cooperative preparation of a third edition of Poole's index under his direction. The indexing of specific titles was assigned to various librarians, with Poole editing. The third edition appeared in 1882 and was followed by a series of supplements whose publication was superseded just after the turn of the century by the H. W. Wilson Company's far more current *Readers' Guide to Periodical Literature*. The *Readers' Guide*, curiously enough, used technically improved stereotype plates of Jewett's "mud catalogue."

Increasing costs and delays in the publication of book-form library catalogs forced American libraries to begin to use catalogs on cards as first proposed, but sparingly utilized, by the French. Harvard University's library introduced a card catalog in 1863, and at that time its book-form catalog had not been updated for 30 years. The first edition of Cutter's *Rules for a Printed Dictionary Catalogue* appeared in 1876 and provided improved standardization for cataloging practices. In the next decade, the size of catalog cards was standardized at 75×125 millimeters, making it possible to exchange standardized cataloging information in a standard physical format. But it was not until 1901, when the Library of Congress began to sell catalog cards containing its own cataloging, that it became possible for American libraries to begin to significantly reduce the duplication of cataloging efforts among their institutions.

As already mentioned, the major abstracting journals came into being in the 20th century, some subsequently absorbing 19th-century titles. In the 20th century, abstracting journals have been able to utilize cooperation among a large number of abstractors for the preparation of entries, much as Poole did for the preparation of the third edition of his index. But there has not been an effective code or standard for abstracts as has been the case for book cataloging, so that the exchange of abstracts among abstracting agencies is hindered by incompatibility.

The application of digital computation to abstracting, indexing, and cataloging during the past two decades has produced some wholly new products and concepts. The pioneering application by the National Library of Medicine of computation to its *Index Medicus* in the form of the Medical Literature Analysis and Retrieval System (MEDLARS) demonstrated the benefits of information retrieval by computer. The subsequent development of the online interactive MEDLARS Online (MEDLINE) system, together with several dozen other online interactive databases, has opened a whole new avenue for attaining the classic objective of abstracting and indexing and attaining it more swiftly and accurately.

Similarly, the development of computerized library networks has made it possible to achieve Jewett's goals of the mid-19th century. These networks provide access in seconds to huge union catalogs and at the same time facilitate cataloging by using the cataloging of other institutions, thereby invoking an economy of scale that reduces costs. Interestingly, these library networks also utilize cooperation for the entry of cataloging data into the central catalog; if a catalog record is not in the online catalog, the cataloging library enters its own record. Currently, these online computerized networks are being designed and operated on a self-supporting financial basis, an economic arrangement that has not heretofore been possible in book cataloging.

These online catalogs of abstracting, indexing, and book cataloging information are entirely new types of catalogs made possible by a new technology. In the case of the Ohio College Library Center (OCLC), the online catalog is not an online card catalog. Rather, it is a collection of more than 1.5 million miniature catalogs, none of which exceeds 32 entries. Similar catalog designs exist in other systems. It appears that this design, consisting of prestructured miniature catalogs that may be subsequently altered by personal interaction to produce a unique catalog, did not come into being largely by deliberate design. Rather, the effort in information retrieval from abstracting and indexing files was to obtain a high percentage of relevance and a high percentage of retrieved items. In the case of the library system, the first goal was to obtain only a single record from a huge file, studies having shown that two-thirds to four-fifths of the use of library catalogs is to retrieve a known item.

These two opposite goals led to the design of what has become recognized as a new and important type of catalog, and the future designers of online abstracting and indexing and library catalogs could well work together for improvements and consequent benefits to users.

The library community has been more successful than the abstracting and indexing publishers in attaining standardization and thereby in facilitating interchange of information. Cataloging standards have been developing for well over a century. In addition, the standardization of the physical format of catalog entries on cards has been translated into the

MARC (Machine-Readable Cataloging) II format of the Library of Congress, which is also a physical format within which cataloging information is imbedded. The abstracting and indexing industry has neither a standard physical format nor generally accepted standards of abstracting, although definite progress has been made in this area in recent years.

The products of abstracting and indexing have been economically viable since the introduction of these activities, and libraries have long been able to purchase the printed catalogs of abstracts and indexes. With a few exceptions, however, book cataloging has not been an economically viable activity. Hence, libraries did practically all their own cataloging until 1901, when it became possible to obtain catalog cards from the Library of Congress. In fact, cataloging was the most expensive activity in a library until the present decade, when online shared cataloging systems were introduced. It now appears certain that online computerized shared cataloging is economically viable.

Cooperation has played an important role in abstracting, indexing, and cataloging. For cataloging, the important aspect of cooperation has been the reduction in cataloging effort among libraries and the consequent reduction in costs. Regarding abstracting and indexing, cooperation by highly motivated people, without fees or with nominal fees, has made possible much of the abstracting publication in the 20th century. Of course, some abstracting operations do not rely on cooperation for preparation of entries.

There is a second level of cooperation, namely, that among networks and among abstracting organizations. The latter have been examining the feasibility of cooperation for some years, and although it is not yet clear that such cooperation is feasible, it still appears desirable. Computerized library networks are so new that there has been little opportunity for cooperation, although at the present time the Bibliographic Automation of Large Library Operations Using a Time-Sharing System (BALLOTS) network at Stanford and OCLC are beginning to explore, at the suggestion of BALLOTS, the interchange of machine-readable cataloging records.

In conclusion, it seems that the abstracting and indexing industry and library book cataloging have never been far apart and are currently coming even closer together, largely because of the new computer technology. It also seems probable that in the not-too-distant future, both types of activity will be providing similar and complementary information in a manner that was not possible in the past.

The online catalog is an entirely new development that will have considerable impact on abstracting, indexing, and cataloging. If catalogs are to continue to consist of miniature catalogs with only a few dozen entries, the requirements for detailed structure in abstracting and indexing publications and library catalogs will be greatly reduced, thereby modifying existing standards and bringing new ones into existence. The obvious user benefits from such catalogs are so great that it is hoped that the abstracting and indexing industry can cooperate with library networks in future development.

Finally, it is now clear that the development of online access to collections of abstracts, index entries, and book catalog records will soon make it possible to provide users with information when and where they need it, with a speed and accuracy heretofore unthinkable.

MARCH 9, 1977

Progress in a Profession

WILLIAM O. BAKER, *Bell Laboratories, Murray Hill, New Jersey*

The privilege of presenting the Miles Conrad Memorial Lecture for 1977 is tempered by the realization that NFAIS's charitable Selection Committee has finally cast caution and tradition to the wind. For the first time — and perhaps the last — it has chosen an amateur. But maybe they have exhibited a special timeliness in the gamble. For the domain of information technology has achieved, in these 20 years of the National Federation of Abstracting and Indexing Services, an important level of professionalism. This is true for the technology of science and technical information processing and especially for the technology of indexing and abstracting. Indeed, after World War II, when the bibliographic automation and levels of research and development that are now commonplace were but distant beacons, we were all amateurs. But some degree of mental sluggishness and a steady distraction by other things are the only excuses for having remained amateurs during these momentous decades. Anyway, perhaps you will soon agree that, whatever the cause, at least one amateur status is secure. I believe I could prove that in almost any feature of what I report to you today. But I shall be doubly certain of it by proposing that the next stage of abstracting will be as radical and experimental as were our theses of automation and pluralistic administration 20 years ago.

To sharpen this perspective, let us look for a moment at how we have fared up to now. Let us see how this priceless resource of professionalism, so much of which is represented here, has not only enhanced our progress in the third quarter of the twentieth century but has given us a strong (if perhaps underused) base for new steps in the final quarter. There was nothing casual in the decision of the Special Assistant to the President for Science and Technology, Dr. J. R. Killian, Jr., and the President's Science Advisory Committee (PSAC) to make the study of our Panel on Scientific Information, "Improving the Availability of Scientific and Technical Information in the United States," their first report after we were taken into the White House by President Eisenhower. At the end of 1957 and the beginning of 1958, we had assessed American science and technology. This was in terms of the cold, hard challenge of Soviet space and missile capabilities, following their mastery of nuclear weapons.

Only a few meetings of the charter membership were necessary to convince us all that the United States had more science and engineering knowledge than it was using. Specifically, we would need to create new systems in defense, space, energy, health, and the like to move in concert with the world awakening to the power of knowledge and techniques. This the president and his advisers were determined to do. So we had to quickly and forcefully determine how knowledge and research and development could best be shared among those public and private organizations that would have to support our national strengths. We undertook the matter carefully but quickly. We remembered that the *information* of science and technology and research and development is the life stream of creativity, engineering, design, and execution, and an essence of manufacturing and education.

Our brief report appeared in the fall of 1958. It was approved by President Eisenhower for release on Sunday, December 7, 1958, reminiscent of another sobering Sunday, December 7, which had impelled us so strongly into an era of science and engineering. This report had, in fact, also been presented to the Cabinet on Friday, December 5. Interestingly, it represented the first and only White House Science Office study formally reviewed. It was not that the study was disliked or ignored, but, as President Eisenhower told me later, the Cabinet, unlike the Senate, is not a deliberative body. The official statement of the episode says, "The report was well received. There were numerous questions and the recommendations were approved by the President."

Something of the span and nature of the report are indicated by the membership of the panel that produced it. Members included Curtis Benjamin, President of McGraw-Hill Book Company, from the private publishers; Dr. Caryl P. Haskins, President of Carnegie Institution of Washington, from the independent research community; Dr. Elmer Hutchisson, Director of the American Institute of Physics, from the national, scientific, and professional societies; Dr. Warren C. Johnson, Dean of the Divison of Physical Sciences of the University of Chicago, from the domain of higher education; Don K. Price, Dean of the School of Public Administration and Littauer Professor of Harvard University, from the scholarly world of policy and public affairs; Dr. Herbert Scoville, who was carefully omitted from our news releases of those days but who was equally carefully chosen as a high official of the Central Intelligence Agency (whose information and literature-processing facilities, representative of those of the intelligence community, were already of high capability); and, finally, Dr. Alan T. Waterman, Director of the National Science Foundation, representing broad federal science and technology interests.

The immediate theme and thrusts of the study, as approved by President Eisenhower, were the application of automation and the sharing of responsibility for the availability of scientific and technical information between the public and private resources. This policy endured and was strengthened over the next two decades (Figure 1) and appears to be very appropriate for the equally revolutionary technical and operational progress possible in the future. Anyway, let us pursue a bit further the implications of the findings and the emerging status of the federal and national programs. (I should note that, although I have copies of the report and there are others in the Eisenhower Library, the text is otherwise not available.*)

The White House release that announced the president's approval said,

The Committee urged that the fullest use be made of existing information services, both public and private, and that the Foundation's Science Information Service supplement rather than supplant present efforts. . . . The President asked that all Federal agencies whose programs involved scientific information cooperate with and assist the National Science Foundation in improving the Government's own efforts in this area.

Reference was then made to approval of . . .

a program calling for the review, coordination, and stimulation, on a nationwide basis, of activities in the areas of primary and secondary publications, scientific data centers, unpublished research information, storage and retrieval, and translation by mechanical means.

Only the final concept remains beyond the present reach.

It is interesting, in view of the complexity of government relationships nowadays, that policies and plans approved by the president after submis-

---

*The original December 7, 1958 report and press release are reprinted as Appendixes A and B to this paper, respectively.

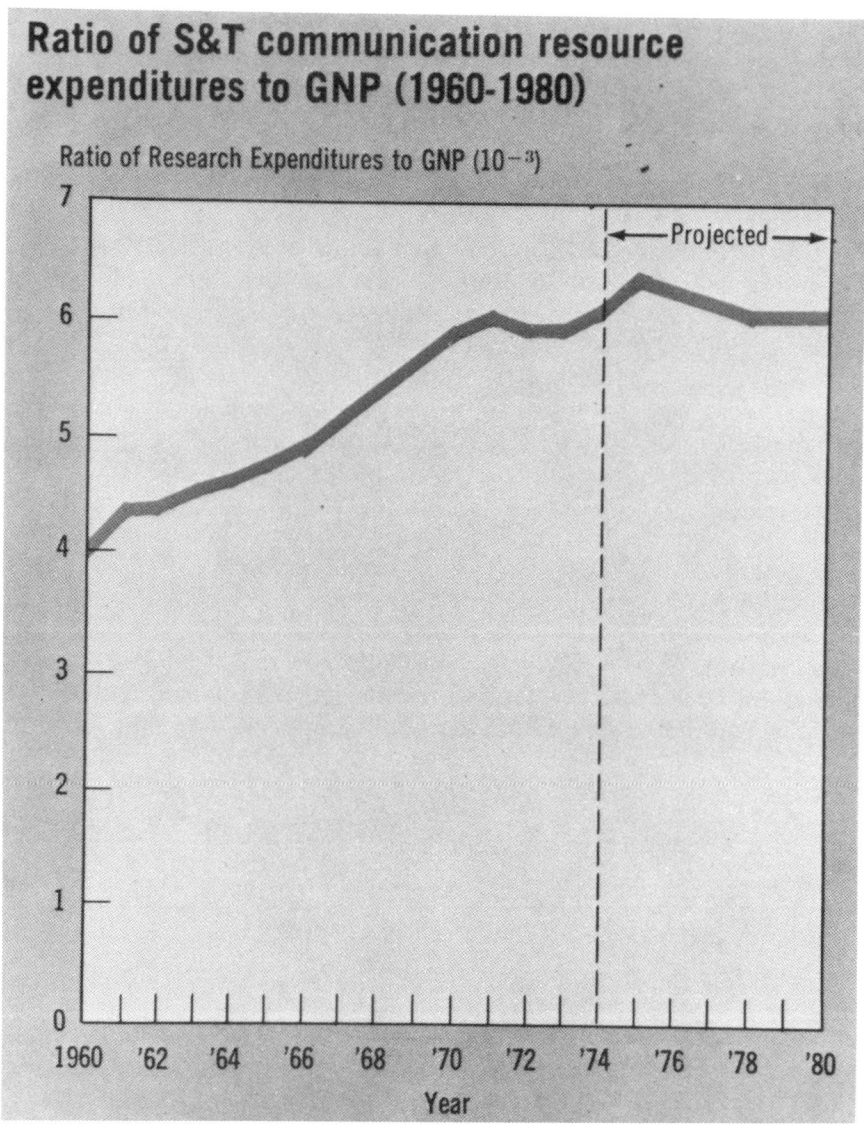

Figure 1 In 1960, the cost of communicating scientific and technical knowledge amounted to 0.4 percent of the Gross National Product. The percentage has increased steadily, reaching approximately 0.6 in the early 1970s. After another increase, it is expected to level off at 0.6 percent by 1980. (Reprinted with permission of King Research, Inc., Center for Quantitative Sciences.)

sion by the panel to PSAC had already been carefully worked out with interested members of the legislative branch. Nevertheless, there was no statutory base for PSAC or any other White House science activity until 1976. We are particularly grateful, however, that our panel was quickly and warmly received during 1958 by the Chairman of the Subcommittee on Reorganization of the Committee on Government Operations, Senator Hubert H. Humphrey. In the winter and spring of 1958, during the course of our intensive study, Senator Humphrey conducted hearings on the provisions of S3126, The Science and Technology Act of 1958. He thereby recognized the vital role of scientific and technical information in connection with the study of reorganization of science activities in the Federal Government. Not unexpectedly, reorganization of science activities is still being pursued through the statute in Title III of the 1976 Act. A reconstitution of the President's Committee on Science and Technology, which has already delved into new options, will likely be announced by President Carter in the near future. Hopefully, it will pursue that mission so wisely foreseen two decades ago by Senator Humphrey.

During 1958, however, one strong and direct statutory responsibility for overall science and technology activities — perhaps the first — was worked out. It designated the National Science Foundation as the coordinating body for the federal effort. I shall jump ahead to say that despite the frustrations and limitations that organization has necessarily encountered in handling such a challenging and complex assignment, it remains, along with its other federal collaborators, one of the prides of the world's science, engineering, and learning communities.

Legislative actions also represented the concurrent theme of strong, independent participation and use of independent resources in concert with federal activities. Senator Humphrey's letter to me, dated April 23, 1958, inviting participation in drafting of legislation, noted that a special meeting of The Council on Documentation Research (held at Case Western Reserve University, Cleveland, Ohio, February 3-4, 1958) was a basic stimulus. The subsequent famous National Defense Education Act of 1958 sought, through the Science Information Service of NSF, to

provide, or arrange for the provision of, indexing, abstracting, translation, and other services leading to a more effective dissemination of scientific information, and undertake programs to develop new or improved methods, including mechanized systems for making scientific information available.

The rest, as they say, is history.

This is a suitable time, for many reasons, to give this distinguished NFAIS assembly a critical assessment of where we have come and where we might be going (Figure 2).

An important point in the first study by our panel was the ranking of

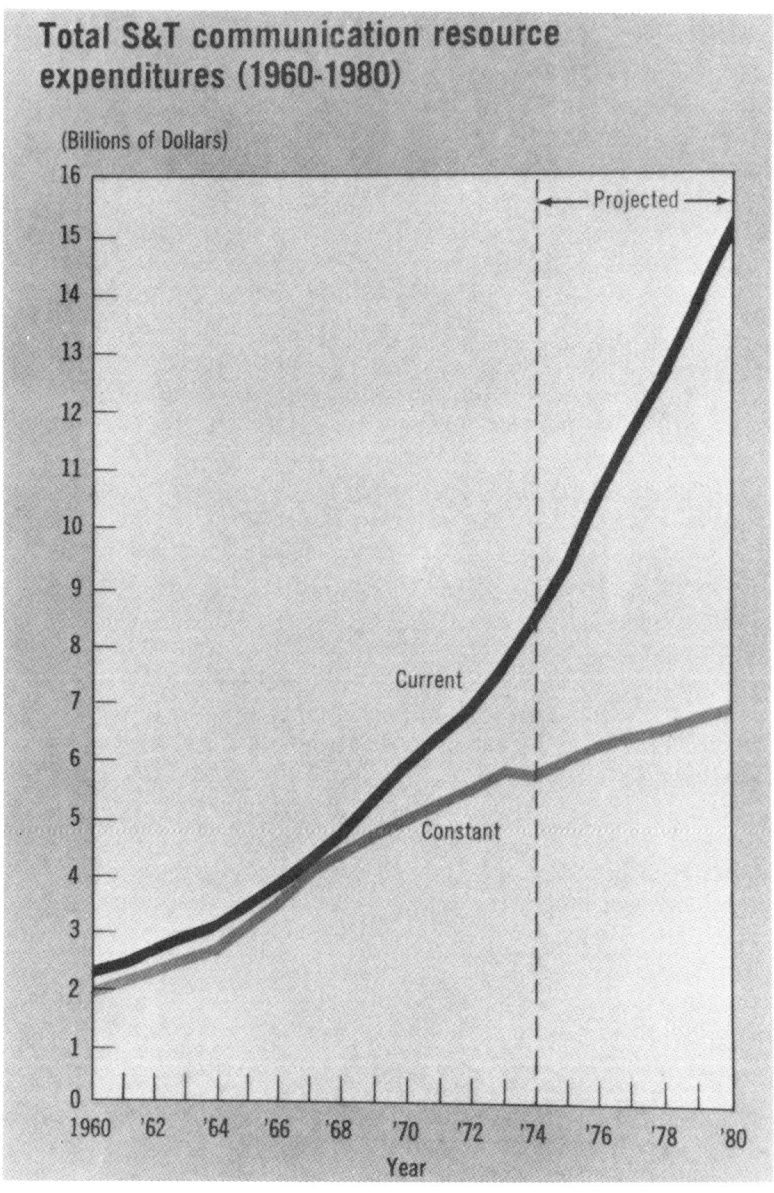

Figure 2 The total scientific and technical (S&T) communication resource expenditures in the United States have increased rapidly in both current and constant dollars since 1960. The total resources expended include the costs by authors, publishers, libraries and secondary services, and users in the production and use of scientific and technical publications, including books, journals, and reports. (Reprinted with permission of King Research, Inc., Center for Quantitative Sciences.)

abstracting journals alongside primary sources, including monographs, as a basis for scientific and technical learning. In somewhat foretelling terms, the report noted that "when adequately indexed, [abstracting journals] permit a searcher to locate previously published papers on any given subject. If an abstract is sufficiently informative, it may serve the scientist in lieu of the complete paper." The report further noted an important early response of the abstracting services—those very ones that comprise NFAIS—to our investigation:

> It should be noted . . . that the 14 major scientific abstracting services in the United States recently indicated that the almost half-a-million abstracts that they issue annually constitute only about 55 percent of what they should be publishing in order to cover literature in their combined fields reasonably well.

(I believe a current assessment would be vastly more reasssuring in terms of the coverage of abstracts.)

So much for the past. What can I add in remembrance of Miles Conrad to the continued progress of NFAIS, considering that you are all competent professionals? Now that your various basic policies have been pursued, following the initial impetus, what worthwhile information can an amateur like myself provide at this juncture? To answer that, I seek your indulgence for some moments of personal reference to connections with our cause.

During this whole period, I have been primarily a user and generator of modest parts of the scientific and technical literature. I haven't been a professional in its management and processing. The earliest and most enduring of my interests have been in work that came from many directions and disciplines. For, as you know, the bases of both solid state and polymer science and technology were built by work in physics, chemistry, applied mathematics, and engineering. This research extended over many institutions, including universities, industry, and government laboratories. Accordingly, in exploring these multidisciplinary and somewhat disorganized arenas, my associates and I were pressed to depend heavily on correlating widely diverse literature sources. At the same time, we sought to use abstracts extensively because of the impossibility of otherwise assimilating the volume of work encompassed, which drew on much of physics, chemistry, and technology of the first half of the century.

It turned out that assimilation of such background material could lead to the formation of new resources in solid state and materials science and engineering. It also induced an era of science and technology of macromolecules that have broad impact on our modern life. These extend from the biopeptides and nucleic acids to the plastics, fibers, and rubbers comprising much of our materials for human use.

Coincidentally, there also emerged out of the solid-state-electronics evolution of the transistor another dramatic advance in science and technology: 20th-century information processing and communications. In particular, this meant the use of digital machines for logic and memories and the ability to apply electronics in handling data, graphics, and language. Therefore, we became simultaneously involved, through these two realms, in gaining knowledge and organizing and stimulating others in ever broader discovery. We were also trying to concentrate and focus that knowledge so that it could contribute to certain national and industrial purposes (Figure 3).

It has been necessary to impose these somewhat biographic details to give perspective to my conclusions and proposals in this lecture. My assessment is, above all, that you have created a national community of professionals in information handling, especially in scientific and technical abstracting and indexing, whose quality is unsurpassed, indeed unapproached, anywhere else. This represents a national capability of merit and value to our continued well-being.

You can see, from the scope of my assessment, why I had to establish the detachment of my occupation in the preceding paragraphs. I am not one of you saying how great we all are. Rather, I am reporting, perhaps for the first time in this context, the admirable advances in the creation and cultivation of such a community, going beyond the wildest dreams of the PSAC report of 1958. Likewise, you are constituting this professionalism at a most opportune time in our national history. This is due not only to the continued role of science and technology and your support of it, but also to the fact that, in the last couple of years (as shown by the careful studies of Dr. Marc Uri Poral of Stanford University, sponsored by the U.S. Department of Commerce and the Institute at Stanford), this nation has turned from the dominant economy of agriculture and manufacturing to an economy dominated—albeit by just a small margin—by the information and communication industries. The Gross National Product is slightly but significantly larger in these activities—which, of course, include banking, education, the media, and entertainment—than it is in the traditional production of goods and the processing of materials.

So goes my assessment. As other realms, such as educational programs, expand, we shall find that our community, now dominated by scientific and technical information missions, will become ever larger and more vital in our total national expertise (Figure 4). But the very success of the new and evident professionalism of the secondary service, the very dependence of our scientific and technical progress on the information treasure that these services marshall, can lead to stagnation and decline. The members of NFAIS are engineers of entropy. In a theoretical sense, you fight constantly, like Sisyphus in his uphill battle, to gain negative entropy against the forces of disorder. These forces, in information hand-

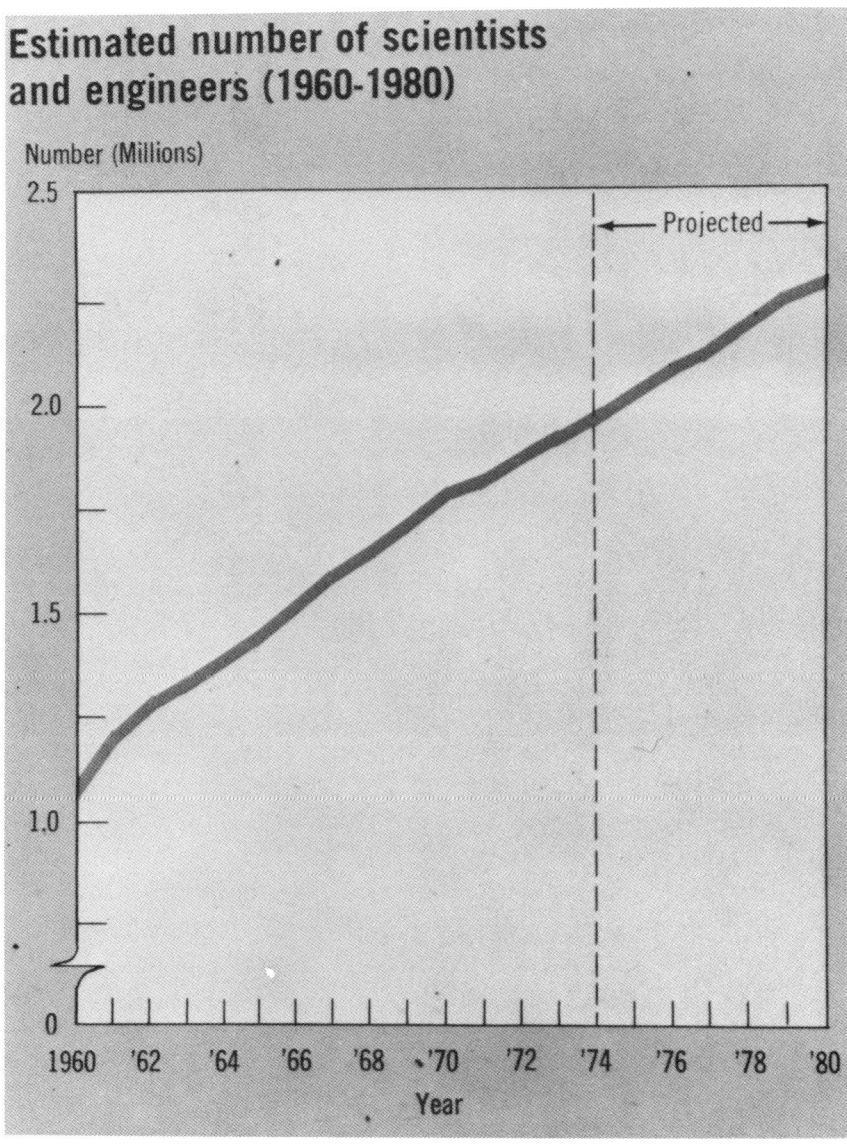

Figure 3 An important factor in the growth of scientific and technical communication expenditures is the increase in the number of scientists and engineers in the United States. The average annual growth rate between 1960 and 1975 was 3.8 percent. (Reprinted with permission of King Research, Inc., Center for Quantitative Sciences.)

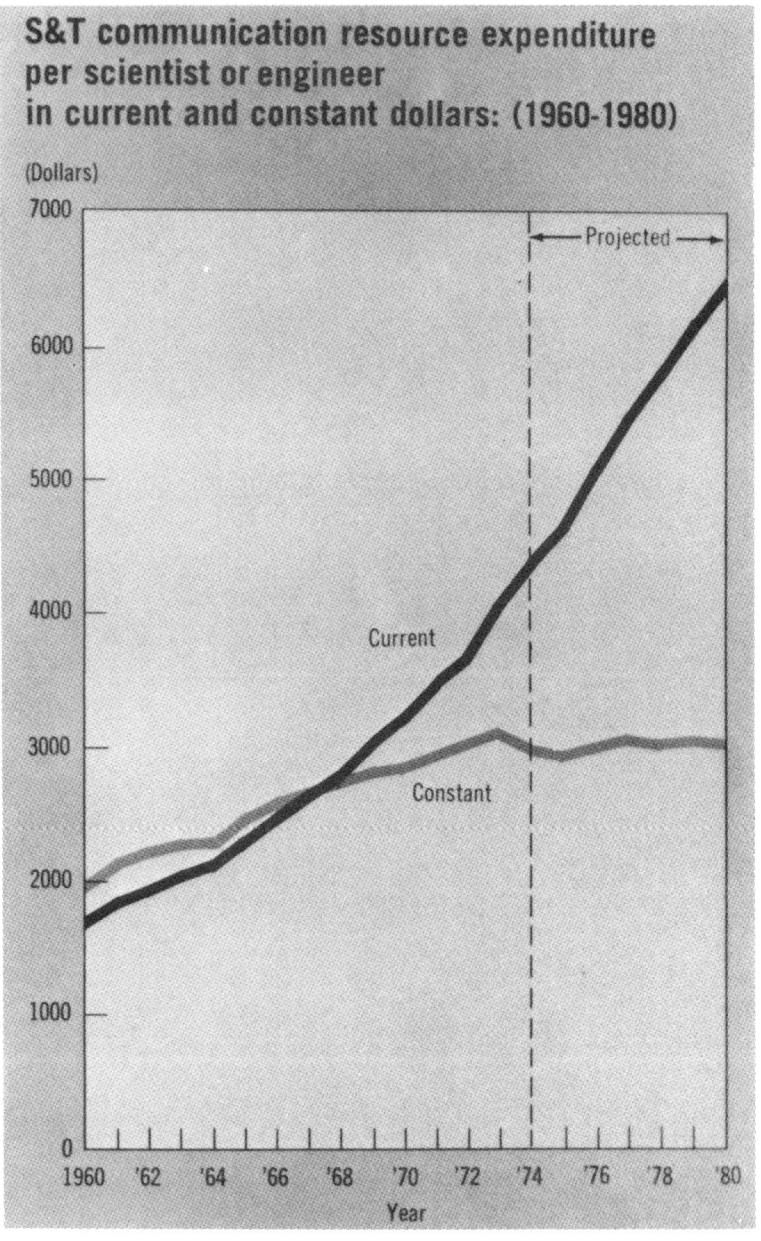

Figure 4 The resources expended per U.S. scientist or engineer on professional communication equaled $1,700 in 1960 and $4,300 in 1974. In constant dollars, this reflects a 50-percent increase. (Reprinted with permission of King Research, Inc., Center for Quantitative Sciences.)

ling, are continuous and relentless. In the course of this successful struggle, you have created institutions, systems, standards, customs, formats, and practices. These use certain technologies. You have, in fact, used excellently the computers, printers, and copiers that were injected into the lofty culture of literature decades ago. But these professional practices always seem to fall out of step unless carefully tended and revised. This is because of the surging growth of new science and technology that apply to these matters. As I said in a lecture at Harvard University, change never comes easily in society, but change involving human sensing of perception, thought, logic, memory, and knowledge may come very hard indeed. These are the essence of human action; the things that, along with spirit and emotions, make us human. They are not likely to be revised casually. Yet they are the very aspects that these profound new technologies most affect. The more expert a culture becomes, the more it favors the *status quo*. Thus, now that you have achieved this professionalism, you must learn to be suspicious of it. Please examine and self-criticize more acutely than some other great professions—biomedicine, for instance—have done during their periods of revolution. I leave to this fine Federation, and to its affiliated professional assemblies worldwide, the responsibility for determining how to exert this self-criticism. But I wish to reinforce my plea by examining quickly a few (doubtlessly inadequate) examples of how rapidly information and communications science and engineering are changing. In fact, it may be seen already (although not very clearly) how greatly these changes will affect the profession in the near future.

I must emphasize that one of the products of information science —indeed one of the manifestations—shows how this new professionalism extends far beyond the traditions of bibliographers and librarians (Figure 5). I am referring to the continuing set of analytic, operational accounts of present activities and status. Good examples are the National Science Foundation's (NSF's) current *Progress Reports*; its sponsorship of various accessory studies, such as the MITRE study referred to earlier; and, especially, the 1960–1980 *Statistical Indicators of Scientific and Technical Communication*, sponsored by the Division of Science Information of NSF with contract to King Research, Inc. These useful studies, as well as approaches being expanded by Dr. Lee Burchinal, Andrew Aines, and their associates, tie in with well-established analogous systems studies carried out by the National Library of Medicine, parts of the Departments of Agriculture and Defense, the National Aeronautics and Space Administration, and the Energy Research and Development Administration, to mention only a few. These give confidence that the systems analysis and administration hoped for in 1958 are being achieved.

Furthermore, we have, in these times, generated some additional

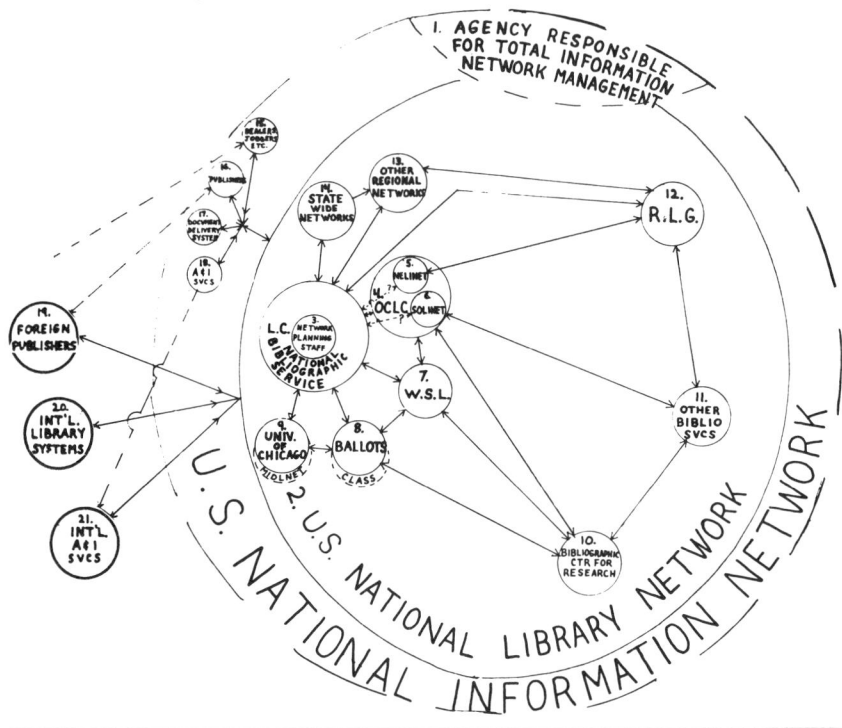

Figure 5 The growing role of library systems in national networks of information handling is reflected in the interactions proposed by the Council on Library Resources. (Reprinted with permission of L. Livingston, Council on Library Resources.)

organizations to help with planning and strengthening the basic national information resources. Some are concerned with enhancing education, and others reflect the increasing contribution of the information industry to our Gross National Product. For instance, the National Commission on Libraries and Information Science has already applied much of the specialized experience of the last two decades in handling scientific and technical information to the broader arena of libraries, education, industrial databases, and other subsystems that might be associated in a national network (see Figure 5). The Library of Congress (Librarian's Task Force) and accessory independent enterprises, such as the Council on Library Resources, have begun important related work.

The proliferation of such efforts is a natural part of good professionalism, too. But the steadily rising industrial-technological growth and the remarkable market economics and economic stimulus that can come from access to knowledge are still in their early stages. Therefore, it is heartening to report that the science and engineering of information processing that we foresaw hopefully, but somewhat dimly, two decades ago is achieving high goals.

The theoretical principles of digital encoding and logic and memory processing are borne out in the astonishing versatility of their electronic implements. While humankind plods along with no discernible change in the 40-bits-per-second average speed of in-go and out-go through the nervous system and the mind, kilomegabit machine speeds—nanosecond (10^{-9}) logic and memory access—are shaping up steadily. One might ask, Is this a natural limit? Is this the goal that will level off as we now use multimegabit and indeed hundreds of megabit rates in present-day facilities? The answer, I believe, is that we still have broad new horizons to study, such as the behavior of exitonic plasmas (Figure 6). Perhaps under more specialized conditions will also come cryogenic Josephson junctions and high-density, high-speed magnetic domain or "bubble" memories. Embodied in these techniques is the wonderful goal of encoding all human knowledge or sensation in pulses or nonpulses (Figures 7A, 7B, and 8). This is happening as the result of independent initiative in industry devoted to still larger objectives of the economy and free-market demands; and, since industry is developing more information products to fill new markets, information processing will continue to decline in cost (and tediousness) (Figures 9 and 10). Hence, we can look to the operational system opportunities I have just noted for wide and lively exercise of human ingenuity. Automated systems will be increasingly distributed among processor-user groups. But, as I shall discuss next, they will appeal also to the generating groups as well.

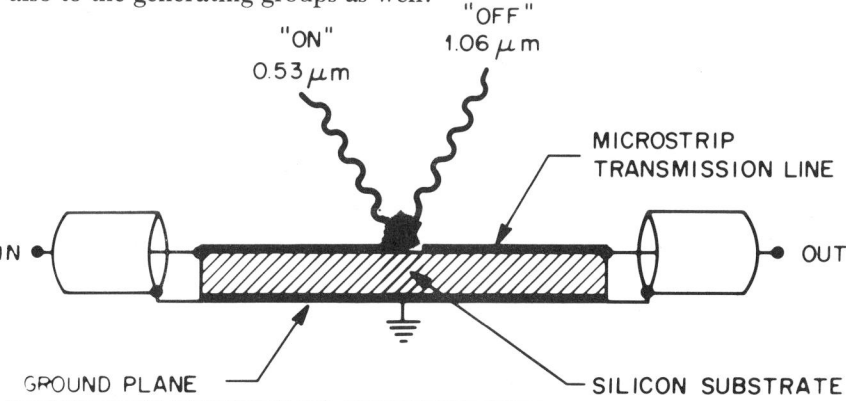

Figure 6 This new optoelectronic switch operates in only 10 picoseconds (10^{-12}). A 0.53-micron laser pulse focused on the gap in the microstrip transmission line increases conductivity near the surface of the silicon substrate and turns the switch on. A 1.06-micron pulse turns the switch off by shunting the line.

170 *Abstracting and Indexing Services in Perspective*

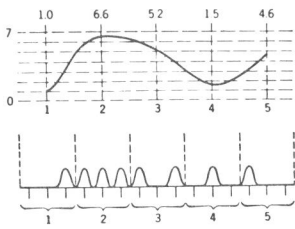

Amplitude	Code
0	000
1	001
2	010
3	011
4	100
5	101
6	110
7	111

Figure 7A Shown here is the digital encoding by electrical pulses (in Figure 7B) of the analog wave of a voice signal.

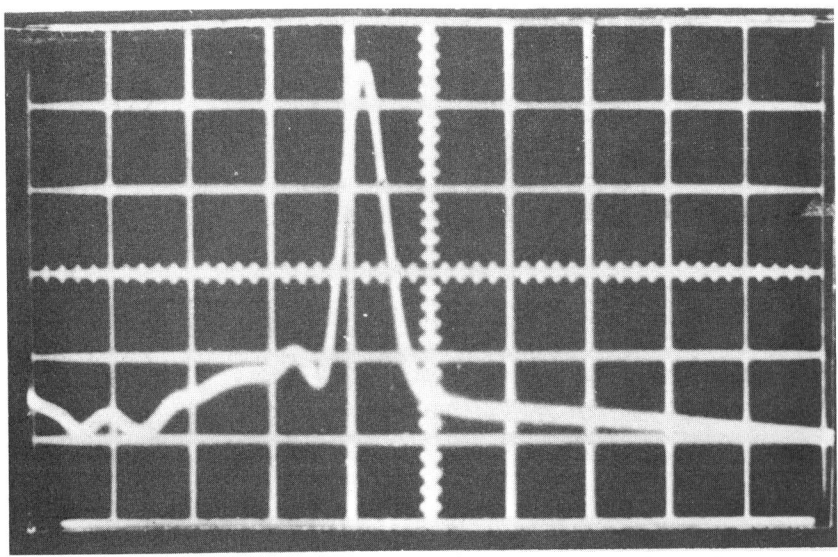

Figure 7B A real electromagnetic encoding pulse, made at the rate of about one billion pulses per second, is shown in an oscillograph image.

The alphabet in 4.7 bits per letter

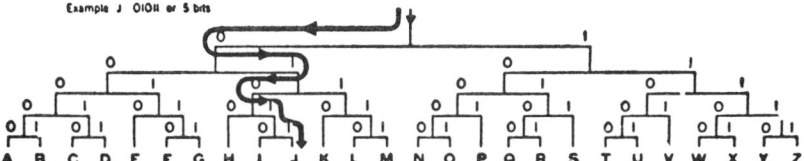

The weather map, bit by bit

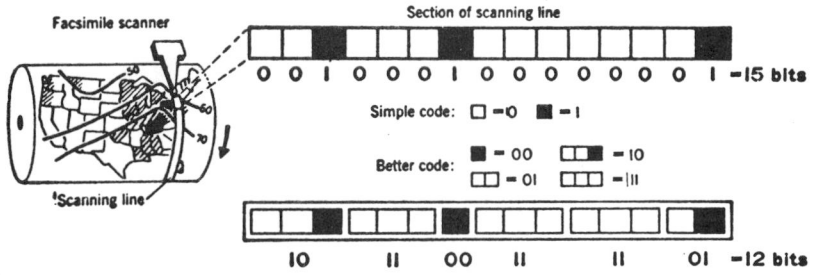

Figure 8 Words and pictures can be expressed in a common code, the binary digital system. With binary codes, all types of information of varying complexity can be encoded.

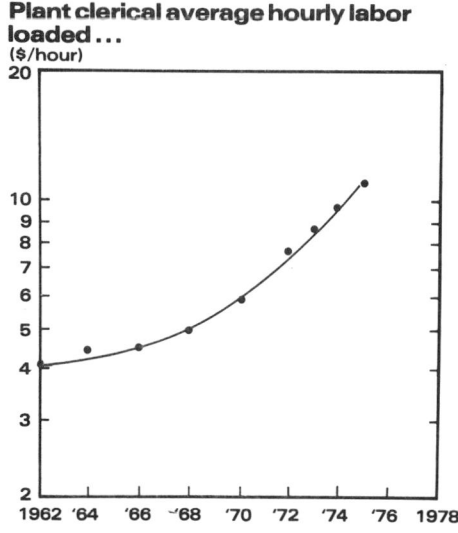

Figure 9 The hourly wage earned by clerical personnel in the Bell System has increased since 1962 at approximately the indicated rate.

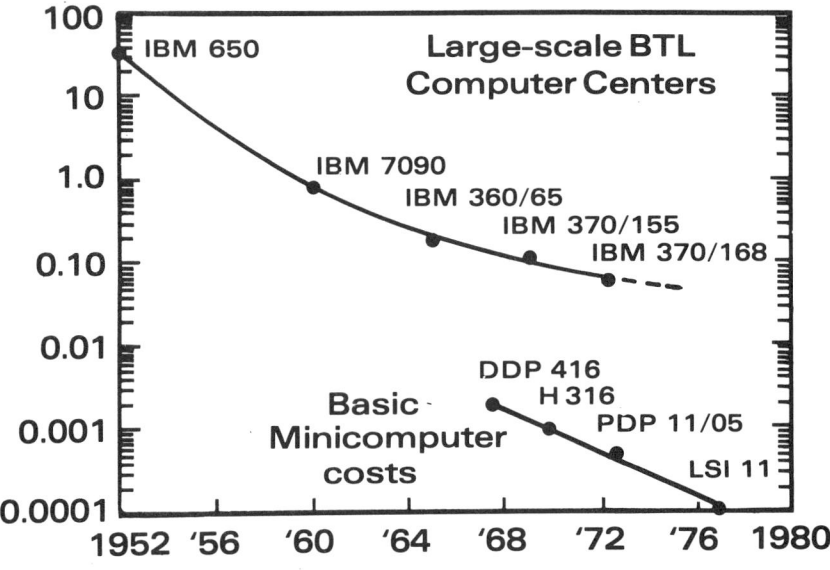

Figure 10 The change in cost of processing information on both large-scale computers and minicomputers is illustrated by these Bell Laboratories usage figures.

We are entering a period when digital processing will at last follow the needs of the mind and body much as the printed book and journal have done for so long. For example, a microprocessor has recently been reported that is less than 1/10th the size of a postage stamp and is powered by 0.1 watt. This "MAC-8" can carry out several hundred different logic functions and can discharge more than 400 instructions at a rate exceeding 100,000 per second (Figure 11). Also, it is equipped with whatever sort of memory one prefers—for instance, a silicon chip unit the size of the head of a thumb tack. This complementary metal oxide semiconductor and n-channel metal oxide semiconductor combination functions with the equivalent of more than 7,000 individual transistors. It will provide a variety of information activities (Figure 12).

With these take-off points, what should be the next steps for the abstracting and indexing of knowledge? A practical hint is given in the fiscal graphs of the *Indicators Study* of the Division of Science Information at NSF. It can be seen that in science and technology, communications

Progress in a Profession   173

Figure 11 Shown here are two MAC-8 microprocessors (foreground) and one of two circuit boards equivalent to the new microprocessor. The MAC-8 is able to execute more than 100,000 logic functions per second, while using only 0.1 watts of power.

Figure 12 The MAC-8, which contains more than 7,000 transistors, is as powerful as a small computer.

resources expenditures have risen since 1960 from just over $2 billion to $9.4 billion, a 6.6-percent annual increase in constant dollars (see Figure 2). It seems that expenditures will continue to rise but at a reduced rate of around 3 percent through 1980. Furthermore, while the cost per scientist and engineer is more or less leveling off in terms of constant dollars (the inevitable result of high technology) (see Figure 4), the total cost of $5,000 in 1976 is projected to rise to at least $6,500 by 1980, and it is those dollars with which the budget competitions in government and the private sector will deal. Most significant is the finding of King Research that the largest part of the costs of publishing and abstracting is that associated with the salaries of scientists (Figure 13), who are both authors and users of information and thus represent the extremes of the information processing cycle. This cost is said to amount to approximately 65 percent of the total expenditures and thus is a multibillion dollar cost.

There is an even deeper issue surrounding this dominant element of the system. In the 1958 PSAC study, it was said,

From a purely practical point of view, it must be remembered that much of the day-to-day work involved in the dissemination of scientific information — that is, the writing, editing, abstracting, translating, and so on — is done either by scientists or people with technical skills of a very high order. Many of these people perform such chores in addition to their regular scientific work, and it is quite inconceivable that they could be induced to affiliate themselves on a full-time basis with a centralized agency.

Having thus derived our theme of decentralization and pluralism from such basic considerations, we should now emphasize that we must appeal further to this generator-user community. We must persuade them to enfold in their abilities and interests the best and newest skills in transmitting, organizing, and abstracting information. Actually, in view of the mounting complexity of science and technology in the last 20 years, and with the curious fluctuations in literacy derived from primary and secondary education, we fear that the always-marginal efficiency of generators and ultimate users probably has declined. But, in any case, it stops far short of its potential.

We now have new generations of scientists and engineers who must strive to master the enormous volume of knowledge accumulated during the middle of this century. That volume will not decrease soon; the scientific and technical communications studies I have cited suggest that the number of scientific articles published in 1980 may exceed 169,000 (151,000 were published in 1974) (Figures 14 and 15). The greatest growth, as in the past, will be in the interdisciplinary, transspecialty fields, such as computer and environmental sciences. The combination of machine-aided word processing and properly led pedagogy applied to

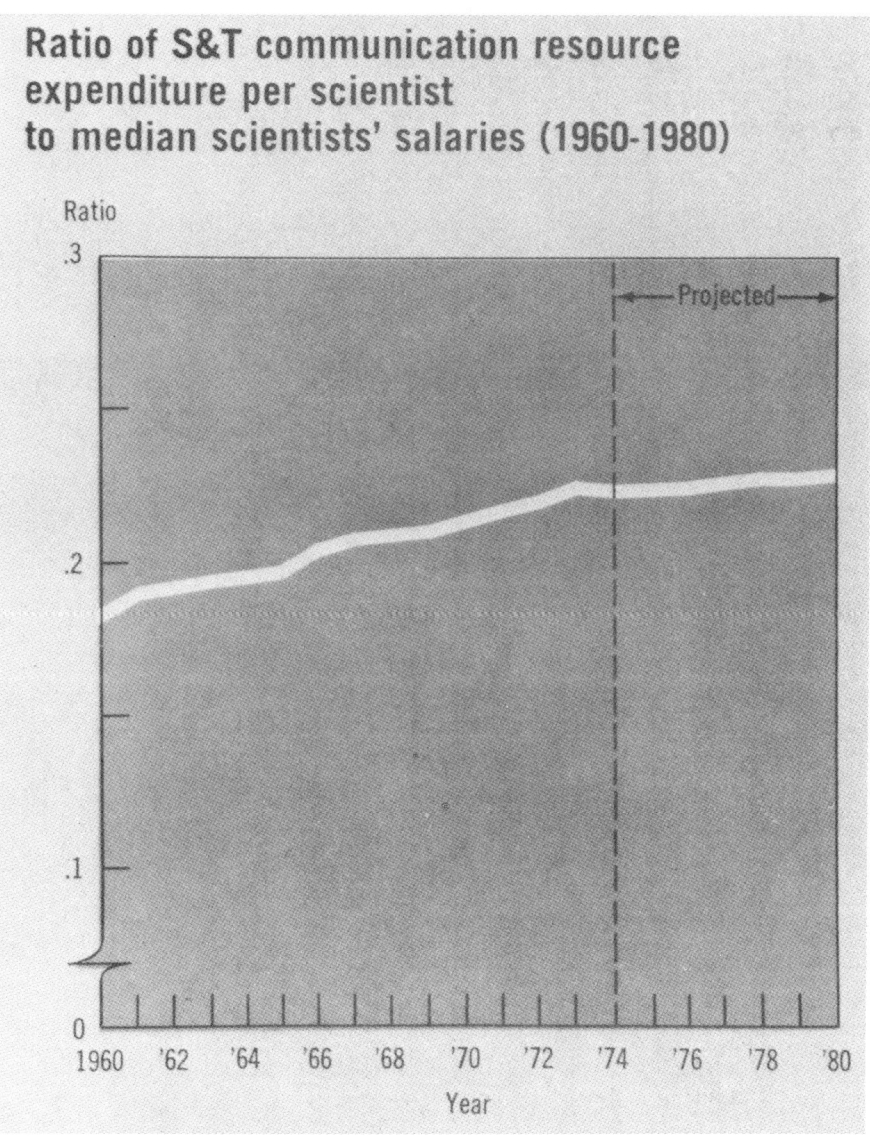

Figure 13 A significant part (perhaps 60 percent) of the total scientific and technical communication resources expenditures is a function of the salaries of scientists. (Reprinted with permission of King Research, Inc., Center for Quantitative Sciences.)

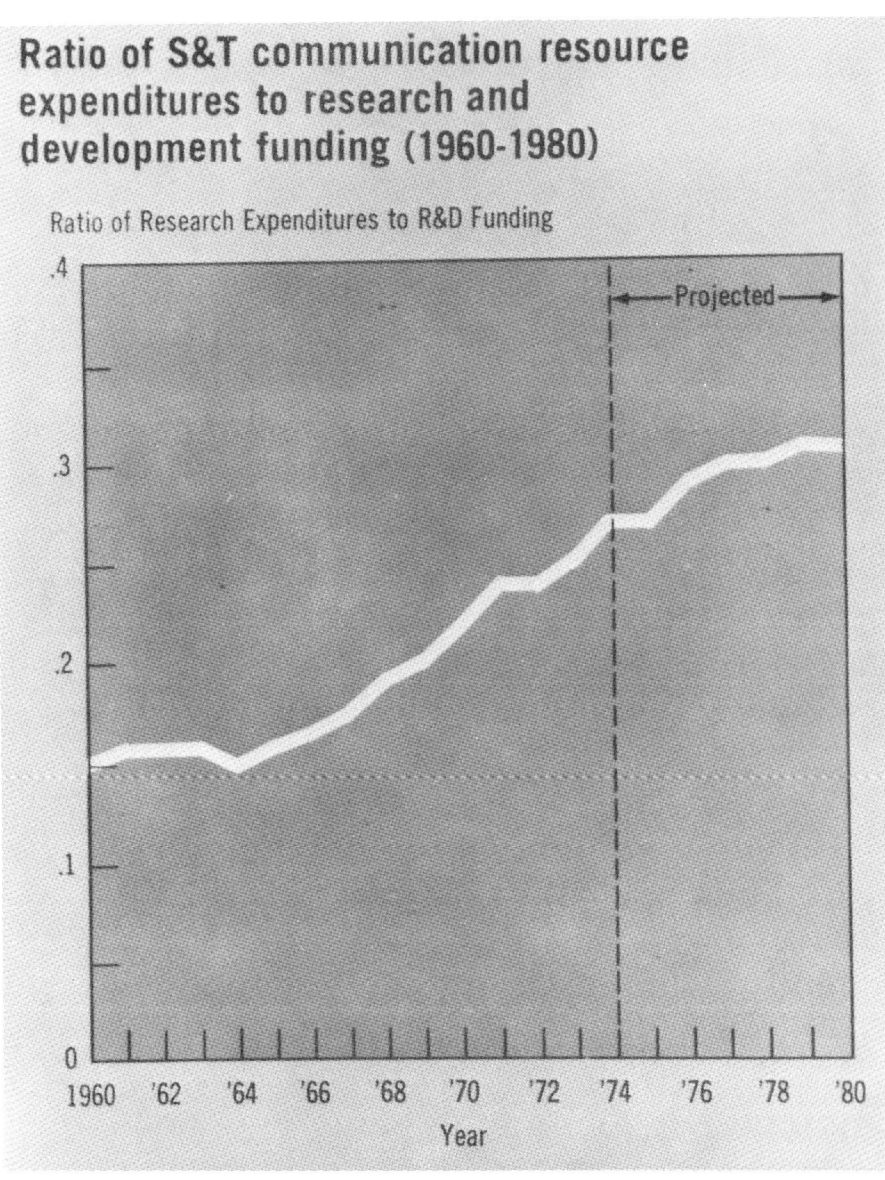

Figure 14 The ratio of communication resources expenditures to research and development (R&D) has risen steadily since 1964. Much of the resources expended in scientific and technical communication comes from R&D funds. (Reprinted with permission of King Research, Inc., Center for Quantitative Sciences.)

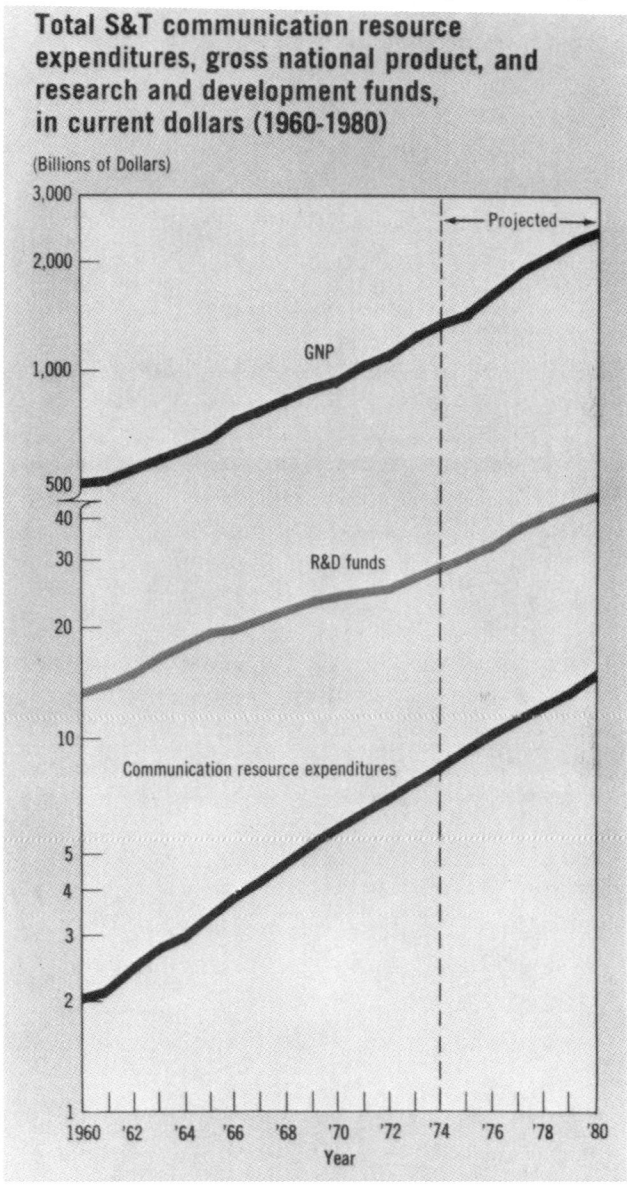

Figure 15 The scientific and technical communication resources expenditures have risen faster than the Gross National Product (GNP) and R&D funding. From 1960 to 1974, the GNP grew 177 percent, R&D funding increased 136 percent, and scientific and technical communication resources expenditures increased an estimated 323 percent. (Reprinted with permission of King Research, Inc., Center for Quantitative Sciences.)

composition and organization could lead to strong advances in the quality and utility of scientific and technical (and ultimately all) knowledge. Mainly, abstracts and indexes offer a fascinating place to start. Already their formatting and style reflect recognized needs. Within those needs, the relatively primitive organization and processing we do now can be developed into simplified, optimally displayed modes of human expression. These will go far to counter the hasty, often confused, gibberish that is so frequently cited as replacing the composition skills expected from early education. Despite excellent and expanding teaching and exercise in the scientific and technical literature, it appears that of the basic skills, elements that could be injected into particular realms of abstracting and indexing have barely been realized.

Let us turn briefly to a set of studies by Dr. L. T. Frase of Bell Laboratories. Dr. Frase applied behavioral rating tests and statistics to manuals for Bell System operations. These manuals have been developed over decades as possibly the most straightforward and simple modes of expression for what are exacting communications for craftsmen, plant engineers, and the like. Despite the best efforts of the generators, it was found that at least 30 percent of all sentences could be reduced in complexity and improved in intelligibility and impact. Some 80 percent of these changes involved such formatting and style as actually enumerating the principal elements of the sentence (e.g., numbering the steps in a given procedure) and specifying sentence elements (e.g., repeating the subject of the sentence). These changes greatly improved the speed and comprehension of assimilation of literature that is similar in many ways to abstracts (Figure 16). To these findings may be added speculative ideas, such as the significance of colored inks and various shapes and shadings of letters. Research at Bell and elsewhere has shown that such factors can have important consequences.

It is hoped that further studies and trials can soon be undertaken. In these, volunteer authors and users of our national abstracts and indexes will begin experimenting with word processing and modification of sentence structure. The objective will be to match newly determined levels of reader and writer comprehension. It cannot be assumed that this study will be easily executed or quickly accomplished. For instance, in an earlier Bell study, E. Z. Rothkopf and later Frase, determined that educators' and reviewers' judgments of effectiveness were often negatively correlated with demonstrated performance of self-instructional materials. Also, Frase found that there is little basis for assuming that readers will eagerly select writing that has been carefully reviewed in terms of actual cognitive qualities or demands. Nevertheless, this anomaly does not mean that the ultimate efficiency of such improvements is not felt; it is just that the reader often does not recognize it. So together we should try to exploit

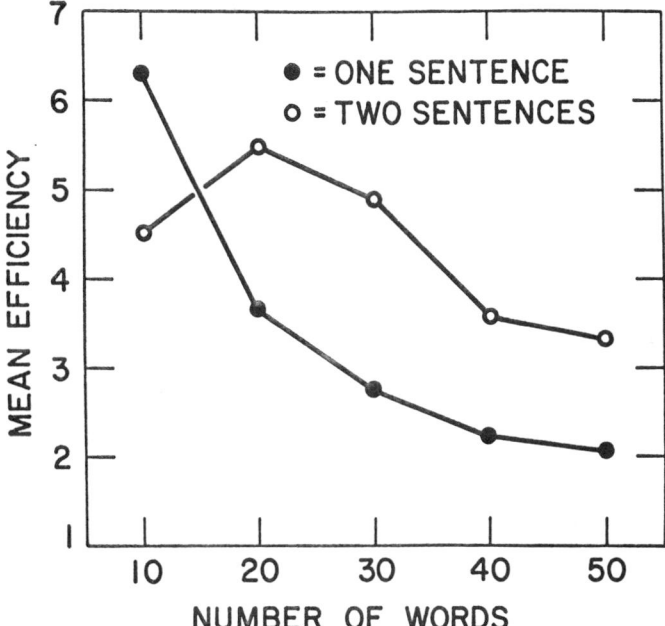

SENTENCE RATINGS WHEN VARIOUS NUMBERS OF
WORDS ARE EXPRESSED IN ONE OR TWO SENTENCES.

Figure 16 The effectiveness of sentences decreases as the number of words increases. Thoughts expressed in two sentences in an experiment conducted at Bell Laboratories received higher ratings than the same thoughts in one-sentence form. When 10 words were involved, however, two 5-word sentences were less efficient than one 10-word sentence. (Adapted from the work of L. T. Frase, Bell Laboratories.)

the new electronics for dealing with knowledge and language so that prospectuses and indexes, and hopefully authors, will creatively use improved structures. These will immediately link the human composition with the machine processing that is eventually applied.

One approach to this venture is through the continuing progress that is being made in word-processing systems. These have already vastly expedited the editing, typing, and assembling of papers. It seems that these systems, if extended for the use of abstractors and ultimately authors, could induce a new level of simplicity and intelligibility of text. At the same time, certain features would be machine coded and processed, thus making available more than the conventional hand-coded inputs that are already so useful for computer retrieval in the literature. Indeed, such inputs have taken hold so strongly, as reported at the American Association for the Advancement of Science (AAAS) meeting in Denver, that there were about 1.2 million online searches in 1976. It was noted that 50 million abstracts and listings from 50,000 journals representing 90–95 percent of the current literature, including that of reports, are now available.

Some feeling for the manipulations of language and usage that are at hand can perhaps be gained from comments on the UNIX operating system developed at Bell (Figure 17). First, it is versatile regarding files (Figure 18). It is effective in injecting consistent nomenclature and data forms as abstracts and original papers are prepared. Likewise, both text and data

UNIX

A Time-Shared Operating System for
DEC PDP-11 Minicomputers

- Compact
  System occupies between 20,000 and 30,000 16-bit words of memory, including buffers
- Simple
  One-man design of main system software
- Low Cost
  Various configurations cost between $40,000 and $250,000

Figure 17 The UNIX system, developed by Bell Laboratories, is a compact, general-purpose, interactive operating system. It offers a number of features seldom found even in larger operating systems.

UNIX FILE SYSTEM

- Uniformly addressed hierarchy
- Uniform file structure
- Device independence

A file is a stream of bytes with
- No idea of records
- No idea of intended use
- No idea of physical hardware parameters

Figure 18 To retrieve a UNIX file, the user supplies the name of the file and the device or program where it is to appear. For example, the file can be typed on a terminal, displayed on a cathode ray tube, written on magnetic tape, or used as input to a program. All files are handled in the same way regardless of their intended use.

TEXT PROCESSING UTILITIES

Word count
Alphabetical sort
Translate characters
Find duplications
Find word or letter patterns
1-, 2- and 3-letter frequencies
Encryption and decryption
...

Figure 19 Listed here are some of the operations that can be performed, either singly or in sequence, on a UNIX text file.

A PROGRAM FOR FINDING "SPELLING ERRORS"

Strip out all punctuation (tr)
Change all upper case to lower (tr)
Place all words one on a line (tr)
Alphabetize the words (sort)
Cast out duplicates (uniq)
Cast out those in dictionary (comm)
4-column printout (pr)

Figure 20 A program that operates under UNIX follows this sequence of operations to identify and print in alphabetical order all the words in a manuscript that are not in its dictionary.

can flow through successive processes. Editing, numbering, and table-making are done without having to store intermediate results (Figure 19). This capability is believed to be peculiar to UNIX, but will certainly be incorporated into others in the near future. A text file can be manipulated many different ways to increase its consistency. Then, for many interesting purposes, the program will identify, in a particular abstract or manuscript, all the words not in its dictionary (Figure 20). This serves to identify misspelled and distorted words. It also points out those words to which the composer should give special attention to ensure understandability.

Likewise, the system will arrange for publication through phototypesetting or other reproduction means (Figure 21). It will provide desired formats that can be developed to improve configuration of concise abstracts. Color can be introduced at this point if desired. Similarly, a Bell-developed language called EQN allows the typist to insert equations in the same terms used in reading the equations aloud. Use of this by authors and abstractors could significantly improve readability and coherence of modern records (Figure 22). Better use of tables, which are now inhibited by both composing and transcribing times, is another demonstrated approach to easy scanning.

Also, the conventional and costly processes of making galley proofs, followed by page layouts and various intermediate checkings, can all be bypassed with these techniques. This will be shown in a forthcoming article in *Science* entitled "Computers and Research," which was put in final published form by UNIX with no intermediate editing. As might be expected, these processes greatly reduce the cost of primary journal publication by up to 30 percent, as indicated in some recent experiments with the American Institute of Physics (Figure 23). Also, better combinations of word statistics are easily surveyed in the course of this automatic assembly. Thus, for all the words in a particular document, a "peculiarity order" is assigned so that attention is quickly called to various anomalies (Figure 24). Again, new values of this may yet be brought out, since the system can be adjusted to clarity scaling as well. Numerous other uses are also possible with this machine system, such as compression of files according to new information content criteria (Figure 25).

TEXT PROCESSING ON UNIX

Document Preparation
- Text formatters
- Global document layout
- Mathematical equations and tables
- Phototypesetting

Statistical Studies of Text
- "Typo" program
- File compression
- Readability studies

Figure 21 UNIX is especially versatile in preparing documents and performing statistical studies on text. Document preparation has been particularly stimulated by the availability of an inexpensive, high-quality phototypesetter.

There are many additional sorts of technologies being developed that will further encourage flexibility and innovation in composing and abstracting reports. For instance, the fragility of paper, as well as its large space usage in storage, is increasing cause for concern. Its transport will become another expensive and difficult process, with comparatively large

EQN — A LANGUAGE FOR
TYPESETTING MATHEMATICS

```
.EQ
x sup 2 over a sup 2 ~+~ y sup 2 over b sup 2 ~=~ z
.EN
```

$$\frac{x^2}{a^2} + \frac{y^2}{b^2} = z$$

```
.EQ
1 over sqrt{ax sup 2 + bx + c}
.EN
```

$$\frac{1}{\sqrt{ax^2+bx+c}}$$

Figure 22 A Bell Laboratories-developed language, called EQN, permits a typist to input mathematical equations in the form used to read equations aloud. Shown here are two equations and the format used to input each.

COMPUTER TYPESETTING
OF TECHNICAL PAPERS

- Document preparation software under UNIX; *ROFF, NROFF, TROFF, EQN, TBL,* macros

- Phototypesetting of Bell System documents, technical papers, and books

- American Physical Society experiment; composition costs for Physical Review and Physical Review Letters $10-$20 per page vs. $25-$30 for typewriter composition and $40-$50 for monotype

Figure 23 Following its refinement in preparing and typesetting Bell System technical documents, UNIX has been used in cooperation with the American Physical Society/American Institute of Physics on an experimental basis. This enterprise now plans to produce *Physical Review Letters* with similar computer aids.

energy costs. Micrographics have now long passed the microfiche/microfilm stage (as valuable and effective as those forms still are). For example, laser writing on metal-covered tape appears to offer, both economically and functionally, much promise beyond higher bandwidth of the cathode-ray tube and conventional slow facsimile. Records stored in this manner should last at least a century, according to accelerated stress tests.

So the challenges and opportunities at the end of the first two decades

"TYPO" PROGRAM

Statistically Unlikely Words from a 100-Page Typescript

☛	17	nd		16	disagreement
	17	heretofore	☛	16	bwirte
☛	17	erroronously		15	violating
☛	16	suer		15	unaffected
	16	seized		15	tape
☛	16	poiter		15	swapped
	16	lengthy		15	shortly
	16	inaccessible	☛	15	mutiliated

Figure 24   The TYPO program looks at the combination of letters in all words of a document, computes for each word an "index of peculiarity" (shown here to the left of each word), and prints the words in order of decreasing peculiarity.

TEXT AND DATA COMPRESSION

ASCII character codes	8 bits/character
Actual information content	
English text	1 to 2 bits/character
Business records	2 to 3 bits/character
Fortran programs	3 to 4 bits/character

Variable length encoding: Letters, digrams, ...

Dictionaries of common "words"

Efficient encoding-decoding programs

Figure 25   Shown here are a summary of studies made on the information content of various files and some of the techniques that can be used to compress files for long-term storage.

of the national bibliographic and informational regime remain unabated. But they are not, by any means, the same ones that we faced earlier, nor can they have the same solutions. Thus, it is a happy occasion, worthy of the memory of Miles Conrad, to be able to look ahead with confidence that we are not yet passivated or even pacified by the past. Having contributed so much in terms of quantity, we must now cope with quality. This means that we must make not only a concerted effort to cultivate better writers and readers, but also that we must expand the quality of usership. New knowledge, especially in science and engineering, must be used earlier and more strongly by social, economic, governmental, industrial, educational, and personal decision makers everywhere. The right abstracts and indexes can do much for this.

NOTE: Unless otherwise noted, all figures are reproduced with permission of Bell Laboratories.

APPENDIX A

RELEASE FOR A.M. PAPERS OF SUNDAY, DECEMBER 7, 1958

Anne Wheaton, Associate Press Secretary to the President

THE WHITE HOUSE

The President today approved a plan designed to help meet the critical needs of the Nation's scientists and engineers for better access to the rapidly mounting volume of scientific publication.

Acting upon the recommendations of his Science Advisory Committee, the President directed that the National Science Foundation take the leadership in bringing about effective coordination of the various scientific information activities within the Federal Government. The President asked that all Federal agencies whose programs involve scientific information cooperate with and assist the National Science Foundation in improving the Government's own efforts in this area.

Today's action by the President strengthens and reinforces the provision of the "National Defense Education Act of 1958" calling for the establishment of a Science Information Service in the National Science Foundation to: "Provide or arrange for the provision of, indexing, abstracting, translation, and other services leading to a more effective dissemination of scientific information, and undertake programs to develop new or improved methods, including mechanized systems for making scientific information available."

The Committee urged that fullest use be made of existing information services, both public and private, and that the Foundation's Science Information Service supplement rather than supplant present efforts.

Dr. James R. Killian, Jr., Special Assistant to the President for Science and Technology and Chairman of the Science Advisory Committee, commented on the growing dimensions of world scientific publication to the extent that it has become a problem requiring action at the national level.

"Science and engineering are largely built on the published record of earlier work done throughout the world," Dr. Killian states. "There are, for example, 55,000 journals appearing annually, containing about 1,200,000 articles of significance for some branch of research and engineering in the physical and life sciences. More than 60,000 different books are published annually in these fields, while approximately 100,000 research reports remain outside the normal channels of publication and cataloging. Within this vast body of world-wide scientific information, published and unpublished, lie the technical data that scientists need in order to do their work. The situation is further complicated by the fact that a large and important proportion of the world's scientific literature appears in languages unknown to the majority of American scientists, such as Russian and Japanese."

In its recommendations, the President's Science Advisory Committee outlined a program calling for the review, coordination, and stimulation, on a nation-wide basis, of activities in the areas of primary and secondary publications, scientific data centers, unpublished research information, storage and retrieval, and translation by mechanical means.

No new agency will be required to carry out the recommended program. Under its enabling act, the National Science Foundation has devoted special attention to the scientific information needs of scientists and has developed a series of programs designed to help meet those needs. At least ten other Federal agencies are engaged in abstracting and indexing, translating, preparation of technical reports, and research related to information needs. These agencies are asked to cooperate in providing or arranging for acquisition and reference programs, clearinghouse functions, and evaluation studies of existing programs. Research on new and improved methods of information-handling will be emphasized and the Department of State will take the lead in encouraging cooperation among the United States, foreign and international scientific information organizations.

The President's Science Advisory Committee considered the whole problem of such importance that earlier this year it appointed a special subcommittee to consider the subject at length. Headed by Dr. W. O. Baker, Vice-President (Research), Bell Telephone Laboratories, the subcommittee comprises the following members: Mr. Curtis Benjamin, President, McGraw Hill Book Company; Dr. Caryl P. Haskins, President, Carnegie Institution of Washington; Dr. Elmer Hutchisson, Director, American Institute of Physics; Dr. Warren C. Johnson, Dean, Division of Physical Sciences, U. of Chicago; Mr. Don K. Price, Dean of the School of Public Administration and Littauer Professor, Harvard University; Dr. H. Scoville; Dr. Alan T. Waterman, Director, National Science Foundation.

In submitting its findings the subcommittee paid special tribute to the work of individual scientists and engineers in selecting, interpreting, and abstracting scientific and technical information. It noted the fact that the services rendered by many of the scientific societies and professional institutions to the scientific community in the information field are world famous for their quality. It expressed the hope that such private groups would continue to cooperate with and assist the Federal Government in the achievement of long-range solutions to scientific information problems.

The subcommittee's conclusions form the basis for the recommendations submitted to the President by the Science Advisory Committee.

APPENDIX B

FOR RELEASE IN A.M. PAPERS, SUNDAY, DECEMBER 7, 1958

Anne Wheaton, Associate Press Secretary to the President

THE WHITE HOUSE

A REPORT OF
THE PRESIDENT'S SCIENCE ADVISORY COMMITTEE

IMPROVING THE AVAILABILITY
OF SCIENTIFIC AND TECHNICAL
INFORMATION IN THE UNITED STATES

WHAT THE PROBLEM IS AND WHY IT IS SERIOUS

The long, hard look we have recently taken at the state of science and technology in this country has brought to light several areas that need to be strengthened and improved. Some of these, notably in the field of education, have aroused nation-wide concern. But another area—also in great need of attention—has attracted little or no public interest. This is the matter of scientific information—the technical data that a scientist needs in order to do his job. Yet our progress in science may very well depend upon the intelligent solution of problems in that area.

All of us use a wide variety of information every day of our lives. We glean it from newspapers, conversation, radio and television, magazines, clocks, books, meters, mail, maps and so on. The scientist, however, is interested in the specialized information that results from scientific research. The publication of research information is absolutely essential to every working scientist for two reasons: (1) It is the means by which he announces significant results in his own work, establishes priority where appropriate and invites the evaluation of other scientists; (2) It is also the means by which he keeps abreast of what others are doing in his field.

The extent to which the working scientist depends upon the work of others has been clearly stated by one of the greatest of all scientists, the atomic physicist, Ernest Rutherford. As quoted by James Newman in a recent issue of *The Scientific American*, Lord Rutherford said:

> I have also tried to show you that it is not in the nature of things for any one man to make a sudden violent discovery; science goes step by step, and every man depends on the work of his predecessors. When you hear of a sudden unexpected discovery—a bolt from the blue as it were—you can always be sure that it has grown up by the influence of one man on another, and it is this mutual influence which makes the enormous possibility of scientific advance.

Scientists are not dependent on the ideas of a single man, but on the combined wisdom of thousands of men, all thinking the same problem, and each doing his little bit to add to the great structure of knowledge which is gradually being erected.

The reason scientific information has become a major problem, particularly since World War II, is that the rapid rate of scientific progress has multiplied the volume of scientific information to a point where it can no longer be published and handled within the framework of existing methods. When one considers, too, that much of what is significant in science is being published in unfamiliar languages, it is clear that the working scientist is faced with almost insuperable problems in attempting to keep himself informed on what he needs to know.

Some idea of the volume of increase may be had from the fact that the science and technology periodical collections of the Library of Congress have doubled approximately every 20 years for the past century and now contain approximately a million and a half volumes, a significant fraction of the Library's total bound collections. The Library is receiving journals in science and technology at the rate of about 15,000 annually, and 1,200 to 1,500 new periodicals are appearing each year. Yet the Library receives less than a third of the 50,000 scientific periodicals that appear in the world list of 1952 and it is expected that by 1979 the total world output will reach 100,000 journals.

The language difficulty is reflected in the fact that Russian-language publications are estimated to account for a tenth or more of all the scientific literature being published in the world today. This Russian total is second only to English.

Reduced to simple terms, the scientist's problem with respect to information is: How can the present volume of research results be published promptly? What is being published now? Where is it? and How can I get at it? The purpose of this paper is to examine these problems and to suggest possible ways in which they can be solved. In particular, it will consider the question of what should be the responsibility of the Federal Government in meeting this crisis.

THE PRESENT SYSTEM

The system by which scientific information is disseminated is the result of evolution rather than any preconceived system or plan. Its defects stem largely from its inability to keep pace with the increasing volume of scientific results and literature and the absence of techniques geared to the newer forms of scientific information, such as Government reports. The situation is further complicated by the fact that a large and important proportion of the world's scientific literature appears in languages unknown to the majority of American scientists, such as Russian and Japanese.

Scientific information appears in several forms. Most significant are the highly specialized technical periodicals, called primary journals, because it is in these that new scientific results are first published. *The Physical Review*, *Journal of the American Chemical Society*, and the *Aeronautical Engineering Review* are examples.

Another important primary source is the monograph, an exhaustive study of some highly specialized phase of science. Because it is of interest to only a limited number of scientists, and because it often includes elaborate charts and plates, the monograph is almost prohibitively expensive to publish. The result is a lack in this country of monographs on many exceptionally important scientific subjects that should be so covered.

A second important category is the abstracting journals, such as *Biological Abstracts* and *Chemical Abstracts*. These contain summaries or synopses of papers that originally appeared in primary journals. When adequately indexed, they permit a searcher to locate previously published papers on any given subject. If an abstract is sufficiently informative, it may serve the scientist in lieu of the complete paper. It should be noted parenthetically, however, that the 14 major scientific abstracting services in the United States recently indicated that the almost half a million abstracts that they issue annually constitute only about 55 per cent of what they should be publishing in order to cover the literature in their combined fields reasonably well. Other important secondary sources include critical reviews, special indexes and indexing services, bibliographies, title lists, collected tables of contents, handbooks of data, and compendia of various kinds.

A recent trend of special interest is the establishment of Data Centers. When the quantity of research data in a given field becomes too great for book publication to be practical, the Data Center offers a solution. Such centers compile, correlate, standardize, and organize numerically, data representing the properties of materials or the characteristics of phenomena. Examples of such centers include the Thermophysical Properties Research Center at Purdue University; American Petroleum Institute Research Project 44 at the Carnegie Institute of Technology, which is concerned with the physical properties of hydrocarbons; the Nuclear Data Project of the National Research Council; and the National Bureau of Standards center on Selected Values of Chemical Thermodynamic Properties.

Falling outside scientific information that is published, catalogued, and indexed in the normal way, is a steadily mounting volume of Government research reports. It is conservatively estimated that upwards of 50,000 scientific reports (at least half of which bear no security classification) are issued annually by the private and Government laboratories that conduct Federally-sponsored research. Many of the newest and most significant scientific data are to be found in these reports.

A smaller body of scientific information not covered by the normal processes is to be found in such material as research findings submitted in satisfaction of Ph.D. thesis requirements, industrial reports and papers presented at scientific meetings and symposia.

At the present time it is not even possible to answer the question with any degree of completeness, "What is being published now?" One would assume that, somewhere in the world, there must be a composite listing of the world's scientific publications — perhaps even arranged by subject fields — but no such compilation exists. The establishment of such a list and its maintenance on a current basis obviously would be a very expensive undertaking, and this is one reason why it has never been done.

The basic answer to "Where can I find it?"—as far as journals are concerned—is the "Union List of Serials,"—in the libraries of United States and Canada. Such a compilation lists periodicals alphabetically and names the libraries where each can be found. But no such union list of *scientific* journals now exists. A Joint Committee on a Union List of Serials covering all fields has estimated that the science and technology portion of a new union list would cost approximately three-quarters of a million dollars. It could be kept up to date only in a relative sense, since such a list is constantly changing. It follows, of course, that no comprehensive listing of the principal secondary publications is in existence either.

Then there is the problem of "How can I get it?" The scientist who needs a particular journal may find himself (if the journal is rare) far distant from the location of the nearest copy as indicated by the union list; or he may find that the article he is seeking is in a language he does not read.

In summation, then, it may be said that both inside and outside the normal channels of scientific communication a mounting flood of scientific data threatens to swamp even the most zealous research investigator. The implications go far beyond the inability of one man, or even a group of men, to keep abreast of developments in their field. *Our very progress in science is dependent upon the free flow of scientific information*, for the rate of scientific advance is determined in large measure by the speed with which research findings are disseminated among scientists who can use them in further research.

HOW ARE WE GOING TO MEET THIS PROBLEM?

The situation has evolved over a lengthy period of time, during which the developing problems not only have been recognized, but have been the subject of attack on a number of separate fronts. These efforts have been handicapped, however, by the lack of overall coordination and sufficient funds with which to support really effective remedies.

What Is Already Being Done?

All along the line there have been sincere efforts to cope with the problems. Primary journals have expanded substantially in recent years and the scientific societies have helped to cover the increased costs by raising dues and subscription prices. In an effort to conserve space, greater and greater condensation of papers is being required, with the result that there is danger of few people besides the author and his immediate colleagues being able to understand a paper. There is constant search for cheaper production methods and many journals levy page costs upon the authors, so that scientists must pay for the privilege of having their research findings published. Such financial help as the Government has given has been limited, consisting largely of short-term emergency grants made to tide a particular journal over a rough spot or to launch a new journal that is badly needed in order to fill a gap. Some agencies pay page costs for their employees and their contractors' employees when they publish.

Federal aid has also been provided in the form of temporary assistance to commercial abstracting and indexing services, including funds to support the establishment of a National Federation of Science Abstracting and Indexing Services, designed to bring cooperative efforts to bear upon mutual problems. A few Government agencies publish or partially support certain secondary publications in subject fields of particular interest to them.

It is generally agreed, however, that the magnitude and seriousness of the problem are such that a long-term solution requires fundamental research into the problem and widespread application of machine methods and techniques. In other words, science must look within itself for a new system that will meet present-day requirements for the location, storage, and retrieval of scientific information.

A number of industrial firms have developed, and are using successfully, mechanized storage and retrieval systems tailored to their own needs. Large manufacturers of business machines and computers are becoming increasingly interested in the application of their equipment to information-processing problems. A dozen or more universities are carrying on research in the information-handling field, including studies of existing patterns of scientific communication in various subject fields, research in mechancial translation, development of procedures for determining how scientists use technical information, and research on actual mechanical systems for information storage and retrieval. Within the Government, the National Science Foundation has supported research on scientific information problems to the extent that available funds have permitted.

Efforts are also being made to improve the availability of foreign scientific information. The emphasis is on Russian research results because Soviet scientific publications are second only to our own in number, and because so few scientists in this country read Russian. Of the 61 Soviet journals available here on subscription in cover-to-cover translation, about 34 are being supported principally by the National Science Foundation, with assistance from the Atomic Energy Commission and the Office of Naval Research. Nine are supported by the National Institutes of Health; the rest are issued commercially.

In the field of unpublished documents the Office of Technical Services, Department of Commerce, lists some 7,500 such documents each year in its abstracting journal, *U.S. Government Research Reports.* Copies of all items so announced can be obtained in original form or in photoreproduction. The Library of Congress is building in its Science and Technology Division an open reference collection of unclassified reports. The National Science Foundation maintains a clearinghouse for Government research information to provide scientists information on Government-supported research in their fields and the reports that are available.

Thus a considerable amount of work is being done on serious scientific information problems. From the standpoint of national welfare, however, these efforts are on far too small a scale to deal with the over-all problem. The question then remains as to how it can be met.

What Should Be Done for the Future?

Two alternative possibilities have been advanced. One would be the establishment of a large and highly centralized scientific information agency, financed by the Federal Government or by government and private industry. A second would be the establishment of a science information service of the coordinating type, which would strengthen and improve the present system by taking full advantage of existing organizations and the specialized skills of persons with long experience in the field. Let us examine the respective merits of these alternatives.

A Single Large Operating Center? The proposal to solve existing problems in the field of scientific information by the establishment of a single large operating center, financed wholly or in part by the Federal Government, may have been suggested by the experience of the Soviet Union with its All-Union Institute of Scientific Information. The organization and operation of the Institute implies that the Russians recognize the magnitude and importance of the problem by their decisive and aggressive attempts to meet it. Available evidence indicates that the Institute operates effectively in meeting the needs of Russian science. But, it must not be overlooked that in planning the establishment and operations of the Institute, the Russians could not call upon the services of scientific information organizations such as we find already in existence in the private enterprise structure of our country, and which have been in operation many years.

The solution the Russians have developed for meeting their own problems in our judgment *would not* be equally effective in meeting ours. The Russian Institute is organized along the lines that are basically compatible with the organization and administration of research in the Soviet Union, which, of course, is controlled by the Central Government. Our own research efforts are organized and administered very differently, and it is illogical to suppose that a highly centralized organization for the dissemination of research information would serve our purposes equally well. Whatever its faults may be, our present system has developed along the lines of individual initiative and private enterprise that are very basic to our institutions.

The primary journals, as well as the abstracting services, are published under the benign auspices of the scientific societies who are in a better position than anyone else to appreciate the information problems of scientists. Existing services, moreover, represent a considerable investment of private capital. *Chemical Abstracts*, for example, which has operated without Government subsidy, had a 1957 budget of approximately $1.5 million. Although most of the journals and services have smaller budgets and many do receive some Government support, the total private investment in the publication and dissemination of results of scientific research runs into many millions of dollars. The mere mechanics of transforming the existing decentralized system of private enterprise into a strong central agency are enough to stagger the imagination.

From a purely practical point of view, it must be remembered that much of the day-to-day work involved in the dissemination of scientific information — that is, the writing, editing, abstracting, translating, and so on — is done either by scientists or people with technical skills of a very high order. Many of these people perform such chores in addition to their regular scientific work and it is quite inconceivable that they could be induced to affiliate themselves on a full-time basis with a centralized agency. Put the matter another way: the case for a Government-operated, highly centralized type of center can be no better defended for scientific information services than it could be for automobile agencies, delicatessens, or barber shops.

A Science Information Service? The second alternative, however, could lead to an integrated, efficient and comprehensive scientific information service that would take advantage of privately supported programs as well as the very extensive work being done by the Federal Agencies—that is, it would strengthen rather than supplant them. Specifically, this solution calls for the establishment within the Government of an organization that might be called a Science Information Service. Such a Service would assist, cooperate with, and supplement the many existing scientific information programs but would "take over" none of them. It would retain the benefits of the existing complex of scientific information services while working at the same time toward remedying its defects. Such a program would be in the best American tradition of private enterprise and Government working together voluntarily for the national good.

The Service would have two important functions: (1) through effective coordination and cooperative effort of public agencies and private organizations to capitalize upon and improve existing facilities and techniques in such a way as to afford immediate relief of short-term problems of a pressing nature; and (2) to encourage and support a fundamental, long-term program of research and development, looking to the application of modern scientific knowledge to the over-all problem through the application of machine techniques and through yet-undiscovered methods.

Under the first category the Service would help to answer the scientist's fundamental questions: How can the present volume of research results be published promptly? What is being published now? Where is it? and How can I get it?

In the area of primary publication, the Service would provide financial assistance where needed for the publication of journals and monographs. It would encourage publishers and scientific societies to experiment with new and streamlined methods of publication designed to increase efficiency, improve services, and decrease costs. Similar cooperation would be encouraged among the producers of secondary publications, and financial assistance provided when necessary.

The Service would provide the answer to "What is being published now?" by sponsoring, and if necessary supporting, the immediate preparation of world-wide lists of both primary and secondary scientific research publications, subject-classified and indexed. It would perform a similar task with reference to a union list of scientific and technical periodicals and provide a clearinghouse of information on abstracting and indexing services throughout the world. It would review the newly developing field of Data Centers, compiling information on those that now exist, analyzing overlaps and duplications, and defining areas where new centers are needed.

The whole area of foreign scientific information would be scrutinized and the translation of Russian science expanded to the extent needed to provide full coverage. Additional translation programs in Japanese and other languages would be initiated as needed.

The Service would give special attention to the area of Government scientific reports by expanding the existing announcement system to include every significant unclassified report. It would also expand and improve facilities for making copies of these reports available upon request. It would foster cooperative projects among the agencies to promote greater efficiency in the preparation, processing, and dissemination of Government reports.

It would seek to expand and improve inter-library exchange agreements throughout the world, photocopying processes, and other ways and means of bringing to the scientist copies of items unattainable through normal channels.

All of these things, the Service, with sufficient funds and backing, could proceed to do at once. For the longer term, the Service should support a continuing program of research and development through grants and contracts, looking to the widespread application of machine techniques to such problems as storage, retrieval, indexing, and on a higher plane, to such problems as translation and abstracting.

CONCLUSION

It is clear that in the realm of scientific information, the scientist has neglected his own needs. As a nation we have readily applied modern scientific knowledge to the solution of much more difficult problems. If the Federal Government will establish a national coordinating service of the type that has been described, we can move toward solution of a problem that is vital to our progress in science.

Fortunately a new agency will not be required to meet this need. The National Science Foundation, whose enabling Act charges it with specific responsibilities for scientific information, already has a pilot program in this field and hence useful experience and special competence. The Foundation plays a coordinating role with respect to basic research and policy matters within the Federal Government. The establishment of the Science Information Service within the Foundation could be easily acheived by the extension of the Foundation's present program.

The Committee therefore recommends that the National Science Foundation expand its scientific information program to constitute a Science Information Service that would serve to aid and coordinate existing governmental and private efforts.

MEMBERSHIP OF THE PRESIDENT'S SCIENCE ADVISORY COMMITTEE

Dr. James R. Killian, Jr., Chairman, Special Assistant to the President for Science and Technology, The White House
Dr. Robert F. Bacher, Professor of Physics, California Institute of Technology
Dr. William O. Baker, Vice President (Research), Bell Telephone Laboratories
Dr. Lloyd V. Berkner, President, Associated Universities, Inc.
Dr. Hans A. Bethe, Professor of Physics, Cornell University
Dr. Detlev W. Bronk, President, Rockefeller Institute for Medical Sciences and President, National Academy of Sciences
Dr. James H. Doolittle, Vice President, Shell Oil Company
Dr. James B. Fisk, Executive Vice President, Bell Telephone Laboratories
Dr. Caryl P. Haskins, President, Carnegie Institution of Washington
Dr. George B. Kistiakowsky, Professor of Chemistry, Harvard University
Dr. Edwin H. Land, President, Polaroid Corporation
Dr. Edward M. Purcell, Professor of Physics and Nobel Laureate, Harvard University
Dr. Isidor I. Rabi, Professor of Physics and Nobel Laureate, Columbia University
Dr. H. P. Robertson, Professor of Physics, California Institute of Technology
Dr. Jerome B. Wiesner, Director, Research Laboratory of Electronics, Massachusetts Institute of Technology
Dr. Herbert York, Chief Scientist, Advanced Research Projects Agency, Department of Defense
Dr. Jerrold R. Zacharias, Professor of Physics, Massachusetts Institute of Technology
Dr. Paul A. Weiss, Rockefeller Institute for Medical Science

MARCH 8, 1978

Information Transfer in a Time of Transition:
The Need for Community, Organizational, and Individual Empathy and Ethics

BEN H. WEIL, *Exxon Research and Engineering Company, Linden, New Jersey*

In choosing to talk on ethics and empathy in connection with information transfer, I claim no personal freedom from error. But I believe that in the midst of the technological and economic changes that are affecting information transfer communities, organizations, and individuals—that are providing enormous opportunities for progress, yet are placing enormous stresses on all concerned—it seems important for a moment to reflect on the consequences of how we are behaving as human beings, individually and collectively, and to consider how much more we can accomplish if we can recognize and rise above instincts that can lead us into actions that are often not even in our own best interests.

EMPATHY

Before I relate these principles to the information-transfer field, I believe it is important to dwell briefly on the significance of the word *empathy*. Dictionaries have several definitions for it; I feel one of the shortest is the most powerful: "sympathetic understanding." To be sympathetic, one must not be carelessly unthinking and certainly not disregardful of consequences, much less intentionally and deliberately hostile. The concept of understanding is even more powerful—it requires one to have or to gain knowledge, to apprehend or to comprehend facts and consequences. Empathy requires really knowing what it would be like to be in the other person's shoes, at which point "ethics" enter. In the direct language of the Hebrew form of the Golden Rule: "Do not do to others what you would not have them do to you."

Now, I am certainly not implying that we students and practitioners of information transfer are uniquely vicious or unthinking or are somehow worse than others. On the contrary, idealism and dedication are normal trademarks of a very high percentage of people in our fields. Empathy, however, is not so well known and, as a consequence, idealism and dedication can all too often carry one to extremes—far beyond ethical boundaries—when some basic belief, practice, or institution seems threatened. At this point, I am sorry to say, some information practitioners have been guilty of dirty tricks remarkably similar to those that are typical of practitioners in less-well-regarded occupations, including crooked politicians and bootleggers, if I may be somewhat objectionable.

I will soon give some examples to demonstrate what I have said, but before that I would like to turn to my main theme. Until now, I have chiefly been laying the groundwork for my subtitle: "The Need for Community, Organizational, and Individual Empathy and Ethics."

INFORMATION TRANSFER

Information transfer begins with the message to be transmitted, whether creative thought, scientific principle, know-how, or hard data. Then a medium is required. In the past, it was either oral or written communication. With the advent of writing came the library and archive, with an evolved distinction based on active use or storage of important records. Since Gutenberg and the later invention of the typewriter, printed communications have predominated, evolving into the present system of typed letters, memorandums, and reports and published (printed) books, journals, magazines, proceedings, newspapers, and newsletters. Most of these, after initial transfer of their messages, have required storage in and retrieval from libraries and archives, more mundane local files, and more elaborate document clearinghouses. In between, they have also required access guides (catalogs, indexes, abstracts) to make it possible for seekers of knowledge to effectively locate specific information or documents from the accumulating mass.

All this information transfer has involved human beings, usually very skilled or specifically educated ones who have also gained from experience. In the early days, these people were chiefly scholars and clergy, set apart by nature and education from the mass of humanity. More currently, and with a good educational background now far more common, this information-transfer work has increasingly involved specialists such as editors, publishers, librarians, archivists, abstractors, indexers, systems designers and implementers, and managers. Some are specially educated in schools of library and information science; many are emigrants by design or circumstance from the tasks more usual for their education (teaching, research, business, industry, or the arts). But regardless, they are still somewhat apart from the mainstream of humanity and are becoming increasingly specialized in a few areas rather than broadly covering information transfer as a whole.

Not surprisingly, this specialization has been fostered and required by the organizations in which information-transfer people work. Few libraries are also primary publishers, and few publishers continuously make available all their own publications, much less the publications of others. Only within some learned societies (those that clearly recognize information transfer as at least one major function) have primary publications and access services both been produced, and even here these functions are still usually handled by very distinct, specialized staffs. Other access services have rarely been provided by publishers or libraries (the national libraries aside), and this situation pervaded even the for-profit area until blurred by business combines and profit-motivated diversifications. Nor has interspecialist communication been optimally aided by the specialized societies that information-transfer people have formed for themselves. I will go no further here than to comment that this is why I, as something of an information generalist, have found it necessary to belong to the American Chemical Society's Division of Chemical Information, the American Library Association, the American Society for Information Science (ASIS), the Society for Technical Communication, and the Special Libraries Association (SLA). My early need for information on abstracting is what initially led to my association with NFAIS.

I am not decrying very real needs for most or all these and other specialized information-transfer societies. My point is that none of us (I say this with some assurance) can keep abreast of many of these societies, no matter how pertinent. Yet even those societies that are functionally related or naturally additive are instinctively or politically resistant to merger. (I shouldn't even mention the ASIS/SLA merger debacle.)

To add to our Tower of Babel, we have the problems of personal and professional status, relative and absolute. To give this subject only a broad (and somewhat offensive) brush, most librarians were, until recently, tagged as book lovers who would rather handle books than practice real professions and who could be underpaid accordingly. Only in recent years have there been many professional (full-time) editors; even today, many of the journal editors in societies have university research and teaching as their primary professions and have been known to look somewhat askance at their publishers (whose policies they greatly influence). Professional abstractors and indexers have only recently become numerically visible; much of their work was, for a long time, done by scientists as a professional contribution or to supplement incomes in a minor way.

It is only fair to add one more rationalization to the factors that may account for some of our behavior: most areas within the information-transfer community and many organizations (certainly in the not-for-profit area) have been, and still are, underfinanced for their purposes and needs. Moreover, the situation shows signs of worsening rather than improving, even with the benefits of modern technology. Money is indeed the root of much evil, but in this case, it is the shortage, not an overabundance, of money.

TRANSITIONS AND UNITY

This discussion has so far presented a little of the past and something of the present for information transfer and its professionals. It is certainly not necessary for me to dwell in any detail on the technological bases for our present time of transition. Advances in computers, micrographics, and telecommunications have touched or altered many of our present operations and are likely to revolutionize most of them within a finite number of years. If we are skillful professionals, many of us and many of our organizations can effectively harness these technologies and can benefit from the changes they will provide or force. I do not mean to point with alarm when I speculate that the paperless office may be followed or accompanied by the paperless journal, paperless access means, and paperless sources of information (can a library be called a library without books?). Skilled professionals are still likely to be needed, whether or not they will be known by their present titles. (More likely, our successors may be called something more like communicators, in recognition of greater unity.) A good many years will pass before we reach any such technological information society, however, and it is within our power to make the transition as smooth as possible or unbearably rough. There are many trite sayings that relate. I'm going to cite a few because they each have their own flavor: "The cowboys and the farmers should be friends"; "United we stand, divided we fall"; "A house divided against itself cannot endure"; "E pluribus unum"; and even "Little birds in their nest must agree."

Now I do not imply that this unity, this application of empathy, will be easy or always possible. The truth is often hard to discern, and there must at least be debate before it stands clear. There will often be honest differences of opinion. The ebb and flow of technological change will certainly affect some of us sooner or more drastically than others. Some of our organizations may not survive (although if we plan wisely, we can salvage the good parts and stay above water as professionals). It is too much to expect that we will all be happy with the future, but I insist that it is not too much to expect that we can do better than we have done in the past when faced with changes.

Of course, it is not possible to predict exactly how, where, and when we might create problems or miss opportunities in the future by not applying empathy and ethics, but the following examples from the recent past and present should illustrate the harm that can be done to our own moral fiber, as well as that of others, when we fail to demonstrate "sympathetic understanding."

BAD EXAMPLES FROM THE PAST AND PRESENT

You will have to bear with me if a good many of these examples revolve around "standards" and "copyright," two areas in which I have been very involved and both areas in which the people concerned seem all too inclined to generate heat rather than light.

Standards

In the area of standards, it is readily possible to build a straw man of misinterpretation and then easily set him on fire. This also is true for the idea of standards themselves. Following are a few quotations from a letter that I recently received from an otherwise respected professional colleague (and personal friend) to whose attention I had casually called a nonstandard use of date-element order (day-month-year instead of year-month-day) that apparently had all the logic of the International Organization for Standardization (ISO)/ANSI standard order, but with its elements reversed. Here are his remarks: "I decided that the ISO/ANSI so-called standard is too back-asswared for simple but honest people. . . . It has all the logic and all the lack of empathy of most decisions arrived at by a committee. . . . You know, 'standard' is an interesting word. One meaning—'generally accepted because of long, widespread use'—is becoming almost extinct. The other, somewhat frightening, use is as a synonym for regulation or rule; for example, a 'standard' way of writing dates because a group got together and said, 'From now on everybody will do it the way we tell them to.'"

This is neither the time nor the place for a lengthy exposé on ANSI's actual procedures for developing voluntary national standards, but my friend could not possibly have been less well informed. Indeed, some of our better informed, but equally intemperate, colleagues are vastly impatient with the committee and subcommittee structures that have been created to ensure community agreement. Such structures include committee reviews for comment; formal votes by the concerned organizations; attempted resolution of negative votes or the requirement for a well-reasoned explanation as to why such votes have to be disregarded; subsequent nationwide public exposure; attempted resolution of further objections; and then—and only then—action by a national board of review. (As it happens, of course, the specific order of date elements adhered to by ISO/ANSI *does* have logic behind it: By beginning with the largest element (year), one can continue on past month and day (when needed) to such smaller time elements as hour, minute, and second.)

Continuing on the subject of standards, we may soon have to bear the consequences of a nearly incomprehensible series of misrepresentations and misunderstandings, plus the all-too-human power struggle that can accompany the approaching end of a benevolent monarchy when there is no mandatory heir-apparent and no fixed capitol/capital (both spellings are all too correct). Specifically, ANSI Committee Z39 ("library work, documentation, and related publishing practices") may well have to suspend operations in the near future, because what might have been a normal transition of administration and funding has become deeply imbedded in controversy. I am not going to go into recent details, but I think it only fair to show how a problem such as this can become major if responsible individuals turn away from empathy and ethics.

Committee Z39 originally was charged with the development of library standards, but during the 1960s it added "documentation and related publishing practices" when it became clear that all these areas were closely related; that is, they were all part of information transfer. In the years that followed, the committee's chairman appointed numerous special subcommittees to work on specific standards in the "new" fields—indexing, abstracting, bibliographic referencing, thesauri, serial codes, report format, report numbering, article codes, microfiche headers, formats for serials and papers, etc., in addition to subcommittees concerned with many fields specific to libraries. The committee was funded equally by the library-development grantor and a federal research foundation, with total budgets that did not exceed $20,000 until a few years ago. Invaluable services have obviously been rendered gratis (except for travel expenses) by subcommittee members, as well as the review committees of the numerous information-transfer organizations that make up Committee Z39.

All ANSI committees report administratively through an ANSI hierarchy involving a secretariat (an appropriate organization) and an ANSI management board and are technically responsible to funding sources (when involved) only for the proper expenditure of funds. Two years ago, however, one of Committee Z39's funders called a meeting because of purported complaints that only library subjects were being handled. This meeting led the secretariat (sponsoring) organization to appoint a study committee. Suddenly, that committee was provided with a document, addressed to the *funder*, which berated Committee Z39 for not having initiated work on 10 specific nonlibrary standards—suggested areas for standards that the organization writing the letter had somehow not bothered to call directly to the attention of Z39. It so happened that Z39 had already considered three of the most important areas on its own initiative, but at that point, who was concerned with facts?

At any rate, the secretariat's study report was quickly deemed inadequate by the funder because it rated the "problem" as largely one of perception. Thus, the funder promptly financed another study, this time by a national commission. While that study was still in progress—replete with such initial inaccuracies as "Until recently Z39 has not had a planning group"—this funder discontinued its financial support on the basis of adverse reviewer votes on a project request for interim funding. (It may be unfair to say this, but it is relatively easy to find reviewers whose viewpoints are predictable.)

I won't go any further, but I believe that the saying "All's well that ends well" is no excuse for actions that were, at the very least, not thought out or not based on appropriate information. Not even if they were only intended to spur action—albeit through careless disregard of channels—were they reasonable. Certainly empathy was not involved, and not much attention was paid to ethics. Yet the individuals involved are highly regarded in the information-transfer field. (Can it be the times?)

ABSTRACTS

The subject of standards brings to mind some early NFAIS debates on the relative and absolute merits of journals of abstracts versus bibliographic-reference-based indexes. At the time, some advocates of the indexes missed no opportunity (and created several) to make it appear that the use of abstracts was unnecessary and, hence, that publication of abstracts was unnecessarily expensive. This controversy has long since died down. Both types of access services are now known to have specific costs and efficiencies, but there was a time when the very preparation of abstracts was threatened by rhetoric instead of facts.

Indeed, there was still a touch of this "virtue out of necessity" advocacy when the ANSI standard on writing abstracts was being developed. It proved impossible to gain acceptance of early versions of the standard because definitions of the different types of abstracts were unacceptable to organizations that prepared bibliographic listings or descriptive abstracts. It was not that the definitions were inaccurate, but rather that these organizations would not accept *any* definition for the informative abstract. Success had to be achieved by an *ethical* "end run." In other words, no definition at all would be given for the informative abstract, but the statement that "An abstract should be as informative as is permitted by the type and style of the document; that is, it should present as much as possible of the quantitative or qualitative information (or both) contained in the document" would be incorporated.

A discussion of abstracts can lead us to an account of some regrettable happenings in the copyright field, where desires seem to outweigh facts, law, or reason by a large factor. Indeed, the copyright status of author abstracts that are parts of papers in primary journals affords us an appropriate bridge to a discussion of this important area.

Copyrights

The new copyright law is not black or white. What it permits or precludes is not right or wrong. For example, its substantial verbiage on photocopying provides room for interpretation, especially because there are at least a few inconsistencies. But even lawyers, understandably intent on interpreting maximum benefits for their clients (at the moment, many of whom are document *users*), can readily lose sight of what the law is intended to accomplish, that is, the promotion of the flow of knowledge by rewarding communicators with some proprietary rights while also allowing certain "fair" uses that will not substantially limit or extinguish that flow. Lawyers can also lose sight of the message of simple statistics, which tells us that a program based on a series of just four interpretations—each of which has an 80-percent chance of being correct—will wind up in the aggregate with only a 41-percent chance (mathematically) of being correct (legal, fair, or whatever). "Great oaks from little acorns grow," and large errors can devolve from a series of small ones.

Many of us have worked hard to improve the quality of author abstracts, with the expressed intention of making them optimally useful not only for initial communication but also for direct use in access services. Both the old and new copyright laws, however, seem to indicate that the copyrights to these author abstracts belong to the primary journals in which they are published, at least in terms of systematic (quantity) use. Any major change in the long-term willingness of primary journals to permit at least the not-for-profit, discipline-type access services to use author abstracts without charge would cause major economic problems, because many such services do use these abstracts. (Those that do not use author abstracts probably do so deliberately to avoid copyright entanglements.)

Unwillingness to face these facts has typified the words (or lack of words) of some access services, perhaps on the basis that "if we don't talk about it, maybe it will go away." This has an element of truth in it but does not justify statements like "we don't use author abstracts" by services that occasionally or regularly do use them. (That many do base their abstracts on author abstracts was demonstrated as long ago as 1958 in a study by Saul Herner.)

Copyright evasions bid fair to be far more important, and far more divisive and damaging, in the area of library photocopying of copyrighted works. Here, the drawn-out debate over omnibus copyright-revision bills, stretching from the 1950s until final passage of a bill in 1976, caused major differences in desires and interpretations between the library community and publishers to be inflated to the extent that a wide chasm now exists between these integral parts of the information-transfer continuum.

It is all too easy to oversimplify the issues, but what is involved has been the continuing desire by libraries to be able to supply—preferably without payment to publishers—at least single photocopies whenever these are required by any of their patrons. Inadequate library budgets and the rising costs of books and journals have been cited as reasons enough for paying nothing more than subscription charges. Moreover, because these subscription charges have been forced up sharply by inflation (including steeply rising paper costs) and by publication of an ever-increasing number of articles, libraries have also wanted freedom to pool their holdings (drop marginal local subscriptions) through "resource sharing" in whatever networks (or even a "national periodicals system") that will enable them to obtain photocopies of needed articles, preferably without specific payments to publishers for this copying.

Not surprisingly, publishers have wanted their copyrights extended long enough to permit them to recoup at least their basic costs of publication ("first-copy costs") through some combination of subscription charges and copying fees in order to permit them to continue publishing (in which libraries certainly have an interest too!). It is only fair to report that many publishers were, for a long time, unwilling to see extensive photocopying continue—even with the possibility of payments—preferring, instead, their historic methods of document delivery. This resistance, however, has recently faded considerably as the technological facts of modern information transfer have become clearer and as it has become evident that a share of operating revenues might be obtainable from copy-free payments.

Congress, beset more by copyright issues relating to cable-TV and publishing technicalities than to photocopying, occasionally listened to both sides. When other issues were finally resolved, legislators decided at last not to permit unlimited photocopying but to permit some photocopying under certain circumstances and to certain extents. It urged authors, publishers, libraries, and others concerned to develop licensing and clearance procedures that would permit (obviously for remuneration) additional vital copying by libraries.

Now, what happened as passage of the law in 1976 gave way to preparation during 1977 for its application and to the advent of 1978 as the first year in which the law had legal weight? Continued drum beating arose by specific elements of the library community who still were not willing to accept anything less than complete freedom to make fee-free photocopies. This was clearly denied them by the new law, and, hence, elements of the library community turned to elaborately reasoned liberal interpretations of the wording of the new law. Not surprisingly, publishers were unwilling to accept most such interpretations, although a willingness not matched by the combined library associations to discuss further guidelines was expressed.

"The publishers won't sue!" says an attorney member of a library association. Also, "When you've exhausted your specific 'Limitations on exclusive rights: Reproduction by libraries and archives' [Section 108], go right ahead with photocopying under 'Limitations on exclusive rights: Fair use' [Section 107]." (The latter is supposedly no more than a codification of a previous limited, strictly defined judicial doctrine.) "Guideline numbers are only minimums, and hence can be exceeded," say some library-association spokesmen. (Regularly, rather than exceptionally?)

Now, the vast majority of librarians are understandably confused by the intricacies of the copyright law and as to whether and when it really requires them to make changes in or payments for their important photocopying. "Everything that was permitted under the old law is permitted under the new one," say some library-association spokesmen. This is correct, but they somehow neglect to point out that this does not mean that all the photocopying that libraries had become accustomed to doing for free is still permitted. For example, some libraries had become used to sending out sets of tables of contents of journals, then backing these up systematically with photocopies of the articles checked.

A few library journals are making instant heroes of librarians who rail against the greed of publishers. These publishers, the librarians say, are not content with only inflating their subscription charges and collecting page charges from authors (collected by less than 20 percent of journals), but are insistent on augmenting their profits by charging exhorbitant fees for photocopying. (When anyone points out that most journals are published by not-for-profit societies, these protagonists shift to attacks on their wasteful publishing practices and on publishers catering to the "information explosion" of worthless papers. Statistics showing level or falling numbers of subscriptions are dismissed as propaganda, even by some libraries intent on establishing journal-sharing networks.) A few supercharged librarians, especially at universities, are even urging authors not to publish in journals "unconscionable" enough to charge for the photocopying that falls outside the law.

"Know thine enemy!" cries a well-regarded library/educator/attorney (to a stir of applause) when he finishes his frequently repeated, usually accurate descriptions of the meanings of portions of Sections 107 and 108 to groups of librarians. "There is little need for a Copyright Clearance Center, because there's little copying that will require payments," say some library-association spokesmen, pointing to a recent study by King Research that correctly shows that a high percentage of 1976-level interlibrary photocopying is permitted for free under the new law and its guidelines. (But this report also shows that interlibrary photocopying was less than 10 percent of the total photocopying of copyrighted material by libraries during 1976, a volume for which only some part is clearly permitted fee-free under the new law.)

I could tell you tales about other attacks on the Copyright Clearance Center that would make your hair curl (if you have more than I do). I will limit this, however, to reporting a series of ostensibly ad hoc presentations, at meetings at which I also spoke, by a past-president of a major library association. These consisted of a remarkably complete collection of adverse rumors and misstatements, so extensive as to be about as easy to answer briefly as a question like "When did you stop beating your wife?" These "truth squad" (?) efforts tailed off only after I incorporated pre-answers to his attacks in my basic presentations. Sir Walter Scott must have sensed something like this when he wrote "Oh, what a tangled web we weave, when first we practice to deceive!"

Incidentally, make no mistake as to my motives in being appalled at the virulence of these attacks on journal publishers. I have spent my entire career in an information-using, research environment, in which I know—and have recently helped to prove—that journals are the most important source of information. Until something better than journals becomes available, none of us can afford to see them killed off by unreasoned and unreasonable attacks or to see publishers forced to provide such lesser substitutes as synoptic journals, which would require users to order the full papers for mail delivery.

Also, I want it to be clear that I am not criticizing the bulk of the library community, but only a certain vocal few who have taken the extreme positions on which I have commented. Indeed, heads of some important libraries support copyright positions that clearly recognize proprietary rights as well as user requirements.

One last caveat: Why haven't I taken the primary publishers more to task for a lack of ethics and empathy? Actually, more examples of a lack of publisher understanding are not hard to find, although publishing houses seem to be trying hard not to antagonize their major customers (libraries) unduly while also trying to stay afloat (and, for the for-profit publishers, to make profits). Some publishers have set disappointingly high initial copy fees. Some are still asking for transfer of *all* copyrights, without regard for in-house needs. But it certainly must have been a lack of understanding (of a different kind) that caused publishers to agree to interlibrary guidelines that exempt from copy fees more than 90 percent of current interlibrary photocopying.

WE MUST DO BETTER

Enough! Where are our information-transfer statesmen? How is it that we, many of us scientists devoted to the search for truth, find ourselves engaged in such polemics? In half truths? Or in deliberate misstatements? Do the ends justify the means? Indeed, what are the ends? The end of publishing? The end of libraries? Will "dirty tricks" really help us to weather the challenges of technology that put information transfer squarely into a time of transition?

There is a chance that certain of my statements may further the existing disunity; I recognize that. But even if I have been impolitic in places, perhaps this will shock some of us into burying our hatchets somewhere other than in each other. Publishers will still be needed, much the same as now, for some years to come and can play other roles in the future if we do not kill them off. Libraries and librarians are indispensable, at least for now; if they are adaptive and ingenious—and if we work to aid their funding—it is not too much to expect them to maintain current leadership. Access services face economic and technological challenges of formidable size, but we cannot do without them, and no replacement is in sight except, perhaps, long-range, full-text searching (and I have doubts about that).

It may not be true that the future will be what we deliberately make of it; perhaps the technological tides will be too strong for us to control. But let us not destroy what we have and ruin major opportunities by continued internecine struggle. Communicators of the world, unite! NFAIS members, help to centralize this effort, just as you presently unite searchers with sources! Professionals in information transfer, practice more empathy and ethics in your daily lives!

The psalmist sang that man is but little lower than the angels. In these more pragmatic times, we know for certain only that there were psalmists, but we also know that some things are "right" and others "wrong" in terms of our relations with our fellow human beings. Are we, then, our brothers' keepers? I say that we are, and I have enough confidence in the quality of our information-transfer community to believe that in the future we can behave, as individuals and as groups, as ethically as we behave in other ways — especially if we keep the need for empathy in mind.

I have no doubt that this Miles Conrad Memorial Lecture will bring some "slings and arrows of outrageous fortune," or at least of outrage. If so, I, along with the many of you whom I know stand with me, will take some comfort from the inspired words of the second stanza of a poem by Maltrie Davenport Babcock: "Be strong! Say not, 'The days are evil. Who's to blame?' And fold the hands and acquiesce — oh shame! Stand up, speak out, and bravely, in God's name."

MARCH 7, 1979

The Information Community: Its Dilemma, Opportunities, and Challenges

DONALD W. KING, *King Research, Inc.,*
Rockville, Maryland

One of the most perplexing issues I have encountered in the past few years is the plight of the information community. There is strange irony in the fact that at a time when our nation is racing into the information age, the information community is encountering many difficulties, some members of the information community are fighting bitterly over such issues as copyright, the information profession seems to lack a clear identity, and the field of information science is at the very brink of extinction. I have had a chance to reflect on this paradox in the past few months and would like to share with you some of my thoughts as to why there are so many crises in the information community.

First, I will try to describe broadly what I mean by the information community, information profession, and information science. I do this hesitantly, because part of our problem has been a self-consciousness caused by our inability to define these areas accurately. By considering descriptions of these terms, however, we can perhaps begin to see where our opportunities lie and what some of our greatest challenges will be in the future. Then I will give examples of problem areas where we can apply our skills and expertise to serve the information community. Throughout, I will attempt to assess the future role of information institutions, particularly abstracting and indexing services.

Evidence of the importance of information to our nation and to every individual is overwhelming. By now we are all familiar with the thesis advanced by Machlup (1962), Machlup and Leeson (1978), Bell (1973), and Porat (1974) that our country is shifting from the industrial age into the information age. Porat recently claimed that nearly 50 percent of the Gross National Product consists of information-related activities. The need for information pervades the lives of citizens in their daily work, formal education, lifelong learning, methods of coping with life's problems, and recreation. Information also affects our society in many less obvious ways. It is at the very heart of government, education, science and technology, medicine, law, finance, business, and so forth. I cannot think of a single sector of society that is not highly dependent on information to function smoothly and efficiently. The concept of information is slowly but steadily becoming a part of our daily way of thinking. Just recently there was a headline in the *Wall Street Journal* stating that "A New Breed of Information System Executive Crops Up at Some Firms." An advertiser in *Time* proudly announced that it was comprised of informationists. I noticed three advertisements on television in which firms refer to themselves as information companies.

Information is recognized by many as one of our country's most important resources. Yet there are serious problems in the information community. Publishers and librarians have recently waged a devastating battle over the photocopying of copyrighted materials. A similar confrontation may be brewing between primary publishers and abstracting and indexing services. Many barriers are being constructed that will inhibit the free flow of information. Also, some information entities are having great difficulty in making a case for themselves. For example, libraries complain that even if their budget increases are keeping up with inflation, they are actually falling woefully behind because of the accumulation of past materials that must be maintained, increases in the amount of new material available, and the ever-increasing number of users to be served. The American Society for Information Science recently barely survived a financial crisis that easily could have forced it into bankruptcy. Most sources of information-research funds provided by the Federal Government in the 1960s have dried up completely and the Division of Information Sciences and Technology of the National Science Foundation (NSF) now has its lowest operating budget in the 15 years since I entered this profession. In fact, it is fighting for its very existence.

Why is all this happening at a point in time when we are most needed? Of course there is no single reason for such a phenomenon, but rather many reasons. First, and perhaps most important, is the size, complexity, and incredible rate of growth of the information sector of our society. On the one hand, these factors present us with exciting opportunities and challenges. Yet it may be that it is these very factors that are overwhelming our formal information profession as we know it. It is very difficult to even define the information community, information profession, and information science. Let me try to demonstrate this fact.

First, I would like to provide one definition of information from among several general definitions available in dictionaries. My definition here is simply that information is a message communicated between or among individuals. Information is distinguished from knowledge, which is the sum of what is known by a person or persons in a certain field. Therefore, new information assimilated, understood, and analyzed by a person adds to that person's knowledge. Wisdom is knowledge applied successfully through insight, good sense, or one's inner qualities. A distinction may also be made between data and information in that information contains meaning. For example, the number 220.1 million is datum but has little meaning outside some specific context. Yet, to say that there are 220.1 million persons in the United States today is information, because the datum, when combined with other messages, is informative.

The information community is comprised of all the entities and organizations, as well as the information workers and professionals, concerned with the transfer of information. The information profession is made up of persons who are engaged in functions performed in information transfer. Such functions appear to fall into five generic groups that are depicted in Figure 1 (King et al. [1978]). The five functions are origination, recording, preservation, end use, and the function that ties the others together—transmission. It seems to me that the information community and information profession should include all those organizations and persons employed in performing activities related to the five functions except the actual originators and end users of information. This means that, in addition to the creator of a work, there may be many other persons involved in origination of information, such as technical writers, translators, editors, and abstractors. The recording function involves publishers of both primary and secondary information materials. Libraries, database systems, and information clearinghouses play a major role in preservation. Information brokers and information analysts in a variety of areas seem to be a new and evolving part of the end-use function since they directly serve the end user. These information professionals all make up the operating part of the information community. Other information professionals are those who perform systems analysis and systems design, educate and train information professionals and workers, and are involved in research and development.

Suddenly one begins to realize that we are talking about a very large number of organizations and people. Should we establish boundaries to reduce the number to a manageable size? I don't know how! One boundary already given is that information is transmitted among individuals

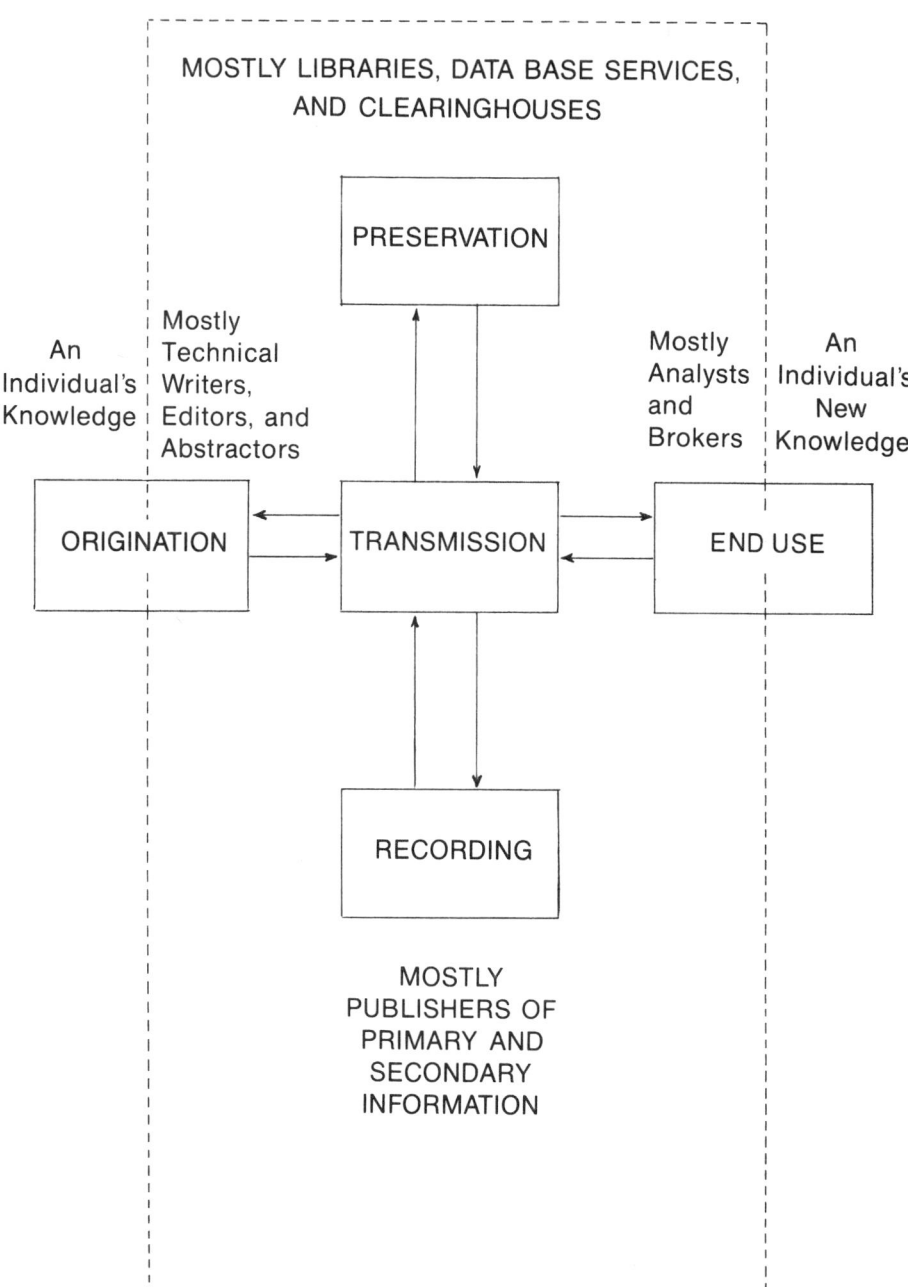

Figure 1 Information functions.

and should add to the knowledge of those individuals. Boundaries on other dimensions are not as clear cut. Some possible dimensions for setting boundaries include the community served, the purpose of use, the level of information, the type of information, the form of information, or the combination of information-transfer functions. There are problems involved in using any of these.

Much of the work and research done by information scientists, abstracting and indexing (A&I) professionals, librarians, and publishers has involved science and technology. This is because of funding by the Federal Government and the drive for growth by industry during the past two decades. As mentioned earlier, however, information plays a key role in nearly every sector of society. The information needs, functions performed, professional activities, and processes are common to some degree in all of them. I can think of no reason, other than to limit its size, that the community served should be a delimiting factor in describing the information community. One boundary might be the purpose of use of information; yet, I don't think, for example, that it should matter whether scientists use information for research, writing, teaching, or their own lifelong learning. Who is to judge which is most important?

Another possible boundary is the level of information that might include primary versus secondary information. A substantial amount of the work and research funded in information science has dealt with bibliographic systems. In the future, however, I feel that it is going to be more and more difficult to distinguish between retrieval of information used for identification of publications and retrieval of the full text of primary information. Because the processes and technology used for online search and retrieval can be used in the future for transmission of full text, the two kinds of retrieval will eventually blend into a single system.

One might also limit the size of the information community by the type of information that could be classified as textual, numeric, or other. Traditionally, the field has been more concerned with information transfer of text than with numeric data or, say, cartographic information. It is clear, however, that there is little difference between many of the functions performed or systems used (or processes utilized in the systems) to transfer different types of information. It is remarkable how similar storage, search, and retrieval systems have emerged for all three forms over the years.

Another delimiting criterion in describing the information community might be the various forms in which information is packaged, such as paper, microform, digital, or audiovisual. I can see no reason whatsoever that form should be a basis for limiting the information community. In fact, it seems to me that one of our most interesting challenges is to begin to seek optimal combinations of these forms for information transfer.

Just as there seems to be a great deal of confusion and lack of clarity about the information community and information profession, there also is some confusion as to the overlap among information science, communication science, computer science, and library science. The simple schema in Figure 1 will help clarify how I think these fields are related to one another.

To me, the field of communication science and technology includes the theories and processes of the transmission function and pairs of information senders and receivers associated with any of the functions performed. It includes such areas as personal conversations involving the origination, transmission, and end-use functions; broadcasting, which has multiple end use; and transmission of online retrieval, which includes the preservation, transmission, and end-use functions. Also, this field involves high technology such as telecommunications. For the most part, communication science seems to include mostly transmission and instantaneous information transfer with little emphasis on recording or presentation; nor is this field of science nearly as concerned with the content and structure of information messages as we are.

Computer science appears to deal primarily with the digital form of information transfer, including structure, processes, and hardware involving specific functions. It is apparent from Figure 1 that transmission (computer science and technology) interfaces with origination (word processing), recording (photocomposition, videodisks, computer output microform, and the like), preservation (videodisks, computer storage and retrieval of bibliographic records and full text, and cataloging systems), and end use (computer terminals).

Library science seems to focus mainly on the preservation, transmission, and end-use functions. Much of the research and published literature in library science is concerned with resource allocation in a library environment, user behavior and trends, organization and control of the literature, and other related activities. Both computer science and communication science form an integral part of some of the research in the field of library science.

Where does information science fit into the information-transfer environment? Maybe the best way to describe it is by what we are now doing. Professor Fritz Machlup (1979), an eminent economist who is studying the production and distribution of scholarly knowledge, has observed that

Our studies concentrate on capabilities of arranging efficient flows of information, some on the machines and devices employed, some on techniques available or conceivable, some on the human skills required and actually or potentially supplied, and so forth. Studies of information are inter-disciplinary or cross-disciplinary in nature and, hence, require a thorough acquaintance with numerous disciplines in the formal and empirical, natural and cultural sciences. Since one cannot reasonably expect that many information scientists or specialists have complete mastery of several, let alone all disciplines bearing on the study of information, collaboration of scholars trained in one or more of the many relevant fields is indispensable for many concrete research projects.

To this, I would like to add that information scientists have also looked into the entire system of functions depicted in Figure 1. No other field is really concerned about all the functions and their relationship to the content, structure, organization, and control of information.

Some members of the information science profession jump through hoops trying to qualify or justify the science portion of our name. Machlup (1979) has expressed my feelings about this very well. He maintains that

The question whether information science has developed or will develop "laws" of its own, either empirical (epistemic, correlational) or theoretical (abstract, postulational), is moot; the professional importance of information science does not depend on its independence from other disciplines and should not be judged by its autonomy or sovereignty. Many sciences are based on applications of basic laws developed in other sciences. Applied sciences are not any less needed than fundamental ones, and their position in a taxonomic or classificatory hierarchy should not give an inferiority complex to those who profess them.

In addition to the scientific fields mentioned above, Mansfield (1979) has pointed out that there are several disciplines that provide a theoretical basis for studying information transfer or its functional components. These are grouped as follows:

1. Logic and Philosophy: Epistemology, Methodology
2. Behavioral and Social Science: Cognitive Psychology, Social Psychology, Sociology
3. Semiotics: Language, Linguistics
4. Mathematics: Statistics, Modeling, Simulation
5. Technology and Engineering: Design, Cybernetics, Human Factors, Systems Theory

Again, the breadth of this multidisciplinary field of information science is very difficult to fully comprehend, which undoubtedly contributes to our uncertainty about it.

One of our greatest hopes for information science in the future lies with the Division of Information Science and Technology at NSF. Its new director, Dr. Howard L. Resnikoff, and his staff have embarked on an attempt to develop a new program that he described earlier in this meeting (Resnikoff [1979b]; National Science Foundation [1979]). Resnikoff (1979a) has also begun to delineate information science through his interpretation of its fundamental problems. A great deal of what he presents is directly appropriate to abstracting and indexing activities. He gives several examples of the problem areas in terms of pairs of inventories such as users and databases. As I look at the future of abstracting and indexing services, however, I envision that his examples of problems can be extended into many other areas of information transfer as well. I will allude to some of these later.

I hope I have begun to show the futility of trying to formally define the information community, information profession, and information science. Yet, knowledge of the number of organizations, professionals, researchers, and technologies involving activities and processes similar to our's seem paramount. This knowledge can provide us with ample opportunities and interesting challenges. Let us take a look at the information community, information profession, and information science and technology as I have very broadly described them and see what opportunities and challenges lie ahead for us.

To begin with, the fact that information is utilized by an extremely wide range of users and for many purposes provides us all with interesting opportunities, if we recognize them. These take three principal forms. First, our profession has successfully developed skills, expertise, research results, and technology that can be usefully applied across a broad spectrum of new areas. For example, many large corporations spend millions of dollars each year on hundreds of marketing research studies. Rarely are these studies available or used retrospectively, because they are not handled properly in an information system. Second, a meaningful professional liaison can be developed with others who have similar interests. For example, I recently was amazed to find that in the field of cartography, a series of systems for retrospective searching of cartographic materials such as maps, aerial photographs, and satellite photographs has been developed. These systems involve online searches of materials that are indexed by several characteristics. Cartographers perform over 0.5 million online searches each year for government agencies, industry, and the public. A National Cartographic Information Center has also been established to provide information reference and referral through means that are well known to all of us. Yet, to my knowledge, cartographers are ignorant of our professional societies — NFAIS, the American Society for Information Science (ASIS), and the Information Industry Association (IIA). My point is that they have operational, research, and technology interests that warrant professional exchange of ideas that are now lacking. Furthermore, the broad range of information communities, organizations, and professionals also have common interests in other areas, including new government regulations, problems of public and private interfaces, and economics of information products and services.

The third form of opportunity is for our community and profession to review and adapt research results and technology that have been developed in other areas. We can learn a great deal from the research performed in a wide variety of information environments like management information systems, artificial intelligence, mass media, and command and control.

King Research recently completed a project for NSF in which it studied the feasibility of electronic alternatives to paper-based publishing (King and Roderer [1978]). Several examples arose from that study that illustrate opportunities for new research and technology. It is abundantly clear that new technologies, particularly those involving electronic processes, are likely to have an enormous effect on scientific and technical information transfer over the next two decades. Yet, most of the significant technology has or will be developed outside this environment. The reason is that such technologies as word processing, intelligent computer terminals, microcomputing, facsimile transmission, videodisks, and telecommunications were all developed for mass markets, which has made them economically feasible for use in Scientific and Technical Information (STI). This suggests to me that one facet of our research must be directed toward monitoring new research and technology developed elsewhere to determine potential applicability to information science.

Now I would like to discuss some of our future challenges. The best way I know to do this is by relating to the current scientific and technical information-transfer system. I will start with end-use functions and progress backwards through preservation, recording, and origination.

With end use, there is a great deal more reading of scientific and technical journals than previously thought. It has been estimated that there are approximately 250 million readings per year (King, McDonald, and Roderer [1978b]). Three-fourths of these are from personal subscriptions to journals. Approximately 75 percent of the remainder come from library copies and separates distributed as preprints or reprints. Of particular interest to NFAIS members is the way in which readers identify the articles they read: 40 percent of the readings are from articles identified by browsing in an issue of the journal, 18 percent are referred by a colleague, 11 percent are cited in another article, and around 25 percent are cited in a printed index. Thus, bibliographic products and services clearly have a significant effect on scientific and technical reading.

The presence of technology is also beginning to be felt in the identification processes. Even though a relatively small portion of the articles read are found by computer search, the amount is in keeping with the estimates made by Martha Williams (1974) of database use, which was on the order of slightly more than one million searches in 1976. This number is growing very rapidly. Nearly four million computer searches are forecast by 1985 based on current trends; however, other factors may make that number substantially larger.

I feel that we must significantly broaden our perspective on serving users. The Arthur D. Little (1978) study group, under the direction of Vincent Giuliano, made a good point when it visualized research as passing through different eras over the past two decades. It contends that we have moved through an initial era oriented toward scientific disciplines to a second era that was mission-oriented and are now moving into a problem-oriented era in which issues regarding the environment, energy, economic well-being, safety, and so forth, will force policymakers to draw on a wide range of scientific and technical disciplines, as well as societal information sources. They lament the fact that most of our information institutions, such as professional societies, publishing companies, and libraries, are still structured around the discipline orientation, which partially hamstrings the information community's capability to serve in the problem-oriented era. I think this makes some sense, except that a new information era must address many kinds of information use, as well as decision making and problem solving. For example, education and lifelong learning are also highly important. So are the user needs of special groups such as medical practitioners, who are not at all well served at the present time.

There are many examples of the need for a broader range of information. For example, in industry, investigation into a new chemical product now requires a much wider range of information sources than in the past. In addition to the traditional research and patent literature, companies also must be concerned with searching the literature on cancer and toxic substances to ensure that new chemicals do not contain carcinogenic properties or toxic substances. They must look into the effects of their operations on the environment and make sure that a broad spectrum of government regulations are met.

Some professionals, such as physicians, require information systems quite different from those now provided for researchers and engineers. Future information systems must adapt to the special needs of such user groups. The problem is that practitioners have very little time to search for materials, yet they need to be highly cognizant of an extremely wide range of literature covering all diseases and other traumas, as well as their diagnosis, treatment, and rehabilitation. Addressing the information needs of such new users presents one more important challenge to abstracting and indexing services.

A further opportunity and challenge for secondary services involves another new era of information use. I found it very revealing that many of the 35 pre–White House Conferences on Library and Information Services held thus far concluded that more information for coping with life's problems was needed (King Research, Inc. [1979])*. Two sources of such information come immediately to mind. The first, of course, is public libraries, if they will serve as community information centers in the future. The second source is the viewdata kind of information system that is now being tested in England (Gaffner [1979]). The skills and expertise found in bibliographic services seem to be very necessary in this area. The ability to organize, structure, control, and access information is basic to such information services.

Let us assume that the Arthur D. Little report is correct and that we are moving into a new information era. Regardless of whether the new information needs are for problem solving or for a broader combination of purposes, the change presents a great challenge to abstracting and indexing services. These services can accommodate such change more easily than any other participant in the information community because of the flexibility inherent in their activities. Authors currently have little control over who reads their materials, and they are somewhat limited in what they can write about. Publishers, particularly those dealing with society journals, are beset by tradition and the structure of the professional community they serve. Libraries also are heavily constrained by their past role of storing large volumes of materials already acquired, organized, and stored by previous conventions. It is not to say that authors, publishers, and libraries cannot or will not change, but rather that mechanisms of change by these participants are potentially much more cumbersome than by A&I services. It is much simpler for A&I services to broaden and deepen their coverage to include social, legal, regulatory, educational, numeric, or any other type of information source or material that may be required by their users in the future. Secondary information, by its very nature, provides the basis for reorganization, control, and access to a multidimensional body of knowledge. But even though secondary information provides the greatest degree of flexibility for adjusting to information requirements and needs as they arise, there must be substantial new research in this area.

It seems to me that bibliographic products and services, particularly online searching, are essential to meeting the information needs of the future. Because of tightened budgets, however, libraries may have to alter their roles. For example, they might have to acquire fewer books and periodicals and reallocate a portion of acquisition and storage budgets to

---

*The White House Conference on Library and Information Services was authorized by P. L. 93-568, signed on December 31, 1974, by President Gerald R. Ford. The law states that the purpose of the conference is to develop recommendations to improve the nation's libraries and information centers and their use by the public.

(Palmour et al. [1977]), the University of Pittsburgh (Kent et al. [1978]), and others (Chen [1972]; Fussler and Simon [1969]) has demonstrated that substantial reductions can be made in library collections without diminishing use. I also think that information intermediaries will begin to assume an ever-increasing importance in the future and that they will not merely perform reference searches but also some interpretation and analysis of the retrieved information.

In preservation, approximately 14 percent of the scientific and technical journals used are library copies (King et al. [1978b]). Yet, there is a trend toward increased interlibrary lending. It was estimated that in 1976, approximately five million interlibrary loans were made (King Research, Inc. [1977]). This represents around 15 percent of the library uses. Because of the economic squeeze, many libraries are looking more and more to resource sharing and networking. This has led to a plan to implement a national periodicals system in the United States (Task Force on a National Periodicals System [1977]; Council on Library Resources, Inc. [1978]; Palmour et al. [1974]).

New technology provides some potential assistance in reducing the library acquisition and storage budgets. One promising possibility is the use of videodisks as a local library storage medium. On the other hand, I am not enthusiastic about the future use of microform as a solution to preservation problems, for various reasons. The principal reason is that journal prices must cover a very large fixed cost associated with prerun activities, including editing and composition. These costs must be recovered whether the journals are sold in paper form or microform. Thus, the price of microform is likely to be only around 5-20 percent less than paper form, depending on the circulation of the journal. Many feel that the trade-off in price and readability will favor paper form. The use of intelligent terminals and minicomputers in libraries should substantially enhance online bibliographic searching and even the possibility of online retrieval of full text or articles. Transmission costs should drop dramatically because of new telecommunications technology and because the receiving terminals will be able to receive, store, and terminate the transmission very quickly. It is just a matter of time before the bibliographic searches of secondary information will be combined with full-text retrieval online.

In the recording function, publishers presently appear to be doing well (King et al. [1978b]), although our analysis suggests that journals with low circulation, say under 2,000 subscriptions, may be headed toward some severe economic difficulties. Many publishers are currently using electronic composition, which provides them with the opportunity to distribute copies by electronic means. Still, they are very reluctant to increase distribution on-demand any more than necessary. The reason for this is financial. Publishers currently receive a very large portion of their income from subscriptions, which means that they obtain funds prior to incurring costs. Thus, cash flow and return on investment are very favorable. This would not be true if they relied on sales of separates on-demand, nor is it true for receipts from royalty payments.

Publishers have expressed a great deal of concern about interlibrary lending and other photocopying by libraries. They probably do not realize, however, that more than six times as many separates are distributed through preprints, reprints, and photocopies provided by authors as by interlibrary loans. There is a substantial amount of distribution of separates currently taking place. I believe that publishers will reluctantly recognize that formal payments will be to their benefit in the long run. This is particularly true of journals with low circulations. Some journal publishers may even relinquish their traditional paper form of distribution and serve their users by on-demand distribution in electronic form. If so, they must enhance the quality of information content through more thorough review processes.

The principal use of indexes and abstracts is to gain access to primary information following an indication of information need by end users. Indexes are (or could be) used as a basis for aggregation and control, and abstracts are used by many to determine whether to look further at the primary source of information. Preparation of indexes and abstracts utilized for these purposes involves skills and expertise applied to a point in information systems that has a relatively low potential payoff compared to other applications. As mentioned earlier, a relatively small proportion of the readings of scientific and technical journal articles are from older articles that must be identified by bibliographic products or services. Yet, there are substantial inefficiencies in the current distribution of journal articles. Publishers in the United States alone distributed more than 2.5 billion copies of articles in 1977 (King et al. [1978b]). Based on our evidence, only 1 out of 8 copies of articles distributed to individuals is read and only 1 out of 20 copies of articles distributed to libraries is read at least once. This inefficiency provides a great opportunity for A&I services. With electronic processes, the abstracting and indexing could take place simultaneously with primary publication. Using bibliographic controls, articles could then be distributed in batches that fit the profile of individual users based on probable immediate use. Copies of articles could be sent to individuals who are highly likely to use them immediately, and articles with less likely or later use could be distributed as abstracts. Such a system requires feedback from users, but this can easily be achieved through electronic means. If the National Technical Information Service (NTIS) can successfully provide multiple batching and distribution for technical reports (in microform), surely publishers can do it for articles with the electronic power they will have at their disposal. Since the number of scientific and technical materials written each year is increasing steadily, such electronic filtering will be even more necessary in the near future. (In the United States during 1977, there were approximately 15,000 books and 380,000 journal articles published in science and technology [King et al. [1978b].)

Some of the most significant usage of modern technology in information transfer has taken place where one might least expect it, which is with authors. Both electronic word-processing or text-editing systems are commonly used by authors. It is forecast that more than one-half of scientific and technical articles will be prepared in digital form during 1980 and 80 percent by 1990 (King et al. [1978a]). This, of course, provides a great deal of flexibility for authors in preparing manuscripts. But the future implications of this are even greater, for it means that we now have within our reach the opportunity for authors to transmit text electronically to editors and publishers so that publishers will not incur a large portion of the costs for input to composition. There are other advanced technologies that are currently being used by authors. Online computer systems are being used more and more frequently as a medium of interpersonal communication among groups of individuals who are separated by time or space. This form of information transfer can upgrade authorship by facilitating much more extensive informal feedback on ideas or research results that might ultimately end up in articles. Also, as mentioned previously, online bibliographic searches probably should increase the quality of background research and, thus, the quality of articles.

The electronic processes provide authors with a great deal more flexibility for preparing information at different levels of detail. For example, authors can prepare abstracts, summaries, and detailed research results that can be processed and distributed by different modes such as online bibliographic databases, electronic distribution, and paper form. At some time in the future, it might be possible to channel portions of the information to different editors and publishers, depending on the potential purposes of use. These channels could be by discipline, but more likely they will be by such purposes of use as research (findings or methods), writing, teaching, research management, or research policymaking.

These recent technological advances provide all the components of a comprehensive electronic journal system. Such a system would provide enormous flexibility in that individual articles can be distributed in the manner most economically advantageous to them. Frequently read articles may still be distributed in paper form, whereas articles infrequently read can be requested and quickly received through telecommunications when they are needed. The trade-off is that resources formerly wasted in printing, mailing, and storage of infrequently read articles would be applied to better identification and retrieval of information, thus reducing cost, improving quality, and increasing efficiency. Furthermore, better systems integration will yield more emphasis on the quality of content, less republication of articles for updates or for different audiences, and better access to and retrieval of information needed in multidisciplinary research.

This comprehensive electronic journal system is highly desirable and currently achievable. I believe that a majority of articles will be handled by at least some electronic processes throughout, but that not all articles will be incorporated into a comprehensive electronic journal system like that just described. Some articles will be processed electronically in different ways, depending on the electronic capabilities of the senders and receivers involved.

There are some major constraints in adoption and use of an electronic journal system. One of the principal constraints to any alternative communication system is the lack of incentive for the communication participants to change. For example, authors are said to publish partially for prestige and recognition, which results in professional advancement. Certainly the "publish or perish" environment that exists in some fields of science and in some organizations creates incentive to publish, and therefore any alternative communication system must meet this perceived need. Many publishers lack a financial incentive for drastically deviating from the current journal publishing practices. Users also present some barriers to new systems that directly affect their behavior. If an alternative journal publishing and distribution system involves direct online communication, some incentives to use it must be provided to users, and their behavior must be altered. Thus, in the future, new users who have been trained on terminals in high schools and universities most likely will find it unacceptable not to have these facilities available for analysis, text processing, search, retrieval, and other forms of information use. Libraries have little incentive to change their mode of operating unless their patrons and funders desire such change. Although many libraries are automated for circulation control, cataloging, and internal record keeping, motivation is still required to change procedures or to provide facilities for electronic processing of articles.

Other constraints are technological. Standards must be set or conversion programs written for word-processing and text-editing output so that publishers can receive it and easily convert it to the appropriate format. A major problem exists in treating nontextual input, including tables, mathematical formulas, and graphics such as line graphs, photographs, and chemical-structure diagrams. Technologically, graphics can be electronically handled now, but the economics are not practical for the high volume of graphics found in such fields as the physical sciences, engineering, and the life sciences. Another requirement is that the cost of telecommunication must continue its downward trend. Equipment for sending and receiving material must be sufficiently sophisticated to permit rapid, and therefore low-cost, communication. Mass storage devices now available could economically store nearly all current literature, but the cost of input and output will remain unacceptable until some breakthroughs are made.

Bibliographic database services have led the information community in electronic processes. What we have learned in the past about electronic processes used with bibliographic databases can now be adapted in the primary literature. I do not think it is merely happenstance, for instance, that the Chemical Abstracts Service is now processing primary journals as well as bibliographic databases. I firmly believe that many journals will be made available online, just as bibliographic data are now; however, I think that the bibliographic services must continue to lead the way in new technology, systems analysis and design, and other areas such as understanding the economic interdependencies among participants.

One can glibly talk about a single mass digital storage of the primary literature. But information researchers must first solve the problems of incompatibility of databases for bibliographic information. It is not yet clear whether the solution will be to standardize input, to develop programs for converting diverse databases into a common format, or to place the burden of searching through the maze of databases on the user. It seems that such problems would be much easier to resolve with bibliographic data than with the primary literature databases, which would be several orders of magnitude larger.

In closing, there are a few thoughts I would like to leave with you. The first deals with the antagonisms that exist among several participants in the information community, namely, publishers and librarians and, more recently, publishers and A&I services. One of the greatest stumbling blocks to advancement in the information community is a lack of understanding of the systemic and economic interdependencies among system participants (King et al. [1978b]; King [1977]). It is quite clear that any perturbation of the system has a ripple effect throughout the entire system. Some understanding of these effects on flow of materials and funds, costs, and use are extremely important, because it enables participants to make operational or planning decisions in view of the effects on other participants, as well as the ultimate consequences to themselves. For example, when librarians cancel journal subscriptions in favor of borrowing, the publishers must react by increasing price, reducing quality, or obtaining income from another source, such as royalties. Any of these outcomes can ultimately be detrimental to libraries or their patrons. I believe in interlibrary lending, but a balance must be achieved. Some of the systemic and economic interdependencies among participants could be more readily resolved with secondary databases than with the primary literature. Such resolutions could provide leadership for the entire information community.

Second, we should try to describe and understand the enormous information community, its potential, and its growth. There is no doubt that we, as part of the information professional community, can contribute a great deal more to the information sector of society through our unique skills and expertise. Thus, we must continually seek new ways of applying these capabilities. Similarly, others in the information profession and fields of science and technology can add to our knowledge and to ways of improving information systems. Regardless, we must be constantly alert to new research results and technology. Both research and technology are moving forward at such an incredible pace that we could take wrong paths and learn too late that there may be far better approaches to information processes and systems.

Finally, abstracting and indexing services have special opportunities in the information age. First, substantial evidence suggests that the future will bring greater distribution of primary information in the form of separates distributed selectively or on-demand. Such systems cannot succeed without strong secondary information products and services. Second, research and technology applied to secondary information have shown the way to similar applications for primary information in the past. This is likely to continue to be true. Third, as we move into the information age, secondary-information products and services may provide the best solution to broadening and redefining needed information for problem solving, lifelong learning, and the many unique user communities not yet properly served.

REFERENCES

Arthur D. Little, Inc. *Into the Information Age.* Chicago, American Library Assn., January 1978. National Science Foundation Grant No. DSI 76-8930.

Bell, D. *The Coming of Post-Industrial Society.* New York, Basic Books, 1973.

Chen, C.-C. "The Use Pattern of Physics Journals in a Large Academic Research Library." *Journal of the American Society for Information Science,* 23(4):254-265, July-August 1972.

Council on Library Resources, Inc. *A National Periodicals Center: Technical Development Plan.* Prepared for the Library of Congress. Washington, D.C., 1978.

Fussler, H. H., and J. L. Simon. *Patterns in the Use of Books in Large*

Research Libraries. Chicago, University of Chicago Press, 1969.

Gaffner, H. B. "Impact of European Data Base Developments on the American Data Base Industry." Paper presented at the Annual Conference of the National Federation of Abstracting and Indexing Services, Arlington, Virginia, March 6–7, 1979. New York, LINK, Inc., 1979.

Kent, A., et al. *A Cost-Benefit Model of Some Critical Library Operations in Terms of Use of Materials.* Pittsburgh, Pa., University of Pennsylvania, April 1978. National Science Foundation Contract DSI-7511840.

King, D. W., "Systemic and Economic Interdependencies in Journal Publication." *IEEE Transactions on Professional Communication, PC-20*(2):106–113, September 1977.

King, D. W., and N. K. Roderer. *Systems Analysis of Scientific and Technical Communication in the United States: The Electronic Alternative to Communication Through Paper-Based Journals.* Rockville, Md., King Research, Inc., May 1978. National Science Foundation Contract NSF-C-DSI 76-15515.

King, D. W., D. D. McDonald, and N. K. Roderer. *The Journal System of Scientific and Technical Communication in the United States.* Rockville, Md., King Research, Inc., November 1978b. National Science Foundation Contract NSF-C-DSI 75Z-06942.

King, D. W., et al. *Systems Analysis of Scientific and Technical Communication in the United States.* Annex 1: *Communication Functions in Science and Technology.* Rockville, Md., King Research, Inc., May 1978a. National Science Foundation Contract NSF-C-DSI 76-15515.

King Research, Inc. *Library Photocopying in the United States: With Implications for the Development of a Copyright Royalty Payment Mechanism.* Final Report submitted to the National Commission on Libraries and Information Science. Washington, D.C., U.S. Government Printing Office, October 1977.

———. *Potential White House Conference Issues: An Analysis of the First 35 Pre-White House Conferences.* Prepared for the National Commission on Libraries and Information Science. Rockville, Md., King Research, Inc., February 1979.

Machlup, F. "An Economist's Reflections on an Institute for the Advanced Study of Information Science." *Journal of the American Society for Information Science,* 30(2):111–113, March 1979.

———. *The Production and Distribution of Knowledge in the United States.* Princeton, N.J., Princeton University Press, 1962.

Machlup, F., and K. W. Leeson. *Information Through the Printed Word: The Dissemination of Scholarly, Scientific and Intellectual Knowledge. Final Report.* New York, New York University, March 1978. National Science Foundation Grant No. IST 74-12756.

Mansfield, U. "The Study of Information. In: *Readings in Information Science.* Edited by E. Trauth and A. Debons. New York, Marcel Dekker, Inc., 1979.

National Science Foundation. "Research in Information Science." *Program Announcement* NSF 78-82. Washington, D.C., National Science Foundation, Division of Information Science and Technology, February 1979.

Palmour, V. E., et al. *Access to Periodical Resources: A National Plan.* Washington, D.C., Association of Research Libraries, 1974.

Palmour, V. E., M.C. Bellassai, and R. R. V. Wiederkehr. *Costs of Owning, Borrowing, and Disposing of Periodical Publications.* Prepared for the National Commission on New Technological Uses of Copyrighted Works. Arlington, Va., Public Research Institute, October 1977.

Porat, M. U. "The Information Sector: Definition & Measurement." Comments prepared for the American Association for the Advancement of Science. Boston, Mass., February 23, 1974.

Resnikoff, H. L. "On the Problems of Information Science." Washington, D.C., National Science Foundation, Division of Information Science and Technology, January 5, 1979a. Draft.

———. "Waste and Scientific Progress." Paper presented at the Annual Conference of the National Federation of Abstracting and Indexing Services, Arlington, Virginia, March 6-7, 1979. Washington D.C., National Science Foundation, Division of Information Science and Technology, 1979b.

Task Force on a National Periodicals System. *Effective Access to the Periodical Literature: A National Program.* Washington, D.C., National Commission on Libraries and Information Science, April 1977.

Williams, M. E. "United States Versus European Use of Data Bases." *NEWSIDIC*, *14*:10-11, October 1974.

MARCH 5, 1980

Surviving the Eighties:
New Roles for Publishers, Information Service Organizations, and Users

CARLOS A. CUADRA, *Cuadra Associates, Inc.*
Santa Monica, California

It has been declared by several observers of the U.S. economy that we are in the Age of Information. The basis for this statement is that information activities are now the largest component of the U.S. Gross National Product, with close to half our labor force involved in these activities. Although the information area of the economy is growing rapidly, I would like to treat the claim that this is the Age of Information with at least a small grain of salt. One reason is that the definition of "information activities" that underlies the claim includes education, research and development activities, computers, and media and communication, as well as information services — a very broad definition, indeed. It even includes the services provided by the cleaning people who sweep up the holes from punch cards. Another reason that I take the information-age claim rather lightly is that I do not want to aggrandize the relatively small part of all information activities that NFAIS, the Association of Scientific Information Dissemination Centers (ASIDIC), the information industry, and the other elements of the nation's library and information community represent. I remember how the great "information explosion" of the 1960s eventually came to be regarded as a cliché. I suspect that the term *Age of Information* has a good chance of achieving that status too.

Cliché or no, it is obvious that as a society we are more conscious of and more dependent on information than ever before. We are also growing more dependent on computer and communications technology, although much of this technology is used for entertainment rather than for information as you and I understand it. Children are being exposed to computers at a very early age, and it is easy to foresee the time when a computer terminal will become a standard tool in most classrooms, just as the small electronic calculator has become a standard tool in the office, as ubiquitous as the pencil sharpener. By the end of the 1980s, we can expect to see young adults who have learned how to identify information resources, how to use them to advantage, and — particularly important — when to seek help in using more complex information resources. This generation will not exhibit the fear and panic that many of us witnessed or felt in the 1960s and 1970s at first confrontations with a computer terminal.

Are we who are in the information business — more narrowly defined — preparing adequately to meet the heightened demands of an information-conscious generation? The safest answer is no, in part because preparation for most things is never adequate, and also because I don't have a crystal ball to be able to predict with confidence what the information environment of the 1980s will be like. On the other hand, there are some areas of the information environment to which I have given considerable thought, and I believe I can identify some problems and challenges in those areas that will take us years to overcome. The areas have to do with the electronic distribution of information through online terminals. The three major groups of stakeholders that I plan to discuss today, in the context of electronic distribution, are publishers, information service organizations, and users.

At the risk of spoiling the fun by telling how the book ends, I will state at the outset that none of these groups is going to become extinct during the 1980s. Their roles and interrelationships, however, will almost certainly change significantly.

SURVIVAL FOR PUBLISHERS

Growing Costs of Operation

It will come as no surprise to NFAIS and ASIDIC members that the costs of many publications have been rapidly increasing. As part of an NSF-sponsored study on the impact of a paperless society on the research library of the future, Lancaster (1980) has documented some of these increases in terms of prices. Between 1963 and 1978–1979, the price for the *Bibliography of Agriculture* rose from $10 to $245; for *Psychological Abstracts*, it rose from $24 to $315; and for *Biological Abstracts*, it rose from $225 to $1,300. Such increases in the prices for secondary literature are mirrored in the primary literature as well. For example, over the 10-year period between 1968 and 1978, the average subscription price for a journal in chemistry and physics rose from approximately $24 to over $100.

Lancaster asserts that such increases have exceeded and are continuing to exceed the general rate of inflation. He points out that where subscribers once tended to be individuals, they are now institutions and, increasingly, only the larger and wealthier institutions. His conclusion is that both primary and secondary literature, in their printed forms, are doomed to extinction. "It is clear," he says, "that the future lies with electronic distribution."

Are there any ways to avoid or forestall the extinction that Lancaster predicts? One possibility is simply to continue raising prices and accept the consequences in the marketplace. Another is for organizations to combine forces—through collaboration or acquisition—to take advantage of whatever economies of scale are available. A third way is to try to increase the efficiency of existing operations through the use of technology. Many publishers have in fact done this, adopting the concept of one-time keyboarding, preparing camera-ready copy through photocomposition, and using minicomputer-based data-entry techniques that improve the speed and accuracy of data entry.

I find it rather amazing that in 1980 there are still a number of major publishers who are preparing publications by setting hot type. Others are using new technology but not using it well. For example, one publisher keyboards the data to produce a printed publication. Then all the same material is keyboarded *again* to produce a magnetic tape for online distribution. I suspect that if the publication field were as competitive as, say, the online services field, organizations operating in such a manner would no longer be in business.

Diversification Through Electronic Distribution

As every businessperson knows, one cannot focus exclusively on cost reduction as a means to improve the bottom line. One must also think hard and work hard at marketing and sales. With respect to the publishers of abstracting and indexing journals, it seems clear to me that they must think hard about ways to generate additional revenues through electronic distribution.

Ten years ago, there was very little electronic distribution of information: the National Library of Medicine was still three months away from introducing its AIM-TWX online service, and the NASA RECON system was still limited to a relatively small number of users. Five years ago, there were fewer than 50 databases online, through a handful of systems. Today there are more than 450 online databases, available through more than 65 online information services serving thousands of users all over the world. Many publishers of abstracting and indexing journals have recognized the signal that electronic distribution is here to stay, and they have accepted the opportunity to begin generating revenues that help to offset some of the first-copy costs. In nearly every case, printed products are subsidizing the online database, and a question that can reasonably be asked is whether or how long this should continue. If, in fact, the future lies with electronic distribution, the revenues from online database access may need to subsidize the printed publications if they are to continue to exist.

New Opportunities for Publishers

The question about revenues from online database access is one of the survival issues for the 1980s, and I will come back to it later. To close the discussion about what publishers can do to relieve their growing financial pains, I would like to suggest that the marketplace for many publications — or for the data that lie behind those publications — is wider than it may appear. For example, 30 years ago, when I was still heavily involved in the field of psychology, I formed the opinion that the publication called *Psychological Abstracts* was about psychology. This is not an unreasonable view, but many of the items that appear in *Psychological Abstracts* are about other things, such as management techniques, law, medicine, and personnel practices, all in addition to psychology. Thus, the database that underlies *Psychological Abstracts* can properly be viewed as a rich resource that can be sliced and packaged for many market areas outside professional psychology.

I do not want to give the impression that this idea has not occurred to anyone before. Some publishers are, in fact, thinking of their holdings as a data resource that can be packaged and sold in a number of segments, as well as being distributed in various ways (print, tape, and online). The *CA SELECTS* series produced by Chemical Abstracts Service provides one of the best examples of this marketing approach. I sometimes think this approach might have appeared attractive to professional societies earlier on were it not for a certain predilection for inbreeding, reflected in the selection and promotion of staff members — including marketers — primarily from those with credentials within the profession.

Roger Summit (1977) stated that more than 90 percent of all significant machine-readable bibliographic data are already online. I might quibble about whether the percentage is really that large, but, even if it is, it is not the end of the line for publishers. A great deal of nonbibliographic data are eminently suitable for online access, and some of it lies languishing on reels of tape—or worse, on sheets of paper—in major U.S. publishing houses. In addition, there are many databases yet to be invented, that will serve various important areas of our society. These databases need not necessarily be an embodiment of an existing printed product.

Some Problems Associated with Online Distribution

Most people believe that, apart from installation problems and minor problems of transition, the use of new technology has largely beneficial effects, and so it does. But it can also have some negative effects on the revenues developed by online service organizations and, in turn, on the resulting revenues earned by publishers as royalties. A case in point is the replacement of an older generation computer with a newer one. If, for example, processing speed is doubled with the new computer, the time that a user must spend online for a given search may be sharply reduced. It will not be cut in half, because not all the time that a user spends online involves computer processing—part of the time he is typing; sometimes he is reading the material displayed at the terminal; and at other times he is checking desk-side tools and thinking about what to do next. Nevertheless, time online could be reduced by at least 10–20 percent and, if the online services were priced primarily in terms of online connect time and the publisher's royalties were also based primarily on connect time, the installation of a new computer could benefit the user and damage the suppliers.

Because selecting and installing new equipment—sometimes with the old equipment kept temporarily in place as insurance—is an expensive process, it would be foolish for an online service organization to undertake such upgrading if it resulted simply in losing revenues. Some organizations that install new equipment adjust their charging algorithm so that, despite the increased computer speed, the revenue levels generated by a specific computer task remain the same. This is relatively easy to do for those organizations that charge users primarily by the type of resources used (CPU [central processing unit], disk accesses, memory, and so on) rather than by connect time. On the other hand, where charges are based primarily on connect time, the only way of keeping the use of new equipment from having a negative impact is to program a specified delay into the computer response or perhaps a variable delay that would result in relatively uniform response time.

Changes in the telecommunications networks and in terminal speeds also impact on the online service and, in turn, on the publisher. In the early 1970s, terminal speed was typically 10 characters per second (cps). Now it is 30 cps and, in a very few years, it will be 120 cps. The telecommunications networks, such as Tymnet and Telenet, which once provided only 30 cps, now offer 120 cps from many cities. In a few years, even higher transmission speeds will be available.

What has been the experience thus far with higher speed transmission? No formal studies have been reported, and the only available evidence is anecdotal and inconclusive. One company that moved from 30-cps to 120-cps terminals found that its searchers did not spend any less time online than they did when they had only 30-cps terminals—they simply did more online printing than before. In contrast, other organizations have reported extensive reductions in online time with the use of 120-cps terminals.

If the use of higher speed terminals really did have no significant impact on connect time, and if connect time were the primary basis for charging, the revenues to the online service and the publisher would be unchanged. On the other hand, if the user were to be charged in another way—in terms of the number of items displayed—the revenues to the online service and the publisher could increase with the faster equipment if users took advantage of the higher speed to display more items. Needless to say, this area begs for hard data on which online services and publishers can make rational business decisions.

The use of more advanced terminal equipment has other potential problems, the most significant of which is the opportunity for the user to copy large segments of a database onto local storage devices for searching at a later time. Some users are already doing this, and, as microcomputers with storage devices become cheaper and more prevalent, the practice will increase, with a potentially sizable impact on revenues to the online service and the publisher. The fact that the use of new technology in this way poses a problem—and it does for most online services and publishers—can be dealt with in several ways. One is to ignore the problem and hope that, if attention is not called to it, it will not become prevalent. A second solution is to forbid it, even though it is difficult to detect and prove violations. A third solution is to develop a special license for this type of use, with fees over and above the normal fees for use of the online system. A fourth solution is more drastic: withdraw the database from the online service and distribute it on a storage medium such as videodisks. At least one database producer has moved in this direction, withdrawing the database from an online service and distributing it on floppy disks. This cannot be considered an ideal solution as yet, because very few organizations have local computer equipment and interactive retrieval programs that provide a suitable substitute for the sophisticated systems available through the commercial online services. By the mid-1980s, however, we can expect many such systems to be in operation on minicomputers and microcomputers, opening the door to new distribution alternatives.

Relationships with Online Users

Publishers have at least three areas of challenge in their relations with online users. The first has to do with prices. Users who were conditioned to $15 per hour or less for MEDLINE and $25 per hour for ERIC, and who know little about the economics of publishing or the economics of operating online services, have sharply questioned the prices for database use, particularly the royalties earned by the publisher. One publisher that raised the connect-time royalty from $20 to $30 per hour received many complaints. Another publisher, whose royalty fee for a database had been $30 for over three years and who then raised it $10, found the database taken off the air by one of the online services, who issued a written announcement to all its users that such a move was in the interest of holding the line on prices.

Clearly, publishers are going through a period of heavy learning. In the early days of online services, they had little or no idea of what revenues they should attempt to recover from online use of their database or what the basis for these revenues should be. As their experience with online services has developed and as they have improved their position to judge the impact of online services on their printed products, publishers have modified their revenue requirements or their conditions of access. Some of the changes have been severe, triggering protests from the online services, the users, or both. The use of the databases involved in these changes has probably not suffered significantly, but, even though the publisher is in a seller's market, keeping the user's goodwill is important. This requires the development and use of a channel of "user education," either through the online service or directly.

The second area of challenge in the relationship between publishers and online users concerns training. As the general level of experience with online systems increases, users are becoming less and less concerned with the "button-pushing" aspects of online system use and more concerned with database content and indexing philosophy. They want to learn about these from the publisher or from the publisher and the online service together. Demand for this kind of training has grown rapidly, placing great pressure on the publishers to provide personnel who understand both the database and its implementation on the particular system being discussed. Not every publisher has the staff or other resources to meet this demand. Such training is relatively more expensive for a publisher with one or two databases to satisfy than it is for an online service supplier, whose staff members can sell an entire "catalog" of databases. In the 1980s, publishers will need to develop more stand-alone, database-specific training aids—in either printed or audiovisual form—that can carry the lesson from the publisher to the user without the labor intensiveness or hit-or-miss coverage of current "roadshows."

A third area of challenge involves the local recording of information in machine-readable form. Earlier, I made reference to the threat of a user copying a file. There are, in fact, legitimate reasons for copying search results. One is to format the output in a way that local users prefer—for example, showing the spelled-out names of fields. Another is to merge output from two or three databases or systems. Still another is to screen the results and remove irrelevant citations. One user—an information broker—devised a system that could do some of these things and asked permission from 35 database publishers to try it out on customers. Seven gave permission, 1 refused it, and 27 did not reply. I think that most of the publishers are following a bad policy—one that puts them in the position of blocking improvements in service to users. I would prefer to see them make strict rules—for example, limiting the time for retention of machine-readable data—and/or charging a fee. But they should not sulk and do nothing.

Impact of Online Service on Printed Publications

The final area of discussion concerning the role of publishers concerns their relationship to online service suppliers. Earlier, I mentioned the problem of the impact of online service use on revenues from corresponding printed products. The evidence of such an impact is sparse and also inconclusive. Stanley conducted a survey of online users in 66 companies and reported that 24 percent of the respondents had entered a new subscription to the hard copy version of a database as a direct result of its availability online. On the other hand, 52 percent of the respondents said that they had canceled subscriptions for the same reason. Summit has challenged these data and pointed to evidence from a study that online access generates more new subscriptions to the corresponding printed products than it loses. Consequently, there is a net gain in revenues.

One of the challenges for the early 1980s is to shed some real light on this issue, because a great deal is at stake for many organizations and many users. Neither the publishers nor the online services have found a satisfactory means of disentangling changes in online and print-product use with changes stemming from general changes in the economy and in the marketplace they serve. Consequently, there has been a great deal of "flying by the seat of the pants." Some publishers have introduced or increased price differentials between print-product subscribers and nonsubscribers, whereas, during the same time period, other publishers have reduced or abandoned such differentials. Some have introduced restrictions in online access, while others have relaxed them. It would be a great service to publishers, online services, and users if a well-conceived study could be carried out to develop some definitive data to help place pricing on a more rational basis.

The current relationship between publishers and online services can best be described as a somewhat uneasy alliance. Both parties are becoming increasingly sensitive to the fact that, with the growing number of companies entering the online service field, the party that controls the data controls the power. In recognition of the fact, some online services are taking tentative steps toward the development or ownership of databases. At the same time, some publishers are taking tentative steps in the direction of operating their own online service. I suspect that both groups are in for some expensive surprises.

SURVIVAL FOR INFORMATION SERVICE ORGANIZATIONS

Information service organizations include libraries, information centers, online service suppliers, custom information services (sometimes called information brokers), document fulfillment services, and others. I plan to focus on two of these: online service suppliers and libraries.

Online Service Suppliers

In the 1980s, online information services will be under increasing pressure from users to make their systems easier to use and also more compatible with each other. Users develop rhythms of system use, and they enter searches and commands almost without thinking, much as a concert pianist plays in phrases, without thinking of individual notes. These rhythms are difficult to develop or maintain when the systems that searchers use have different or even contradictory protocols. For example, on the ORBIT system of System Development Corporation, one can enter SCOTCH AND SODA OR BEER and the system interprets this just as well as a good bartender does. ORBIT gives the AND operator priority over the OR operator, so it will search for the two well-known drinks. Users of DIALOG Information Retrieval Service will get exactly the same results because it follows the same rules of logic. On the other hand, if users of LEXIS enter SCOTCH AND SODA OR BEER, they could be searching for a strange drink — scotch and beer — because LEXIS gives the OR operator priority over AND.

Users can, of course, learn about the different priority sequences, as well as other differences among systems, if they have formal training and online practice and/or if they study the user manuals carefully. But the distinctions that one can remember about two or three systems begin to blur when one must learn and remember six or seven systems. Since there are now over 65 different international online database services, the problem takes on very sizable proportions.

Without too much fanfare, some online services are converging toward more compatible search modes and commands. For example, DIALOG,

LEXIS, and BRS (Bibliographic Retrieval Services), along with some other systems, permit users to enter parentheses to make the search logic clear, in spite of such differences as the priority of AND and OR. If users learn how to use parentheses correctly, they can ensure that SCOTCH AND SODA OR BEER will mean the same thing to any of the major bibliographic systems they use. On the other hand, there are some system features that are not easily changed. If, for some reason, DIALOG wanted to change the numbers on its print formats so that the numbers 1 to 8 would represent a continuum from the skimpiest information (i.e., accession number only) to the full record, the programming change would be trivial but the impact on users' habits—their rhythms—might be devastating. To some extent, each system is the victim of its own history, and the more databases it has online, the less freedom it usually has to introduce changes in database elements and formats.

I mentioned earlier that some publishers are moving toward distributing their own data electronically, that is, online. They do not necessarily have to develop such distribution systems from scratch. Rather, they can purchase an online service organization, like Dun & Bradstreet did in acquiring National CSS, Inc. or McGraw-Hill in acquiring Data Resources, Inc. Neither of these online service companies currently has the type of computer programs required to handle massive bibliographic and textual data. But more and more organizations are learning how to build such programs. Indeed, the information service organizations that provide online access to bibliographic and textual data are going to have a growing amount of company.

I also noted the possibility of publishers distributing their data on videodisks or other comparable storage media for use on local, small computers. One can, in fact, envision something like a chain of information stores that sell databases to users: "I'll take one MEDLINE, please, and one Encyclopedia Britannica, and one Chemical Abstracts."

If this comes about, what will be the role of the present online service companies? I believe they will continue to have a very important role in our information economy, for a number of reasons. The first is fairly obvious: they provide great economy of scale. They buy and use data storage by the billions of characters, at prices that mini- and microcomputer storage devices cannot approach, and they ensure that the costs of this storage are shared by hundreds or thousands of users. In effect, they can render the cost of storage almost trivial from the standpoint of an individual user.

The second reason that online service organizations will continue to be needed is that they provide an unparalleled means for searching a wide variety of data sources in a single sitting, from the same terminal and using the same protocol. The major U.S. bibliographic retrieval services provide a means by which a user can formulate a search strategy and then apply it to scores of databases. In a world of information that knows no sharp boundaries between disciplines, this is a vitally important factor in information access. Decentralized use of databases on videodisks could actually be regressive, putting users back in the mode where limitations in the acquisitions budgets force difficult either/or purchasing decisions regarding individual databases. The centralized online service organizations reduce the need to make such choices.

The third reason that online service organizations will continue to be needed has gone almost unnoticed. It is that, without coercion, they have brought a high degree of standardization, from the user's perspective, to data created by more than 100 different publishers who operate with great independence and who will undoubtedly continue to do so. I remember well the early days of online information services when online databases exhibited a wide variety of labels for the same type of information. Documents were referred to by document number, accession number, identification number, and probably by numerous other labels, too. The fields containing subject-descriptive information were variously called descriptors, identifiers, keywords, index terms, and so on. In the early 1970s, the user needed to learn and remember all the many ways in which the same type of data were referred to in different databases, even on the same system. Why the differences? In large part, it was because few of us could foresee the likelihood of having 100 or more databases available on the same system, and the problem of disparate labels did not loom as large as it should have. But the more important reason for the disparity was that, in the early days (that is, 10 years ago) it seemed important to have online databases mirror the language and labels of the printed products to which they corresponded. To put it bluntly, keeping faith with the publisher outweighed the idea of making the search task as easy as possible for the user. This imbalance has now been corrected, and, at least for the bibliographic online services, a high degree of standardization has been achieved.

What, then, is the challenge for the 1980s? There are actually two major challenges. The first and most difficult is to develop systems that are easier to use. Some recently conducted studies suggest that many searchers are not using online systems effectively because it is too difficult to do and/or because they do not know that they are not using them effectively. But, for every online searcher who is working with existing systems, there are countless potential users—many of them individual scientists, engineers, businesspersons, administrators, and ordinary citizens who are not information specialists—for whom online searching is still many years away. We must greatly simplify online systems for such users and even for information specialists who do not use these systems frequently enough to maintain a high level of skill.

The second challenge is to bridge the large gulf that now exists between the handling of bibliographic and textual data and the handling of numerical and other nonbibliographic data. With very few exceptions, the systems that are capable of processing bibliographic data cannot also handle nonbibliographic data and vice versa. This limitation in current systems capabilities prevents users from drawing with equal ease on different kinds of information resources, but the gulf can be narrowed through the efforts of either the time-sharing companies, whose systems are best suited to numerical data, or the online service companies that specialize in bibliographic and textual information. I hope it will be the latter: the online services have developed from an information tradition, rather than a computing tradition; they have a greater sensitivity to information science issues and research; and they understand better the need for bringing about greater uniformity in the structure of online databases to facilitate their use by all types of users.

Libraries

Severe challenges also are faced by a very different type of information service organization: the library. Many libraries are encountering serious financial problems, some that have been linked with Proposition 13-type public attitudes but that are really more long-standing and pervasive. One reaction to these problems has been to cut back services to an ever-increasing extent in order to live within existing budgets. I characterize this — somewhat unfairly, I must admit — as a "going-out-of-business" approach. To be sure, the libraries that have elected or been forced into this mode are hoping to find new sources of support at all levels of government. They are appealing to Congress and to the public — most recently through the White House Conference on Library and Information Services — to recognize the importance of libraries as unique and vital institutions in a democracy and to increase their funding so that they can play a proper role in keeping the public informed.

Many libraries have been taking a different approach to dealing with the same financial problems. They are attempting to develop new services and, in marketing terms, improve the product. I think of this as the "going-into-business" style. In public libraries, it is exemplified by the development of information and referral services, which guide citizens to the kind of information needed for coping with day-to-day problems. In academic and special libraries, it is exemplified by the use of online information systems to provide more rapid and comprehensive service to their clients and a more market-oriented approach to selling these services internally to their management and users.

Most of the information that even these more aggressive, enlightened, and/or well-financed libraries provide is bibliographic, and full advantage has not yet been taken of the wealth of information available in other types of databases. This is because it is very difficult to learn what kinds of nonbibliographic databases are available, who provides access to them, and how to use them. Also, nonbibliographic databases typically permit, invite, or require some degree of manipulation in addition to the pure searching function. Therefore, to use these databases, librarians must not only learn new skills, but they must also be willing to move into a new role. It is one thing to respond to a reference inquiry by indicating the appropriate section of the stacks or by identifying references to the needed information at a terminal and then pointing to the sources or placing orders for them. It is a very different thing to go online and do the searching and manipulation necessary to produce the actual data being sought.

This challenge in role perception is not confined to nonbibliographic data. It also exists for bibliographic searching and is reflected in the mechanical, quick-and-dirty, antiseptic approach to satisfying user inquiries. Clearly, one of the challenges for libraries in the 1980s will be to decide how far they are willing to move away from the repository and referral role and toward a research-support role.

To move a bit afield, there is presently a great deal of interest associated with videotex systems (which some of you will recognize better as viewdata). This interest is associated—depending on one's point of view or market position—with the concept of a terminal in every home and with huge volumes of business and large profits. One report predicted a market size of $150 million by 1986 and $2.8 billion by the early 1990s.

Some people, when looking at the almost nonexistent role of people involved in library science in the development of the British viewdata system, see the information-directly-in-the-home concept as a great threat to libraries. I am not ready to take that view. I think that as long as the American public is willing to pay for entertainment, it will not be enthusiastic about paying for information, particularly if that information can readily be obtained in the public library at much less cost. In any case, it will require a number of years of planning, development, and marketing before there is a terminal in every home, ready to use to acquire information. I see a remarkable opportunity here for libraries. By being one of the first organizations in each community to have public-access-type online systems in use for some of the more consumer-oriented databases that already exist and those yet to come online, and by taking an active part in educating their clients in using this resource, libraries can play a major role in the introduction of terminals to the public. Part of the message emanating from the White House Conference on Library and Information Services was that libraries should be regarded as an educational resource. What better opportunity could there be than to actually function as educators, helping patrons to understand and use the new information technology before taking the next step of bringing it into their homes?

Another major challenge for librarians involves changing their concept of the library as a collection and viewing it rather as a resource. The financial pressures on both libraries and publishers will very likely accelerate the movement toward electronic distribution of material. In an information environment in which electronic distribution plays a major role, libraries and other information service organizations will increasingly be evaluated on the basis of the resources that they can reach, rather than the ones they have on hand.

I recently had occasion to speculate about a hypothetical periodicals access system (which I dubbed the Carlos A. Cuadra National Periodicals Service) that consisted of a small office and one or two computer terminals from which one could place orders to the Ohio College Library Center (OCLC) libraries, the National Library of Medicine, the British Library Lending Division, the Center for Research Libraries, and half a dozen other organizations, including commercial document-provision services like University Microfilms International and the Institute for Scientific Information. Of course, the office would also need a telephone or two, or a teletype, for taking incoming orders. The main thing that this periodicals access system would *not* have is a collection. I speculated, and several librarians concurred with my estimates, that this hypothetical periodicals access service could easily fulfill over 95 percent of all orders placed.

As some of you know, I am on record as being opposed to the bill introduced into Congress last year to create a National Periodicals Center. That also places me in opposition to NFAIS, which has endorsed the concept of a National Periodicals Center. I do not plan to use this platform to discuss the pros or cons of such a center, except to note that part of the controversy surrounding such a notion involves the distinction between holding information and being able to obtain it. As computer, microform, and communications technology improve, this distinction is certain to become less important. I do not know how well libraries will manage to shift their emphasis from a collection orientation to an access orientation, but I believe that their survival depends to some extent on their success in doing this.

SURVIVAL FOR THE USER

So far, I have discussed survival issues related to the publishers and survival issues related to information service organizations. Are there any survival issues related to users? Probably not. Users are a hardy lot and they manage to survive almost anything. Besides, publishers and information service organizations are continuing to improve the user's information standard of living by providing new sources and new forms of information and by increasing the speed of access to this information. Nevertheless, there are some challenges that are being posed to users, and perhaps those who respond to these challenges will fare better personally and professionally than those who do not.

I should probably distinguish between the two types of users of information services. One is the professional who acts as an intermediary between the end user and the information resource. I have already commented on some aspects of the intermediary's role. The other type of user is the end user. The primary challenge for the end user is to develop awareness and skill in using new technology, not only to produce more satisfying results but also to reduce the demands on the intermediary, which have grown sharply since online searching was introduced a little over a decade ago. Several years ago, Judy Wanger's (1976) study of the users of 10 online bibliographic retrieval services produced the finding that 45 percent of the libraries and information centers that were conducting online literature searches had never before performed any kind of literature searches for their clients. For them, online searching did not supplant manual searching; it actually introduced a service that had never before existed in these institutions. Literature searching had, of course, been done, but it had been done by the end user. Online services have allowed the users, in a great many institutions, to off-load more of their literature-searching work onto the intermediary.

Because online searching has been faster, more comprehensive, and more precise than previous searching methods, and because the ability to use online systems has improved the image of the library and the librarian (or other information professional), the shift has been largely beneficial to all parties concerned. It has been particularly beneficial where the user has stayed in the act long enough to help the intermediary develop the right search strategy and to help evaluate the results, sometimes right at the terminal. On the other hand, the intermediary's job is, in many ways, growing more difficult every day. Ten years ago, the number of online databases could be counted on one hand. Today, there are over 450 such services, and the number is growing by nearly 50 percent each year.

I know some talented searchers who have found it difficult to remember exactly how to use a dozen different databases, particularly when they do not use them on a daily basis. Imagine how much more difficult it is to remember the details of 20, 30, 50, or 100 databases—details such as the range of content, the scope of sources covered, the types of documents included, the years of coverage, the elements or fields of the record, the vocabulary and indexing policies, the type of vocabulary control, the frequency of updating, and the relationship to the printed product, if there is one. These are not the only aspects a good searcher must remember about a database, but they are enough to illustrate that, as the number of online databases grows, the task of the intermediary grows. This is why the end user must develop some capability to use online systems directly.

You may well ask, if online searching is getting so difficult for the experienced professional intermediary, how can one possibly suggest that end users get into the act? One answer is that it may be necessary to involve end users from a financial standpoint. If part of the overall online searching task can be distributed among 1,000 users in an organization, it can reduce the demands for skilled intermediaries. Also, most end users do not need to use 20, 50, or 100 databases. Their range of interests is typically fairly narrow and may be encompassed by a very few databases. Finally, end users have a better command of the concepts and language of their subject area than most intermediaries are likely to have.

The idea of end users doing their own online literature searching is by no means new. Some online service organizations, such as Mead Data Central, have been promoting it for years, and it is an article of faith for the LEXIS service. Still, it is easier said than done. For all the claims of easy use, online systems are really difficult to use *well*, even for information professionals. So the exhortation for end users to develop more skill in fending for themselves must be accompanied by an exhortation for the online services—or others—to develop user interfaces that are designed specifically for end users or infrequent users.

Ten years ago, I was honored by the American Society for Information Science by being named Distinguished Lecturer for 1970. In this role, I traveled around the country, discussing the promises and pitfalls of online information services. At the time, there were no commercial online retrieval services in operation and, although the company I worked for was operating an online service in support of the National Library of Medicine, I had not conceived of anything like the SDC Search Service. During the talks I gave that year, I discussed the requirements for a good retrieval system and took a dim view of the kind of systems that forced the user into a lock-step, 20-question type of interaction. Interestingly enough, some of the modern systems that are well tailored for the end user use the 20-question approach, which is now referred to as the "menu" approach. Videotex- or viewdata-type systems epitomize this approach because they give the user a series of hierarchically arranged options that can lead, at some point, to the desired information. What is different today from the situation 10 years ago is that the systems behind the menus are much faster and more responsive; some are also more sophisticated and flexible in the paths open to the user. So while a 20-question system was indeed maddening in the days of six-character-per-second teletypes and not-very-intelligent programs, it is a perfectly acceptable approach for many of today's users, now that we can make better programs and can fill an entire screen with information in a split second at a relatively low cost. Therefore, with some supportive research, some clever, user-oriented design and programming, and more uniform and better structured databases, end users can be provided with the tools they need to do more of their own literature searching.

What will this do for the information intermediaries? For one thing, it will give end users a better understanding of information resources and information technology. Therefore, when they need to bring difficult requests to the intermediary, they will be able to better articulate them and to provide vocabulary leads, suggestions, limitations, and other aids to more cost-effective searching. Also, the intermediary will become an educator, rather than simply a searching machine. Finally, intermediaries will be able to extend their skills and services into the area of nonbibliographic databases, which they have so far neglected or avoided.

Nonbibliographic databases as a whole are extremely underused. One of the reasons for this is that they are dispersed over so many different systems. Where it is possible in the United States to access nearly 90 percent of the internationally available databases with only four systems, more than 30 different systems would need to be learned to achieve that level of access to the nonbibliographic databases. Another reason for the underuse of nonbibliographic databases is the narrow perception of the market by the organizations that provide access to them. Just as a database such as Psychological Abstracts is misperceived if it is thought to be only about psychology, so are certain nonbibliographic databases misperceived as being of value only to specific groups or units such as corporate planners, accountants, or attorneys. In some companies, one organizational unit may use a nonbibliographic database such as BI/DATA without any awareness that it could be of use in other parts of the organization. The unit is not opposed to such use; it is simply not part of its function to concern itself with the information needs of the entire organization.

One reason to involve intermediaries—specifically the library or information center personnel—more in nonbibliographic databases is to take advantage of their information-gatekeeper skills. These individuals are in the best position to serve as a focal point for educating scientists, engineers, businesspeople, and others in their organization about the use of all kinds of relevant information. They also can identify potentially relevant information sources and arrange for suppliers to make presentations to both the information professionals and the end users to help all parties concerned to better assess the potential value to the organization of a certain information resource.

Bringing more nonbibliographic data resources into an organization does not necessarily mean that the intermediaries will do all the searching. Some databases, such as those that are closely tied to modeling capabilities, are better suited to end users than to intermediaries. But the intermediaries should, I think, consider it part of their responsibility to learn about such resources and, where possible, learn how to use them, so that they will be in a better position to function in the full-service mode. Of the 450 online databases available on an international basis, approximately 170 are bibliographic and 280 are nonbibliographic. In suggesting that intermediaries consider it part of their responsibility to develop greater understanding and skill in the nonbibliographic area, I am posing a very considerable challenge. They must learn how to use many more databases and many more systems. But they should welcome that challenge as part of a going-into-business style.

Another important challenge to intermediaries is to improve their skills in using their current resources. Online searching is a highly individualized process that permits 30 different searchers to come out with 30 different sets of references. This has led some to believe that there are no right and wrong answers and no good and bad ways to use online systems. This is not true. Searching the wrong database is bad. Searching only one database is bad if other databases contain relevant material. Being satisfied with whatever comes out of the terminal first is bad. So are using inappropriate search terms and not taking the time to find out what it is that the user actually wants. In short, there are practices that are demonstrably bad and there are questionable practices that are not far from being demonstrably bad.

Intermediaries can and should do one thing immediately. They should develop greater intolerance for certain aspects of online service. In a recent study sponsored by the National Library of Medicine (Wanger [1980]) Cuadra Associates reviewed the online printouts of around 200 searchers who had taken part in an extensive experiment. It was discovered that some of them had encountered line noise but, instead of hanging up and trying to get a better line, continued with the search and obtained results that included a great deal of unreadable material. The line noise caused an even worse problem. It interfered with the searchers' ability to determine how satisfactory the results were and whether additional effort or a new tack was needed.

I have known of searchers who would sit for 15 minutes at a silent terminal without trying to determine whether the system they were using was operating. There is a tendency for consumers of all kinds to accommodate themselves to poor service when it is too difficult to fight back, but sometimes they do not even know how to recognize that the service is poor. Intermediaries should make it their job to learn how well any tool or service they use ought to work; then they should be intolerant of any lesser level of service. They should also learn how to diagnose problems so that they can have them corrected and thus make better use of the system.

INFORMATION, PRODUCTIVITY, AND THE USE OF THE PRIVATE SECTOR

I foresee, in the 1980s, a greater realization that an investment in information resources of the right kind can lead not only to greater user satisfaction but also to greater productivity. Recently, Robert Hayes, Dean of the UCLA (University of California at Los Angeles) Graduate School of Library and Information Science, presented the results of a study he had conducted on the relationship between capital investment in information and various measures of productivity. He concluded from empirical data that those industries in the United States with high productivity per worker tend to be those with high investment in information and that, while the co-occurrence of two patterns never proves that one causes the other, labor and information seem to be interchangeable. The more we use information, the more productive we are. This is a heartening message for those of us in the information field.

One question that might be asked is whether it makes any difference who does the investing in information products and services. Some believe that it does not matter whether the investor is the government or the private sector. (Incidentally, the term *private sector*, as I am using it, includes all organizations not directly supported by tax monies.) Others believe that it is better for our economy if the government does the investing. They argue that, when the government has money to spend, it spends all of it; but in the private sector, some of that money will instead be saved. Therefore, there will not be as much money to recycle, reverberate, and otherwise contribute to our Gross National Product.

On the other hand, some people believe that the private sector should make the investments in information products and services. I count myself in this group. Most of the population of the United States works in the private sector, and it is there that most of the products and services we use on a day-to-day basis are generated. More specifically, the private sector has long had a role in the provision of library and information services by virtue of its production of books, serial publications, office equipment, bookmobiles, electronic computers, and telecommunications networks. It has also had a role in the direct distribution of information, most obviously through the communications media, particularly newspapers.

What the private sector is very good at is fostering the invention of new products and services by many different people who are willing to risk money on their convictions and leaving the acceptance or rejection of its products and services to the consumer. This mode of operation is not tidy, it is not organized, and it certainly does not take place in accordance with a grand plan. Yet it produces an enormous variety of goods and services and gives Americans an enormous variety of choices. It also has another important feature: a built-in mechanism for determining when and if a given product or service is no longer needed. In recent years, we have seen the introduction of zero-based budgeting and sunset laws as an organized means of determining when government agencies and their services are no longer needed. The marketplace does not need such laws or regulations. A product or service is no longer needed when the public chooses to spend its money elsewhere.

I do not want to give the impression that the private sector can do everything alone and that there is no role for the Federal Government in the information arena. Far from it. Many of the successful information products and services that now exist in the marketplace owe some part of that success to government-sponsored research and development, to the availability of information resources developed by the government, and, in some cases, to a direct subsidy. The Federal Government has even sponsored tests to determine the readiness of the marketplace for particular information services (an example is the use of online services in public libraries) with the expectation that the private sector would carry on if it became apparent that there was a market for some service. These are just several of many instances of productive symbiosis between the government and the private sector. I, for one, would like to see more in the 1980s.

What I think is not productive is the establishment of new tax-supported information services that either duplicate existing services or that, by their existence, act as a disincentive for the private sector to invest in areas occupied by government service.

I believe that our economy in the 1980s will be healthier and that our citizens will be provided with better information products and services, at lower costs, if we can find ways to take full advantage of the diversity, know-how, creativity, and financial resources of the private sector without impacting adversely on services, such as public libraries, that will continue to require the financial support of federal, state, and local government. Creating the most productive balance between the private and public sectors in the information environment of the 1980s will likely be our greatest challenge. I hope we will be equal to it.

REFERENCES

Lancaster, F. W., et al. *The Impact of a Paperless Society on the Research Library of the Future.* Urbana, Ill., University of Illinois Graduate School of Library Science, 1980. (A report to the National Science Foundation Division of Information Science and Technology, NSF Grant No. DSI 78-04768.)

Stanley, W. G. "Changing Revenue Patterns from Online Use." Paper presented at the National Information Conference and Exposition, NICE III, Washington, D.C., April 1979.

Summit, R. K. "The New Age of Computer Aided Information Access." Presentation at the American Association for the Advancement of Science Meeting, Denver, Colo., February 23, 1977.

Wanger, J., C. A. Cuadra, and M. Fishburn. *Impact of On-Line Retrieval Services: A Survey of Users, 1974–75.* Santa Monica, Calif., System Development Corporation, 1976. NTIS: PB-268 591.

Wanger, J., et al. *Evaluation of the Online Search Process: A Final Report.* Santa Monica, Calif., Cuadra Associates, and Rockville, Md., King Research, Inc., 1980. NTIS: PB 82-132 565.

MARCH 4, 1981

Abstracts, Who Needs Them?

RUSSELL J. ROWLETT, JR. *Chemical Abstracts Service, Columbus, Ohio*

I am an avid reader of mystery stories, and I like the suspense of waiting until the last five pages to discover "who done it." In spite of this, I am not going to keep you in suspense for my answer to the question: "Abstracts, who needs them?" I am going to challenge you at the outset with my reply. Every searcher who tackles any sizable subject needs either today's abstract or a suitable future abstract substitute. The word *never* is not one of my favorites, and I will not say that abstracts will never disappear. But, I do not see the need that abstracts serve disappearing. Nor do I foresee, as yet, any combination of computer-derived or online services that will replace this need.

The popular press in the field of information science is filled with predictions about our evolving information-transfer technology. Recently, I asked two dozen of you, as NFAIS members, what you thought was the future of abstracts in this "new world." I was not surprised to receive a few predictions of the demise of abstracts. I was heartened by many who supported strongly the continuing value of the task abstracts perform. Some replies were, "Abstracts will continue to serve as the minimum units in acquisition of knowledge." "Abstracts are the least common denominator derived from journal articles at not too much cost in time and money." "We need some form of synthesis and condensation of the individual article." "Usefulness is not likely to diminish for years to come."

Abstracts originated to provide scholars with a quicker and easier method of keeping up with the growing literature in their subject fields. It was an alerting need that abstracts first filled. The historical development of abstracting in general has been documented thoroughly by Skolnik (1979) and that of specific abstracting services by Collison (1971), Baker et al.(1980), and many others. The growth of the use of abstracts has paralleled the growth of the subject literature. As the latter became very large, annual and collective indexing was demanded. Such indexing of both the abstracts and the corresponding original documents established abstracts as an indispensable tool for retrospective searching. It is this retrospective need that determines the long-term requirement for abstracts or a very suitable substitute. This retrospective need is so large and so persuasive that any future alerting uses can ride along as incidental benefits. I rest my arguments for the need for abstracts entirely on their substantial use in retrospective searching.

In reviewing the instructions for abstracting of 20 NFAIS members, there is almost unanimous agreement that an abstract provides only access to the original document it attempts to describe. It is not a surrogate. It does not stand in place of or replace the original document. It should not be the final source of precise or complete data. It is an accessing tool. I particularly like one comment: that the abstract "reflects accurately the substance of the article." Others declared that the abstract "provides more rapid means for deciding whether the document is pertinent to professional needs"; "enables readers to identify the basic content and to decide whether they need to read the document"; and "gives a firm idea of whether the reference is relevant." My definition of an abstract draws an analogy with a simple chemical process. The abstract is a well-used filter that the searcher uses to identify those documents that are most pertinent to the particular topic and that must be read in detail. It allows to pass through the filter the many documents that need not be consulted. I suggest that certainly today—and in my opinion, far into the future—an abstract or a very suitable substitute will continue to be needed for this important purpose. Without it, far too many original documents will have to be consulted.

The different types and variations of abstracts have been described by Borko and Bernier (1975), Rowley and Turner (1978), Weil et al. (1963 a,b), and others. The types have been categorized by many terms, including informative, indicative, descriptive, terse, critical, and modular, and by several other representations, such as author, purpose, and form. I will confine my attention here to what I consider to be today's typical informative abstract as defined in the American National Standard for Writing Abstracts developed so thoroughly and expertly by Ben Weil and Subcommittee 6 of the Z39 Committee of the American National Standards Institute (ANSI). Such an abstract is, in ANSI's words, "an abbreviated, accurate representation of a document without added interpretation or criticism." In my survey, 17 NFAIS members who use abstracts in their services adhere very closely to this standard. It is interesting, however, that only one of these services mentions the standard in their statements of abstract purpose or their instructions for abstracting. Perhaps one way to extend the use of good standards is to acknowledge those we use.

I agree with Ben Weil and the ANSI standard that "an abstract should be as informative as is permitted by the type and style of the document." Therefore, when I speak of an abstract, I am considering only informative abstracts. I recognize there are other varieties, but they have purposes other than retrospective searching.

An important point in understanding my reply to the question "Who needs abstracts?" is that I consider myself to be a user of abstracts, as well as a producer. In fact, I was a user before I became a producer and, in my total experience, have used far more than I have produced. In 1946, as an industrial research chemist, I became a volunteer abstractor for the late E. J. Crane, then editor of *Chemical Abstracts* (*CA*). The pay for preparation of abstracts in 1946 was only four cents per line printed. It was said to be "a labor of love." During that year, *CA* published abstracts for 39,578 documents, and 100 percent of them were prepared by volunteer abstractors from around the world. In 1980, *CA* published 12 times as many abstracts, and only 6.4 percent of the 475,739 abstracts were produced by volunteers. If I had continued "my labor of love," I would have been out of a job. NFAIS members in 1980 produced abstracts for almost 2.4 million documents. Why am I quoting these statistics? Because you and I, who today are producers of abstracts and indexes, must adopt the posture of users if we are to understand fully the abstract needs for the future. Users face selection of a few choice pertinent references from a universe of millions of documents. It is a staggering and sometimes repulsive assignment.

Although I have been editor during the production of more than half the 8.5 million abstracts published by Chemical Abstracts Service (CAS) since 1907, I cannot recall editing a single word in a single abstract. I have, however, written and spoken hundreds of thousands of words to and with users, trying to understand their needs and to improve the services they require. Users were aware of the tremendous numbers of references included in the traditional printed services; however, they faced subsets of the total in annual volumes or relatively small collections. Mentally, the large numbers were not so apparent, and human intelligence, sometimes unconsciously, weeded out the less important. Today, with some services having been available online for more than 10 years, users can be inundated, almost at the push of a button, with thousands of answers to relatively simple questions. In the July-December 1980 *CA General Subject Index*, there were nearly 7,300 entries under the single index heading "Proteins," more than 3,000 under "Wastewater Treatment," 2,500 under "Nuclear Magnetic Resonance," 2,200 under "Soils," and more than 2,000 under "Blood Analysis." Multiply these numbers by 20 when you are interrogating a 10-year collection online. Certainly, there are modifying phrases for some of the index entries and logic that can be used in connection with associated subjects to reduce retrieval, but the task is still formidable.

Three years ago, in his Miles Conrad Lecture, Ben Weil (1978) reminded us of the early NFAIS debates on the relative and absolute merits of journals of abstracts and bibliographic-reference-based indexes. As Ben pointed out, this controversy died down and both types of access services have been known for all these years. The debate is reappearing, however, as large amounts of index material are becoming available online and vendors of such services are asking why searchers can't go directly from index entries to original documents. Users can't go directly from indexes to documents simply because there are just too many documents. An additional filter is needed, and the abstract is the tried-and-true tool. Until a more effective tool is devised, I don't think we are going to reject the abstract, which has served us so well.

There is much discussion about the availability of the full text of primary documents in computer-readable form and what this portends for abstracting and indexing services. Yes, we are going to search some full-text documents online, but, frankly, I do not see this replacing the use of some form of an abstract. I continue to see abstracts as a means to determine which full-text documents we will search. In fact, we will learn to search full text by first searching abstract text. Having reviewed our abstracts by either reading them or searching them by computer, we will select the most pertinent original documents. Then, if these documents are available online, we will search their full text for specific information, which we confidently expect to locate because of our index and abstract reviews. Abstracts will continue to play an important role in limiting the amount of search of the original documents. This will be true whether the documents are being read by humans and/or by computer. Abstracts will continue to save time and to provide a more effective search.

My retrospective search scenario for the future is straightforward. We will address an index of some type—online or something even better (or a print index if we are in an underdeveloped country). We will select the probable abstract references of interest, using our computer or mental logic, and we will review the retrieved abstracts either by reading or searching on the terminal. Finally, we will address the most pertinent original documents in full text online (or in print if the required computer technology is not available in our geographical area). Remember, there are large areas of the world where the freely available printed page is still somewhat of a luxury. All our emerging computer technology and information transfer will be in evolutionary stages worldwide for years to come. This scenario continues to include full use of an abstract or a suitable effective substitute. Online searching of the full text of documents will not replace the use of abstracts for retrospective searching and it most certainly will not replace the use of indexes. Even with very-low-cost computer storage, we must keep in mind the proportional differences in the sizes of files of index entries, abstracts, and full-text documents. On an approximate scale where the computer-storage space for the average number of index entries for one document is established as 1, the space for an abstract is 2, and, for the full-text document, it is 40. This last value does not include mathematical, tabular, and graphical materials, which, in today's systems, are not yet searchable. The attractiveness of the abbreviated abstracts and indexes is obvious.

The majority of retrospective searchers can be categorized into two groups. The first includes those who seek one or several items of data or facts about a relatively small subject. These users are generally in a hurry and do not necessarily require the latest information or all the information, but they do seek information in which they have confidence. They often look for information published by a particular author, laboratory, or institution. They proceed rapidly from a few index references to a few abstracts, from which they select the one or two original papers in which they confidently expect to find the data they seek. Examples of such searches in chemistry are for a quick method of preparation of a substance, a numerical property, quantitative data on a user or a property, and a given investigator's findings.

This group of searchers comprises many of those who today ask why our abstracting and indexing services cannot provide the data directly, without the searcher having to actually read the original documents. The answer is inherent in the manner by which these searchers approach the files. They have a built-in mental evaluation defining their quick searches by author, language, institution, and even appraisal of the index entry as they read it. Thus, they locate rapidly the data that fit their individual parameters. In essence, they evaluate the data while they search, a feat that abstracting and indexing services will not be able to accomplish completely ahead of time and package individually. Perhaps there will be means by which we may assist in such searches when the technology is fully available.

There is an additional reason why abstracting and indexing services alone cannot provide "the data": the staffs of these services have thorough subject backgrounds and expertise, but they are separated from current research and technology. They are not conversant with day-to-day developments in a research environment truly on the cutting edge of a subject. To perform good data analysis, to be in a position to select the "best" data, one has to be in such an up-to-date research atmosphere. An isolated abstracting and indexing staff is not. Cooperation between a service and an operating data analysis center is practical, however, and several such efforts are currently under evaluation. In such a way, a bibliographic information service could alert its users to the availability of numerical data in a parallel data-analysis service. Via computer networking, such actual data could be retrieved from the analysis-center files and transferred through the bibliographic service. This is the only practical means today to supply data through an abstracting and indexing service.

The second group of retrospective searchers are involved with the comprehensive assignments—those where relatively large amounts of information are sought on subjects with which the searcher is not very familiar. Such assignments comprise literature studies that precede new research programs, state-of-the-art reviews, prior art-patent searches —exhaustive studies for whatever purpose. It is in such instances that the informative abstract performs its greatest service: it provides the best filtration by removing a large volume of less-relevant references and leaving a small residue of more pertinent references. This is where today's abstract, or some future substitute for an abstract, is most essential. We cannot omit this very productive step in any large search, no matter what the subject area.

Again I direct your attention to statistics that the user must comprehend as available online files continue to expand. The last 10 years of CAS files include 3.8 million abstracts that are accessible via online index entries which have reached the following astronomical totals: subject index entries, 25.5 million; author names, 10.6 million; and chemical formulas, 7.4 million. The grand total is 43.5 million major access points, plus patent numbers, structural ring fragments, registry numbers, and the like, which I have not included. If it were possible to search all CAS files back to 1907, these numbers would just about double in size. Even the most carefully constructed profiles, limited in scope, will retrieve large numbers of potentially interesting references. A second-order filter, an abstract, is going to be absolutely necessary as these files continue to grow. We expect in the next five years that chemistry and chemical engineering will produce 2.6 million additional documents and, therefore, 2.6 million additional abstracts. Hence, some 17.5 million more subject index entries will be created. Online availability of files prior to 1970 also will increase. We will be seeing large growth at both ends of the chronological scale.

I have discussed the definition of informative abstracts and their continued use in retrospective searching. Now, what about the future form of this thing we continue to call an *abstract*?

One of the better replies to my inquiry contained the following interesting thought: "Some forms of abstracting come close to indexing." I would like to turn this phrase around to read, "Some forms of indexing come close to abstracting." When we consider going directly from indexes to the original documents, we may in the future use index entries that in themselves include a one- or two-sentence abstract. The filtration step will continue to occur as part of the review of the index entry. Although such index entries may be quite different from those seen today, there are some examples from current indexes that are almost one-sentence abstracts. These in no way actually substitute for abstracts, but they demonstrate the future potential. I will illustrate with a printed format, but the same principle applies to computer-readable and -searchable formats. Here are four examples from recent *CA* indexes:

Soups
    Carrot, nutrients of, infant diarrhea treatment in relation to,

This entry was derived from the following thought: "Infant diarrhea treatment in relation to nutrients of carrot soup."

Behavior
    Locomotor
        Lead effect on, of newborn, after maternal administration, brain development in relation to,

Interpreting this to a continuous idea, we have "Effect of lead on brain development in relation to locomotor behavior in newborn after maternal administration." This index entry contains enough information to almost be called a miniabstract.

Plastics
    Anticorrosive and waterproofing insulation for construction, development prospects for, in Poland,

This entry came from the thought, "Development prospects in Poland for plastics as anticorrosive and waterproofing insulation in construction."

Stars
    Birthrate and initial mass function of, in solar neighborhood,

Finally, an entry from the stars that originated from the phrase, "Birth rate and initial mass function of stars in the solar neighborhood."

CAS has developed a computer technique (Baser et al. [1978]) by which these one- and two-sentence ideas may be entered into the computer and then converted automatically to several appropriate index entries. The process has not yet been implemented but has been tested and shown to be cost-effective. It is conceivable that full sentences may be expanded and/or improved in the future to serve in a similar manner to today's abstracts but actually be incorporated within the index entries. Again, I am referring to such uses for retrospective searching. The availability of index entries online, in the same time frame as abstracts, does provide some alerting capability, and expanded index entries might enhance this function.

A word of caution is in order on this suggested use of expanded index entries to include the filtration step now supplied by abstracts. Many documents require multiple index entries to fully describe their significant contents. For example, the document on plastics in Poland also could describe development prospects for synthetic fibers for purposes other than construction. An index entry under the alphabetical heading "Plastics" would provide a miniabstract for only this specific part of the document's content. It would not indicate that the document also deals with synthetic fibers. It is the full abstract that brings out the whole content of the document in context. Admittedly, this problem exists only for users of printed services. In online retrieval or browsing, all such miniab-

---

88: 184616b **Insecticidal dusts: grain protectants during high temperature–low humidity storage.** LaHue, Delmon W. (Grain Mark. Res. Cent., ARS, Manhattan, Kans.). *J. Econ. Entomol.* 1978, 71(2), 230–2 (Eng). Diatomaceous earth dusts impregnated with 4.5, 6.0, and 7.5 ppm *pirimiphos-methyl*

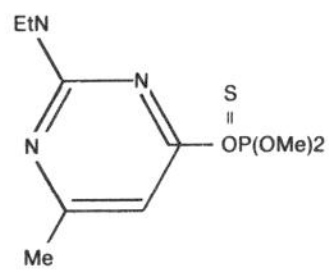

(I) [29232-93-7] and with 5.0, 7.5, and 10 ppm *malathion* [121-75-5] were tested as protectants against insect attack on hard winter wheat (11.2% moisture) stored at ca. 33.4° and 40% relative humidity. The dusts were applied at a rate of 0.5 kg dust/metric ton wheat. Sprays prepd. from emulsifiable concs. and the dust base alone were used for treatment checks. Dust formulations were more effective than sprays that contained equiv. doses and were much more effective than diatomaceous earth alone. I was more effective than malathion.

Figure 1   Original *CA* abstract.

88: 184616b Dust formulations of diatomaceous earth impregnated with pirimiphos-methyl effective as grain protectant during high temperature-low humidity storage. LaHue, Delmon W. (Grain Mark. Res. Cent., ARS, Manhattan, Kans.). *J. Econ. Entomol.* 1978, 71(2), 230–2 (Eng).

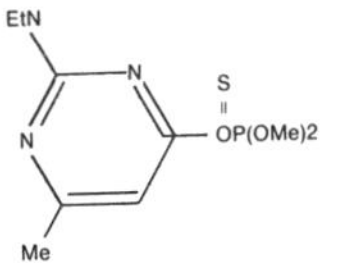

Figure 2 Title-only abstract: title has been expanded with more information; bibliographic citation is the same.

stracts for index entries from a single document could be displayed and read as the total contents of the document in question.

Many suggestions have been made for modification of our present format for informative abstracts. After all, the format used by most services is almost identical to that with which we began our services 50–75 years ago. Some of the ideas suggested have included an expanded title-only bibliographic citation; an abstract with all "excess words" removed; the bibliographic citation plus a listing of the index entries in lieu of a formal abstract; a one-sentence summary abstract; and a terse miniabstract. Examples of these suggestions have been constructed. I present them here only as illustrations and do not personally endorse any. The examples are all built on the content of a typical CA abstract, which is reproduced as Figure 1.

In an evaluation of these examples, an advisory group expressed keen interest only in Figure 6. This example uses the idea of terse sentences and expressions as described by Bernier (in Collison [1971]) in a number of publications. Figures 3, 4, and 5 were rejected not only because the abstract must be sufficiently informative, but also because the user must be able to read, scan, or browse easily through the text. It seems to be the nature of human apprehension, or understanding, that full sentences, properly formulated, are easy to grasp and retain. We may outgrow this stage, but we are not ready to accept telegraphic style in abstracts. From an operational standpoint, production of abstracts as shown in Figure 6 will be more costly in terms of the analyst's time than production of current abstracts. More important, the concise or terse format may be good for alerting purposes but does not always fit my criteria for a useful filter in retrospective searching. In such services, the abstract must provide sufficient information to enable the searcher to decide whether to consult the original document. A useful filter must be easy to apply.

88: **184616b Insecticidal dusts: grain protectants during high temperature–low humidity storage.** LaHue, Delmon W. (Grain Mark. Res. Cent., ARS, Manhattan, Kans.). *J. Econ. Entomol.* **1978,** 71(2), 230–2 (Eng).

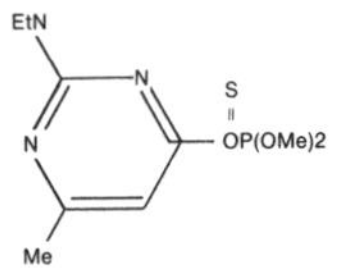

Diatomaceous earth dusts impregnated 4.5, 6.0, 7.5 ppm *pirimiphos-methyl* (**I**) [**29232-93-7**], 5.0, 7.5, 10 ppm *malathion* [**121-75-5**] tested protectants insect attack hard winter wheat (11.2% moisture) stored 33.4° and 40% relative humidity, applied 0.5 kg dust/metric ton wheat. Treatment checks: sprays emulsifiable concs., dust base alone. Dust formulations more effective than equiv. sprays, much more than diatomaceous earth; **I** more effective than malathion.

Figure 3 Abstract and bibliographic citation with all excess words removed.

88: **184616b Insecticidal dusts: grain protectants during high temperature–low humidity storage.** LaHue, Delmon W. (Grain Mark. Res. Cent., ARS, Manhattan, Kans.). *J. Econ. Entomol.* **1978,** 71(2), 230–2 (Eng).

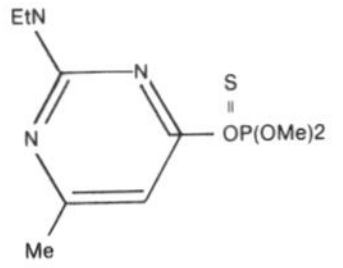

Butanedioic acid, [(dimethoxyphosphinothioyl)thio]-,*diethyl ester* [**121-75-5**], stored grain insect control by
 Phosphorothioic acid, esters, O[2–diethylamino)-6-methyl-4-pyrimidinyl] O,O – dimethyl *ester* [**29232-93-7**], stored grain insect control by
  Insecticides, for stored grain
  Sitophilus oryzoe, *Sitophillis zeamais*, *Tribolium castaneum*, control of, in stored grain
  Wheat, insect control in stored

Figure 4 Bibliographic citation plus a listing of index entries in place of a formal abstract.

88: 184616b Insecticidal dusts: grain protectants during high temperature–low humidity storage. LaHue, Delmon W. (Grain Mark. Res. Cent., ARS, Manhattan, Kans.). *J. Econ. Entomol.* 1978, 71(2), 230–2 (Eng).

<pre>
       EtN
        \
         N
        / \\
       N   \\   S
        \\   \\ ||
         \\---- OP(OMe)2
        /
       Me
</pre>

A diatomaceous earth dust formulation impregnated with *pirimiphos-methyl* [29232-93-7] was more effective as protectant against insect attack on hard winter wheat than the dust impregnated with *malathion* [121-75-5].

Figure 5 Bibliographic citation plus an informative one-sentence summary abstract.

88: 184616b Insecticidal dusts: grain protectants during high temperature–low humidity storage. LaHue, Delmon W. (Grain Mark. Res. Cent., ARS, Manhattan, Kans.). *J. Econ. Entomol.* 1978, 71(2), 230–2 (Eng).

<pre>
       EtN
        \
         N
        / \\
       N   \\   S
        \\   \\ ||
         \\---- OP(OMe)2
        /
       Me
</pre>

Diatomaceous earth dusts impregnated with *pirimiphos-methyl* (I)[29232-93-7] and with *malathion* [121-75-5] were tested as protectants against insect attack on hard winter wheat. Dusts impregnated with I were more effective than those with malathion which was more effective than diatomaceous earth alone or sprays that contained equiv. doses.

Figure 6 Bibliographic citation plus a terse miniabstract.

I have one final point to make about the future of abstracts. This NFAIS membership has been discussing for most of its 23-year history various forms of cooperation among discipline-oriented services. Several services cover the same documents producing similar, if not duplicate, abstracts and index entries. Several have measured this so-called overlap and reported it, but have not come to grips with the basic question: Will users accept a single abstract and a single set of index entries prepared by one

Example 1

BIOSIS

13226. ACKART, W. B.*, R. L. CAMP, W. L. WHEELWRIGHT and J. S. BYCK. (Res. Dev. Dep., Chem. Plast., Union Carbide Corp., Bound Brook, N. J., USA.) Antimicrobial polymers. J BIOMED MATER RES 9(1): 55-68. 1975. [In Engl. with Engl. summ.]— A number of carboxyl-containing ethylene copolymers were prepared which exhibit long term antibacterial and antifungal properties. These materials, containing antimicrobial agents bound to the copolymer backbone as carboxylate salts, were tested for their applicability to hospital products as a means of providing "self-sanitizing" articles. Tests showed that these materials, although not bactericidal, do inhibit microbial growth. Investigations of the compatibility of these polymers with commodity polymers were made and water emulsions of the polymers were tested for applicability as components of product protectant coatings.

Example 2

BIOSIS

40206. MIYAJI, Y. AND K. KATO. (Kurita Cent. Lab., Yokohama, Kanagawa, Jpn.) Biological treatment of industrial waste water by using nitrate as an oxygen source. WATER RES 9(1): 95-101. Illus. 1975. [In Engl. with Engl. summ.].— It is known that nitrate can be used as a chemical O_2 source for biological decomposition of organic matter. In the dissimilatory reaction of nitrate, nitrate is reduced to N_2 gas and at the same time, O_2 as a reaction product is utilized as a final H acceptor in the electron transfer system for the oxidation of organic substances. Compared with usual O_2 supply by the aeration method, the use of nitrate as an O_2 source is easier because of the extremely high solubility of nitrate. A satisfactory biodegradation of organic matter may be carried out through static contact between microorganisms and waste water containing nitrate. Industrial waste water, especially from petrochemical plants, sometimes contains a large amount of nitrate as well as highly concentrated organic matter. The application of a biological treatment method was studied for the treatment of such waste water by utilizing nitrate as an O_2 source and several benchscale tests were conducted to clarify the basic purification behavior in this treatment method. This biological treatment method may prove useful for N removal and consequently help solve the eutrophication problem. This method may also reduce organic matter, causing a decrease in organic loading on the unit that follows. A pilot plant study on the site of a petrochemical plant was made in order to examine treatment ability and practicability. COD [chemical O_2 demand] removed had a linear relation to nitrate nitrogen removed in the reaction tank. If it was supposed that all the nitrate removed had been utilized as an O_2 source, it was found that there was a certain relation between COD loading and O_2 consumed per unit COD removed. Pellets of sludge with a diameter of 1-2 mm were formed in the upflow reaction tank of the sludge blanket type.

Abstracts, Who Needs Them? 265

CAS

144928z. **Antimicrobial polymers.** Ackart, W. B.; Camp. R. L.; Wheelwright, W. L.; Byck, J. S. (Res. Dev. Dep., Union Carbide Corp., Bound Brook, N. J.). *J. Biomed Mater. Res.* 1975, 9(1), 55-68 (Eng). A no. of carboxyl-contg. ethylene copolymers were prepd. which exhibit long term antibacterial and antifungal properties. These materials, contg. antimicrobial agents bound to the copolymer backbone as carboxylate salts, have been tested for their applicability to hospital products as a means of providing "self-sanitizing" articles. Tests have shown that these materials, although not bactericidal, do inhibit microbial growth. Investigations of the compatibility of these polymers with commodity polymers were made and water emulsions of the polymers have been tested for applicability as components of product protectant coatings.

Ei

059417 ANTIMICROBIAL POLYMERS. A number of carboxyl-containing ethylene copolymers have been prepared which exhibit long term antibacterial and antifungal properties. These materials, containing antimicrobial agents bound to the copolymer backbone as carboxylate salts, have been tested for their applicability to hospital products as a means of providing "self-sanitizing" articles. Tests have shown that these materials, although not bactericidal, do inhibit microbial growth. Investigations of the compatibility of these polymers with commodity polymers have been made and water emulsions of the polymers have been tested for applicability as components of product protectant coatings. 3 refs.

Ackart, W. B. Union Carbide Corp., Bound Brook, NJ; Camp, R. L.; Wheelwright, W. L.; Byck, J. S. *J. Biomed. Mater Res* v 9 n 1 Jan 1975, p. 55-68.

CAS

174891z. **Biological treatment of industrial waste water using nitrate as an oxygen source.** Miyaji, Y.; Kato, K. (Kurita Cent. Lab., Yokohama, Japan). *Water Res.* 1975, 9(1), 95-101 (Eng). Compared with the usual O_2 supply by aeration, NO_3^- as an O_2 source was easier because of its high soly. A satisfactory biodegradation of organic matter occurs by static contact between microorganisms and waste water contg. NO_3^-. The application of a biol. treatment method for industrial wastes, especially from petrochem. plants with, sometimes, a highly concd. org. matter, was tested by use of NO_3 in several bench-scale tests. To det. whether this biol. treatment would remove N and contribute toward soln. of the eutrophication problem, in addn., by decreasing the organic loading on the unit that followed, a pilot plant study was made on the site of a petrochem. plant. The COD removed had a linear relation to nitrate-N removed in the reaction tank. Assuming that all the NO_3^- removed had been utilized as an O_2 source, there was a certain relation between COD loading and O_2 consumed/unit COD removed. Pellets of sludge with a diam. of 1-2 mm were formed in the upflow reaction tank of the sludge blanket type.

A. W. Hofer

Ei

069293 BIOLOGICAL TREATMENT OF INDUSTRIAL WASTES WATER BY USING NITRATE AS AN OXYGEN SOURCE. The application of a biological treatment method was studied for the treatment of waste water by utilizing nitrate as an oxygen source, and several bench-scale tests were conducted to clarify the basic purification behavior in this treatment method. A pilot plant study was made on the site of a petrochemical plant to examine the treatment ability and the practical application of this method. 10 refs.

Miyaji, Y. Kurita Cent. Lab., Yokohama, Jpn; Kato, K. *Water Res* v 9 n 1 Jan. 1975, p. 95-101.

service and used by several services? We don't really know that a biologist, for example, will accept an abstract prepared and indexed by a chemist, or that the chemist will accept the biologist's abstract. Even if each service did its own indexing from its own perspective, it is not known if the same abstract could be used in several services.

The two examples on pages 264 and 265 illustrate the present situation. Example 1 is a paper on antimicrobial polymers covered by BioSciences Information Service (BIOSIS), CAS, and *Engineering Index (Ei)*. The abstracts are so similar that they are almost identical. I suspect that each was derived from the same author abstract.

Example 2 is an abstract on water pollution. Either there was no author abstract or else it was unsuitable, because each service prepared its own abstract. The abstracts have similar content but very different depths of information. The question must be answered from a user point of view as to whether one of these abstracts could suffice for all services. If the answer is "yes," then the services should consider seriously how overlap could be reduced and potential savings realized, if such savings exist. Logically, the elimination of overlap should result in significant savings in production costs and in user search time. But in today's environment of different production processes, different time frames, and different policies and standards, it is not known if the potential savings are real or if the users would actually be served better. Serious consideration and practical studies are needed.

Abstracts, who needs them? You do, if you are ever a retrospective searcher. Your users do, if you are a producer of a service that supplies retrospective-search capabilities. Your customers do, if you are a vendor of search services that are going to deliver an ever-increasing volume of hits from an expanding information file. If I have left anyone out, I am certain I can think of reasons why you also need abstracts or a suitable substitute.

I have described three areas of future work, but only three of many. These are improved abstracts from the standpoint of both content and format, potential use of expanded index entries as pseudoabstracts, and practical cooperation between discipline-oriented services to reduce costs and improve service to users.

REFERENCES

Baker, D. B., J. W. Horiszny, and W. V. Metanomski. "History of Abstracting at Chemical Abstracts Service." *Journal of Chemical Information and Computer Science*, 20 (4):193–201, November 1980.

Baser, K. H. et al. "On-Line Indexing Experiment at Chemical Abstracts Service: Algorithmic Generation of Articulated Index Entries from Natural Language Phrases." *Journal of Chemical Information and Computer Science*, 18(1):18–25, February 1978.

Borko, H., and C. L. Bernier. *Abstracting Concepts and Methods*. New York, Academic Press, 1975.

Collison, R. *Abstracts and Abstracting Services*. Santa Barbara, Calif., ABC-Clio Press, 1971.

Rowley, J. E., and C. M. D. Turner. *The Dissemination of Information*. Boulder, Colo., Westview Press, 1978.

Skolnik, H. "Historical Development of Abstracting." *Journal of Chemical Information and Computer Science*, 19(4):215–218, November 1979.

Weil, B. H. "Information Transfer in a Time of Transition: The Need for Community, Organizational, and Individual Empathy and Ethics." 1978 Miles Conrad Memorial Lecture. *NFAIS Newsletter*, 20(2):18–28, April 1978.

_____. "Standards for Writing Abstracts." *Journal of the American Society for Information Science*, 21(5):351–357, September/October 1970.

Weil, B. H., I. Zarember, and H. Owen. "Technical-Abstracting Fundamentals. I. Introduction." *Journal of Chemical Documentation*. 3:86–89, 1963a.

_____."Technical-Abstracting Fundamentals. II. Writing Principles and Practices." *Journal of Chemical Documentation*, 3:125–132, 1963b.

MARCH 3, 1982

Abstracting and Indexing Services: The Business and the Science

SAUL HERNER, *Herner and Company, Arlington, Virginia*

I am privileged to help honor today the memory of my friend and colleague, Miles Conrad. I thank you for the opportunity.

When I first entered this field in 1947 as a chemical reference assistant at the New York Public Library, abstracting and indexing services were not called nor thought of as "services." They were called "publications," "periodicals," or "journals," and they addressed themselves almost exclusively to relatively narrow, easily defined, and primarily scholarly constituencies. They have changed drastically in these 35 years.

Until the late 1940s, most abstracting and indexing publications were unidisciplinary and compact enough to be contained within one or a few volumes a year. Even the literature of applied sciences such as engineering was containable and manageable. A whole year's abstracts, indexes, or both could be consulted at an individual's desk, and an entire run of the major abstracting and indexing publications in his field could be stored in his office. This was very frequently the case.

In 1950, the bulk of the existing abstracting and indexing publications were produced by nonprofit organizations—primarily scholarly and professional societies. In 1980, a slight, but growing, majority of American abstracting and indexing publications—now metamorphosed into services—were produced by profit-making organizations (Herner [1980]).

In 1950, the price of an annual subscription to *Chemical Abstracts* (*CA*) for members of the American Chemical Society (ACS) was $10. The total individual and institutional circulation was 21,627. In 1966, when the special subscription price for ACS members was discontinued, the base subscription price of *CA* had risen to $1,200; its circulation had fallen to 6,672, and it's subscribers were almost exclusively institutional rather than individual (Donnell [1982]). The base subscription price of *CA* in 1982 was $6,200. In the early days, *CA* was used as a current-awareness tool. It has long since changed to a publication of record, used primarily for retrospective searching.

PROLIFERATION AND SUBDIVISION OF INFORMATION TOOLS

In 1952, as part of a study of the information-gathering habits of scientists, I interviewed the chairman of the Biochemistry Department at the Johns Hopkins University. One of the questions I asked him was what abstracting and indexing publications, if any, he had consulted in the recent past. His answer was "none." Since the entire wall behind him was lined with unbound copies of *Chemical Abstracts*, I asked him why. His answer was threefold. First, *CA* was becoming too bulky and cumbersome to scan conveniently; second, even though *CA* was cheap at the time, he did not want to have to receive and store an increasing number of volumes that dealt with aspects of chemistry that were of no immediate interest to him; third, he had better ways of finding out about useful sources of information in his field, namely, word-of-mouth communication from colleagues and cited references. He did, however, continue to use *CA* on rare occasions for searches on subjects that were not central to his interests and less familiar to him (Herner [1954]).

In 1962—partially in response to complaints from people like my 1952 interviewee and partially to get the consumer price down and broaden access and markets—*CA* spun off a separate biochemistry section; in 1963, it spun off an organic chemistry section. It presently offers 123 separate sections, each bringing together everything on a given topic, regardless of where in *CA* it appears (Donnell [1982]). This proliferation is by no means unique to *Chemical Abstracts*. Between 1970 and 1980, the number of abstracting and indexing services increased prodigiously. In 1970, it was about 1,500; in 1980, it was 2,500 (Bearman [1978]; International Federation for Documentation [1969]). Some of this growth is the result of the subdivision of existing abstracting and indexing services; much of it comes from the birth of new services—mainly for-profit services.

ADVENT OF ONLINE SERVICES

Perhaps more significant than the increase in the number of abstracting and indexing services is their increasing accessibility via remote online terminals. Although exact dollar amounts are hard to come by, it is clear that online services are a growth industry. As of 1979, there were 528 machine-readable databases, the bulk of which were accessible online (Williams [1979]). About 60 percent of these online databases were produced by private-sector organizations, indicating that, in addition to being a national resource, the abstracted and indexed contents of publications are a formidable source of national revenue (Bearman [1978]). How formidable is perhaps indicated by an article in a recent *IDP Report* (1982), which indicated that the revenues of electronic publishers were up 30 percent between 1981 and 1982. Obviously, this is one field that is not experiencing a recession.

ECONOMIC RAMIFICATIONS OF ONLINE SERVICES

In addition to producing revenues for database producers and online vendors, this new form of access makes available, even to the smallest library and information center, vast collections, in most fields of research, development, and scholarship, that have heretofore been beyond their physical and financial means.

While this is subject to debate, I suspect that if one were to do a careful cost-benefit analysis, he would find that, on the average, online searching is cheaper than manual searching. In our own shop, for instance, we have found that the total cost of an average online search comes to approximately $35. This includes our in-house set-up and search-programming costs, connect charges, royalties, and the like. In our case at least, a manual search requiring two hours of a mid-level professional's time — not counting the time required to go to other libraries when necessary — would cost around $50.

Unfortunately (and probably inevitably), there is a black or gray side to the otherwise-rosy online picture. There is increasing talk and concern about possible adverse effects of online access on the sale of print versions of abstracting and indexing services. Originally, the common assumption was that searchable tapes were merely by-products of computer production of printed abstracting and indexing services and that revenues realized from sales or online searches of these tapes would be a welcome bonus. But no one assumed that online access would be as heavily appreciated and used as it has been. The tail is beginning to wag the dog.

Smith and Knapp (1981), writing in the *Journal of Academic Librar-*

ianship, present the case fairly well, albeit from a slightly biased viewpoint. They describe the problem as follows: "What eight years ago [in 1973] seemed a highly specialized service for the elite of the research community is now recognized as an important new dimension to the public service programs of most larger academic libraries." The same can be said of special libraries, government libraries, and most other types of libraries.

Smith and Knapp suggest that "library administrators must seek appropriate ways to increase financial resources available for the support of database services; [and] producers and vendors must make strong efforts to hold down costs." This presents an interesting dilemma, which will have to be resolved. Theoretically, the larger the number of people who use an abstracting and indexing service, the lower the cost per use and the easier it should be to amortize the cost of the print and tape versions of a given abstracting and indexing service. But if the users, or any significant portion of them, expect, for whatever reason, to pay nothing or significantly discounted charges for this service, this formulation won't work. There is, perhaps, possible compensation in the findings of a recent British study of the use of the MEDLARS database and *Index Medicus* that online searching may have the effect of increasing use and purchase of the printed version of the database being searched (Childs and Carmel [1981]). But this will require further analysis. Meanwhile, as a protective measure, many producers of print and computer-accessible databases are charging heavier tariffs to online searchers who do not subscribe to the printed versions.

I suggest that the ultimate solution probably lies in the universal application and enforcement of service charges, such as those long in use for subscriptions to H. W. Wilson publications, in which the price to a given organization or institution is based on the size of its overall collection, its budget, and how many users it serves. As Karl Marx (1933) said, "From each according to his abilities, to each according to his needs." I would add—putting a slightly capitalistic face on it—"and to his ability and willingness to pay." Someone *does* have to pay the freight.

ABSTRACTING AND INDEXING IMPLICATIONS

Leaving the economic or capitalistic realm, there are many other ramifications and implications of online services that are far more subtle and, in many respects, more important and challenging.

Prior to the entrance of computers on the abstracting and indexing scene, we lived quite contentedly with two types of indexes: unit record, as exemplified by the library catalog card, and inverted, such as the indexes in the backs of books. We went through stages or eras in which we experimented with, among other things, "free" indexing based on terms taken from the texts being indexed; "semantic factoring," which attempted to develop a basic indexing and retrieval language for each field or discipline; "roles" and "links," which indicated the form or purpose of usage and the syntactic context of index terms; and KWIC (Keyword-in-Context), which helped establish usage and context of terms in or taken from titles.

For many years after the beginning of the general application of computers to abstracting and indexing services, we continued to search by the two basic methods: unit records, which was rather slow and cumbersome in that one had to scan a whole file for a given subject or combination of subjects, and the more efficient inverted index, or back-of-the-book index, which permitted direct access to the subject being searched.

With the advent of text searching—a product of faster and cheaper computers with greater storage capacity—we no longer search inverted indexes but inverted *concordances* to texts. Theoretically at least, "free" indexing has been replaced by "free" searching. This provides much greater flexibility and comprehensiveness in searches, but it also poses various inflexibilities and problems. Consider, for instance, the following. A firm rule or convention among library catalogers is that you do not alter or edit the titles of publications, although it is all right to alter abstracts. In systems that don't use abstracts, this can pose a significant problem for text searching. For instance, if a searcher was interested in *fetuses*, he could lose all papers on the subject in British journals, since they spell the word *foetuses*. This could be remedied via a translation table, but it must be remedied and borne in mind if text searching is to work.

As far back as the Royal Society Scientific Information Conference in 1948, it was proposed that published papers include author abstracts as a means of summarizing contents and as inputs to abstracting and indexing publications or services (1948). And they have indeed been used as inputs to abstracting and indexing publications or services. Russell Rowlett (1981) noted this use of author abstracts in his 1981 Miles Conrad Lecture. In a study my wife and I did in 1957, we analyzed the treatment of a sample of several hundred papers in the major abstracting and indexing journals of the time. We found, almost without exception—even when the abstracts were signed—that they were faithful replications of the author abstracts (Herner and Herner [1959]). The only items that did receive original abstracting were letters to the editor, which did not contain author abstracts. Editors of abstracts, whether author-generated or original, had better keep the "foetus" problem well in mind and standardize and control spelling, usage, and terminology as never before if their products are to be retrieved via text searching. And incidentally, much the same case can be made for cited references, given the growing use of citation indexes. If they are inaccurate or incomplete, they could be lost in searches.

META VERSUS REAL LANGUAGE

Theoretically, a person invoking a system via text searching—especially an expert in the field being searched—should be able to think of a word describing what he is interested in and run a search on it. Assuming that the system is made up of abstracts written in the author's language, this could work fairly well (if provisions were made for differences in spelling and usage among nations). The searcher would, in essence, be interacting with colleagues who speak the same technical language.

That's not exactly how things work, however. First of all, for the time being, and until Atari games have had their full impact and terminals become more available, the average searcher will probably delegate this task to an information specialist. This specialist will undoubtedly translate the searcher's words into the closest equivalents contained in a thesaurus. As a rule, thesauri are based on past indexing terms and decisions, not the language of the original texts, and not necessarily on decisions relating the instant material being indexed. Most thesauri are in what Goffman and his co-workers (1964) termed *meta* language, as opposed to *real* language. There is a varying degree of coincidence between meta and real language, which is one reason for the high levels of intra- and inter-indexer inconsistency.

This use of thesauri or search menus derived from meta terminology can pose some problems in text searching. It is ironic that Hans Peter Luhn (1959) had something quite different than what we now know as the thesaurus when he first introduced its use into this field. What he was proposing was thesauri based on the actual words in the texts to be searched. Although he was working in the late 1950s, Luhn was tacitly predicting text searching and a means of implementing it.

Luhn had another idea, which essentially closes the text-searching circle. This idea was to use the word-frequency and co-occurrence counts on which his thesauri were based to create abstracts of texts (Luhn [1958]). He demonstrated how this could be done in a series of reports and papers. I know it works because I tried it out on, of all things, transcripts of psychiatric interviews (Herner et al. [1966]). Using Luhn's method, we were able to produce very respectable and cogent abstracts of our specimen interviews. Rest assured that routine papers and publications are much easier to deal with. If we were to adopt Luhn's auto-abstracting and thesaurus-development techniques, many of the problems inherent in text searching would be solved. The searcher and the original author would be talking the same language and communicating directly, rather than through surrogates speaking in meta tongues.

THE MICRO-STUDY OF USER IMPACTS

There is one final problem (or opportunity, depending on how we look at it) that has to be addressed. Quite prominent, but rarely mentioned in discussions of Shannon and Weaver's *Mathematical Theory of Communication*, is an introductory chapter by Weaver (1964) in which he lays the groundwork and explains the significance of the theory, which is largely the work of Shannon. Weaver postulates three levels of communication problems: the *accuracy* of transmission of the symbols of communication; the *precision* with which these symbols convey the desired meaning; and the *effectiveness* with which this meaning, once received, and hopefully perceived, affects the receiver.

We have concerned ourselves very much with the first two problems, accuracy of transmission and precision of symbols, but we still have done very little about the third problem, impact on users. This is not to say that no contact is being made with the user, or that his information-use patterns are not being studied. In addition to continuing user studies, which are becoming more and more repetitive and tend to emphasize only the most general aspects of the use of information tools, techniques, and resources, practically all producers and vendors of information services conduct market-research programs to determine how best to sell their wares. But we still don't understand, for instance, when abstracting and indexing services are used and when they are not. We are still not certain of the impacts of these services under varying circumstances of need. We still don't know what really works for the user, and how and why, so we continue to do everything that the technology permits, in the vain hope that something will work.

If we could stop thinking cosmically in our analyses of the reasons, methods, and impacts of the use of the information products and services we generate, and start studying on a case-by-case, incident-by-incident basis, we might eventually determine the true significance and meaning of what we are doing, and we might be able to institute changes that would make us more truly responsive to our audiences.

Just as the "technology is there" for transmitting messages with accuracy and precision, it is also there for determining whether and in what ways these messages change or benefit their recipients. We are overloaded with statistics and data about our users. It's time we found out what makes them tick, and where our tools and services fit into their picture.

There are well-established critical-incident methods for finding out what goes on, on a minute-by-minute, day-by-day basis, in the use of information tools and techniques. There are even well-founded decision-theoretic methods for determining the dollar value of the use of information sources in different circumstances and settings (Decision Science Consortium [1979]). The next step is for us to understand and apply these potentially powerful techniques. If we do, we might make our products and services more useful, and saleable, than ever.

REFERENCES

Bearman, T. C. "Secondary Information Systems and Services." *Annual Review of Information Science and Technology*, 13:179–208, 1978.

Childs, S., and M. Carmel. "Effect of Online Services on Purchases of a Printed Index." *Aslib Proceedings*, 33(9):351–356, September 1981.

Decision Science Consortium. *Research on Information and Decision Making*. Reston, Va., 1979.

Donnell, E. P. Personal Communication. January–February 1982.

Goffman, W., J. Verhoeff, and J. Belzer. "Use of Meta-Language in Information Retrieval Systems." *American Documentation*, 15(1):14–22, January 1964.

Herner, S. *A Brief Guide to Sources of Scientific and Technical Information*. 2nd Edition. Arlington, Va., Information Resources Press, 1980.

———. *A Brief Guide to Sources of Scientific and Technical Information*. Washington, D.C., Information Resources Press, 1969.

———. "The Information-Gathering Habits of Workers in Pure and Applied Science." *Industrial and Engineering Chemistry*, 46(1):228–236, January 1954.

Herner, S., and M. Herner. "Subject Slanting in Scientific Abstracting Publications." *Proceedings of the International Conference on Scientific Information*. Washington, D.C., National Academy of Sciences – National Research Council, 1959, pp. 407–427.

Herner, S., H. A. Segal, and E. Leyman. "Application of Automatic Literature Analysis Techniques to Psychiatric Interviews." Washington, D.C., Herner and Company, December 1966. AD 657 789.

International Federation for Documentation. *Abstracting Services*. 2nd Edition. New York, International Publications Service, 1969.

Luhn, H. P. "Auto-Encoding of Documents for Information Retrieval Systems." In: *Modern Trends in Documentation*. Edited by M. Boas. New York, Pergamon, 1959, pp. 45–48.

———. "The Automatic Creation of Literature Abstracts." *IBM Journal of Research and Development*, 2(2):159–165, April 1958.

Marx, K. *Critique of the Gotha Programme.* New York, International Publishers, 1933.

"Revenues Up 30% for Top Electronic Data Publishers." *IDP Report,* 2(24):1,6, February 1982.

Rowlett, R. J. "Abstracts, Who Needs Them?" *NFAIS Newsletter,* 23(2): 26–36, April 1981.

Royal Society Scientific Information Conference. *Report and Papers Submitted.* London, The Society, 1948, pp. 200–201.

Smith, J. B., and S. D. Knapp. "Data Base Royalty Fees and the Growth of Online Search Services in Academic Libraries." *Journal of Academic Librarianship,* 7(3):206–212, July 1981.

Weaver, W. "Introductory Note on the General Setting of the Analytical Communication Studies." In: *The Mathematical Theory of Communication.* By C. E. Shannon and W. Weaver. Urbana, The University of Illinois Press, 1964.

Williams, M. E. *Computer-Readable Data Bases: A Directory and Data Source Book.* Washington, D.C., American Society for Information Science, 1979.

MARCH 2, 1983

STI, A Psychohistorical Evaluation 1983: "CHIMO"

JOHN E. CREPS, JR., *Engineering Information, Inc. (Retired)*
New York, New York

It is with some fear and trepidation that I undertake the task of delivering this annual Miles Conrad Memorial Lecture, for it is a great honor. In reviewing past subjects covered by this series, I noticed that much of the vocabulary used to express the concepts of the lectures included such words as *progress, change, perspective, hope, development, transition, dilemma,* and *survival*. These were key words used to describe the nature of the industry or events affecting the industry during the past decades. Certainly, it is a profession full of excitement, challenge, and growth.

Although I believe the profession continues to maintain these attributes, I feel I must avoid such active words, since they seem also to denote a day-to-day participation in the ongoing activities and workings of the profession; and we all know, I have not had such hands-on participation for more than a year and a half.

Therefore, when I accepted the responsibility of presenting this lecture, I realized I had to adopt a much more low-key approach, one that can be viewed from a "laid-back" point of view. Thus, I chose to evaluate. I hope you agree with me that "evaluating" at least seems to connote a relaxed review and contemplation of events — a quiet time to observe the meaning and perhaps the outcome of these occurrences. Of course, I am aware that this procedure has a very active role in day-to-day functions and activities, in systems, in departments, and the like. I want to make it quite clear, however, that I will not assume to deal with such active aspects of our profession in this paper. I intend to call attention to the longer range aspects of information activities. I will step back and try to see the whole, with the press of today's decision-making process completely out of mind. I want to be free to undertake the contemplation of the work of Paul B. Kantor (1982), who, in the *Annual Review of Information Science and Technology*, presents a fine discussion of the place of libraries, databases, management files for storage and retrieval, and the use of information mechanics as the method of analysis. After his thorough coverage, he ends his review by saying, "As we move toward a paperless society I hope that the value of traditional libraries (i.e., cabinets, and rooms filled with books and paper), will be measured, documented, affirmed, and accepted. . . . The printed word and the library repository have played a unique role in the evolution of civilization as we know it." I feel very strongly that our profession cannot continue to evoke such cries from the producers/users of information without receiving some response.

To accomplish this goal, I have chosen a relatively new and untried method of evaluation. In fact, I am sure that many of you, having read the title of this lecture, wonder if this method has its grounds in science fiction. You may well feel that it is somewhat questionable to use this method in a serious lecture. But if you will bear with me, I believe the psychohistorical method will prove adequate and perhaps even illuminating.

First, let me be very clear about the scope of this lecture. As you know, I must deal with matters that concern the entire profession—something that is everyone's business—without falling into that old saw, "that which is everyone's business is no one's business." To define the method I will be using, I quote the definition of *psychohistory* from *The Encyclopedia Galactica*. Psychohistory is "that branch of mathematics that deals with the reactions of human conglomerates to fixed social and economic stimuli" (Asimov [1951]). To elucidate why I chose this method, I direct your attention to the words *mathematics* and *conglomerates*.

I suggest that mathematics is a pure science devoid of all human emotions and that it may be possible to describe with mathematics any or all aspects of human activity or being. We are somewhat aware of this possibility by our knowledge, however limited, of $E = MC^2$. The only limiting factors in this matter are our personal understanding and ability to follow all the equations such as those that stand behind $E = MC^2$. Since only the laws of probability limit the accuracy of mathematics as used in psychohistorical methodology, we may assume a 92-percent probability. Although this may seem very high, I must hasten to add that the saving factor is understanding the use of the "conglomerates."

The definition of psychohistory in *The Encyclopedia Galactica* goes on to point out that "Implicit in these definitions is the assumption that the human conglomerate being dealt with is sufficiently large for valid statistical treatment." I hope that you will agree with me that the totality of the information industry is large enough to be considered a conglomerate. Television commercials trying to sell us goods from the "knowledge industry" certainly depict it as a very large conglomerate, in the best sense of the word.

With this in mind, let us think about the evolution of the knowledge industry in such a way that we can postulate mathematical equations to express something complex simply and thus view possible conglomerate activities with a high degree of probability. In other words, let us review the conglomerate as it has been to see why it has become what it is. If we do this, we may even be able to predict possible breakthroughs without limiting these predictions because of individual matters or forces.

I present for your consideration the equation $N = P/T$. In this equation, N denotes needs. Needs may be expressed in the equation $N = n_1 + n_2 + n_3$. Here, n_1 stands for the needs of the industry involved in the preparation of information for use. No need may be ignored. Since n_1 signifies all producer needs, however, it is not necessary to detail the usual expressed needs such as literature sources, manpower, management expertise, systems development, and the like. It is understood that these needs are real and must be met as well as any other set of needs producers feel. We already have an entire blackboard of equations devised to express those needs that are (or ought to be) understood. Thus, n_1 actually represents that understanding and its continual growth. N also includes n_2. Again, any set of needs as defined by any subset of equations is assumed in $n_1 n_2 n_3$. Thus, we apply the principle of our chosen method, to develop a simple equation to express the complex.

In like manner, P and T are conglomerate concepts. P denotes packaging — any and all packaging used to deliver the information. Any package must be considered and tested in the equation. T denotes time — the time necessary to create the information, to package the information, to use the information, and the time covered by the information.

Now that the equation $N = P/T$ is clear, let us leave pure mathematics and discuss the implications and use of the equation in nonmathematical concepts. Ever since I can remember, there has been general agreement among the different elements that make up our information conglomerate that meeting needs is a key element in fulfilling information industry goals. Let us observe how one set of needs were met in a given situation and how it might have been possible to predict the necessary action in that situation if the equation $N = P/T$ had been known and applied.

Last May, I was visiting the Traquair House in the Borders region of Scotland. This is said to be the oldest continuously inhabited house in Scotland. It has one of the finest libraries I have ever seen in a private home. In fact, I was so taken with the library that I spent some time talking with the guides about its development. They told me that the owner/builder had given considerable thought to its construction and decoration. Research into the nature of the books of the day led the builder to have the shelves built to meet the specifications of the printing industry. Thus, the top shelves were five inches tall and the height of each lower shelf grew slightly larger until, at floor level, the shelves were enormous. This permitted the owner/builder to store his books according to their height. As you might suspect, this scheme conserved a great deal of space and permitted the storage of many more books. It was space efficient and was a response to the *package* of the *time*. Unfortunately, however, the size of the books did not relate to the contents of the books, nor to the authors of the books, nor even to the titles of the books. Shelving was determined only by size. Retrieval was a difficult task and required a great deal of time. The *needs* of the *package* had been met, but the user was assumed to have unlimited *time*.

A solution to lessen the time required to find a book was sought. It was noted that the owner/builder of the Traquair House had adorned his library with wall paintings of historic scholars. Over each five-foot section of shelves had been painted a portrait of one scholar. Therefore, each portrait denoted a section of shelving, since the vertical lines of the shelving were the borders of the paintings. A journal of titles and another journal of authors relating the portraits as guides to locations within sections of the library were developed. Thus, there was the Plato section, shelf 1, book "x." When a book was wanted by author or title, the journal was consulted. Rather ingenious, don't you think?

The relationship of the elements of our equation are well illustrated in this anecdote from the past century. The design of this information package was the result of a former need. That need was considered to be a buy/sell motivational force important to the economic life of the information producer. Furthermore, the package was a product of the technological development of the time. It was the dominant element in the information community of the day, so much so that the construction of the depository was designed to fit the package. This balance of the elements of our equation might best be expressed as $P = N/T$. T, time, to meet N, needs, was unlimited.

We might better understand this situation from the excellent lecture given by Paul G. Zurkowski some years ago relating the development of the information dissemination process.

You may recall in Zurkowski's account that the early holders of information were officials of the church. This, of course, placed time in a rather eternal mode and information in a fixed-set amount. Since all information of value was God-given in the canonical books, time was used to adorn the information in beautiful packages. This was the conglomerate state of the information industry at the time, so $P = N/T$. In fact, time was never really considered by the monks, priests, or officials, nor by their later information counterparts, the owners of libraries. Our psychohistorical evaluation, if used by the information producers/users of that century, could have suggested a breakthrough for the system; namely, the development of a system to deal with time as a factor in user need fulfillment.

The interrelationship of the conglomerate elements of N-P-T may be observed in even greater exaggeration—almost to the point of absurdity—if we consider Charles Darwin. Darwin is recognized as the creator, the packager, and the disseminator of a very early scientific information system. The expressed need that motivated the eventual creation of the system was a response of the British Navy to the orders of the monarch to acquire economic and military information about much of the world. The medium for acquiring such information was a royal voyage around the world. The stated purpose was the mapping of land masses in parts of the world for navigation. The secondary purpose was to collect specimens from land and sea. Thus, Darwin was appointed to join the voyage. Darwin's original packages for the information were crates in which specimens were stored. These original packages were sent to friends in England and later converted into descriptive statements about the specimens. These writings subsequently were made into notes and lectures, letters to colleagues, and later yet into books. The time element was five years for the initial collection, five years more for the preparation of the first set of descriptions, another five years for lecturing and letter writing, and a lifetime for book writing. You might describe the equation $N = P/T$ of this system as need oriented, in which the packages were influx and time limited only by life itself.

I have presented these well-known examples of information systems from the real world to support my contention: $N = P/T$ expresses the conglomerates that make up any ideal system and therefore can be used as an evaluation tool. The equation forces us to evaluate in such a way that we may characterize a system as a need-oriented system requiring a breakthrough in the area of packaging or time, or a package-oriented system needing a rethinking of the needs or the time, or a time-oriented system requiring the understanding of needs or packaging. When the system is in balance, it is seen that the elements of the equation relate to each other without creating a static that interferes with the use of the system. On the other hand, when balance is not present, or at least not without great difficulty, the system is in contest with itself, and the efforts of the producer/user to ignore the imbalance tend to endanger the life of the system.

There is one question yet to be considered: Can this simple equation be applied to a modern information system? It is easy to talk about packages when books, or at least printed matter, are the forms to be packaged. It is easy to talk about time when you have from here to eternity. It is easy to talk about needs when history is available to confirm what was. In other words, it is simple to be a Monday morning quarterback. But now that the complex is developed beyond our wildest dreams, and needs may not even be felt in time to be met, now that time is measured in fractions that require strange names, and a device known as a CYBER 205 can perform 400 million calculations per second (1 million times faster than the personal computers that are moving into our homes), can the complex be so simply expressed? I suggest that it is not only possible but quite practical.

Today, in every home, is an information system that uses complex packaging, deals in complex time, and meets a very complex need, that is, the need to know what the weather will be each day. The system to provide weather information for our needs has developed alongside man himself. From the beginning of time, weather has affected man and therefore interested him. The evolution of the system is the perfect example of $N = P/T$. The need has never changed; it only became more complex as more information was learned. The packages have gone from word of mouth to almanacs, to weekly newspapers, to daily newspapers, to the present-day instant reports. Time has diminished from "wait till the sun comes out," to the last instant. Through it all, $N = P/T$ expresses the process completely.

Consider the present systems. Data from around the world are required to provide the input that is used in the equations that predict the coming weather in all regions and in local communities. The data are constantly changing and require a system capable of updating itself by the second. The need to know the weather for any single moment, to the projected conditions six months from now, is as varied as the human condition. It may be as critical as flight weather information or traffic weather information, or as seemingly unimportant as knowing what to wear out in the evening or whether to plan a picnic for next week. The delivery of the information encompasses all ranges of speed, yet the most important one is instantaneous. So we see that the balanced system has instant input, instant calculation, and instant output.

Modern technology and some planning sense has given us the capability of providing the weather information system with just that balance. Time has been controlled by the gathering methods and computer calculations. The central operational office in Atlanta, Georgia makes it possible to receive and compute the data in a usable way. The package is a 24-hour dissemination system that transmits the data to any user anywhere in the United States who has cable television. This cable weather station allows one to see and hear what the weather has been for a day, what the developing patterns look like, and what may be expected by afternoon, evening, and the following day. The three elements $N = P/T$ all work in harmony to further prove our equation.

Let me now explain how these seemingly obvious observations relate to the stated purpose of this paper. What breakthrough is likely and why is it likely? It has always been my contention that the balance of an information system as expressed by $N = P/T$ not only enables us to identify system conditions but enables us to predict the elements of the equation that are due for change. I propose to undertake such a prediction with regard to our own beloved online systems. The system that takes up most of our planning time is, in reality, quite young and has grown very rapidly. If we evaluate this system by using our method of psychohistorical analysis, we can say that the system was the application of available technology to meet the growing need to shorten the time required to search a file. These time constraints seemed to be caused by the packages available to use for distribution of the file. Thus, the online system has adopted some of the characteristics of television while ignoring others. Now let us view the present situation in light of our equation and see what changes are needed to bring online systems into better balance.

An early indication of our professional concern for improvement in modern systems was the attention given to file creation. It had been an individual process since the beginning of our work systems. On the other hand, the thought of a conglomerate file construction was not new — at least as a subject of study. The International Council of Scientific Unions Abstracting Board (ICSU AB) examined the matter more than 15 years ago. The details of that activity are now available to every member service organization as part of long filing systems and may be studied at leisure. (The creation of the serials file, however, was only one step in the agreed-upon solution, the "input plan." This plan seems to have been dropped or overtaken by other possible solutions or by production needs.)

Ways to shorten time of search and time of production were issued in another manner after the input plan cooled and developments became package oriented. It was believed that a new package could overcome the time constraints that were perceived as producer/user needs. This change in direction was the first step in the development of online systems. But few, if any, tapes (the present first package in the online distribution process) were created to decrease the time factor of our book package distribution systems. Tape was an improvement to speed the production of books. Thus, the beginning of online systems was an attempt to improve our book package creation.

These attempts to improve the book-production system launched us into the use of 20th-century technology and at the same time created some very vivid side effects in our understanding of producer/user needs and packaging. The most obvious effects in the early stages were institutional, and not system related. The adoption of computer input and word processing also created some interesting effects on the institutions creating the systems. Every graduate school of library and information science had at least one student studying the effects of computers on all aspects of the information producer community. It is easy to recall the studies of cost and cost/benefit and management development and evolution. I remember my own involvement in the early effects of computer usage and the development of the present-day online systems. The least I can say is that there was no thought of such development or use and thus it was not well planned. Some dreamers and computer-types who were outside the information system to which I belonged came to me and asked for copies of our tapes for use in what they called a "batch search system." My answer was an emphatic "no." But from such simple beginnings grew an organization of information dissemination centers, an organization with a history and involvement in online that, to my knowledge, had not been predicted. What had first been seen as a new book production system became a batch search system that produced profile outputs. These outputs became individualized and were run on a monthly basis to become a new print package in the information system. Certainly the short history of this innovation in packaging indicates what imbalance in our equation existed, not to mention the growing pressure of new needs.

The batch systems quickly gave way, for the most part, to online dissemination. New distribution means became a new package mode in the system. With the new package mode came new problems and new concerns. The interdisciplinary nature of user needs was understood as a demand to acquire the most number of files by the new group of distributors. The package was assumed to be right, and central processing as a distribution means became the order of the day. With this, of course, came yet another set of needs for producers. Contracts with distributors were no longer bookseller boiler plates. They required new legal reviews and new pricing understandings. The development of new user studies by the distributors as marketing tools for the products of their systems became weapons, as well as producer tools for increased services. Files were evaluated against files, with the end user being loudly heralded as the most important system mover, only to be pushed from pillar to post. Learning as many systems as became available, attending as many workshops as employers would pay for, and joining groups to become better known became an even greater force in the systems to push for progress. Input difficulties as once studied by ICSU AB were now in the hands of the users, and the needs of production became the user group parlor game of the day.

The package—a hardware receiver connected to phone lines hooked up to computers that provide interactive search capability—is a far cry from the good old book package. This is the cry so clearly heard from Paul B. Kantor, recorded earlier in this paper. Far from requiring a cry, however, the response to this new packaging situation could well be the sign of a new breakthrough for the package itself. The package you see has taken on a negative user characteristic. The material in the package is forever in a magnetic flux. The input and the output forever require interface with one or more files. Clearly, the way to use the file must be to turn on the clock. Turn on the clock for the telephone company. Turn it on for the computer/distributor companies. Turn it on for the producer company. Turn on the clock and sit before a machine and search the file to produce your own package to read. I submit that herein lies the problem of the balance of the equation. The package ignores the reality of the many time frames of the user of technical information. It is not the weather about which they see information, nor is it the stock market. It is not an instant need, but clearly has longer time frames. The package ignores the producer need for direct user interface, and I submit that all the online training sessions in the world do not really overcome this situation. In other words, the package is wrong. The equation $N = P/T$ is out of balance.

The present technology drive in our industry seems to ignore the next breakthrough. During the past few years, while online has become the hot new package, another technology—optical videodisk—has been developed and introduced to the market. Of course, the present systems are mostly entertainment oriented. Even the research done by our industry has not yet made an impact on our planning programs. In October 1982, it was announced in *The Economist* that a disk the size of a long-playing record would hold 6,000 pages of text or still monochrome pictures. Add to this the search capabilities of most computer packages of the present systems and you just may have a new package, one that has the potential of providing the needed balance in the information equation.

Consider the advantages of this package in our equation $N = P/T$:

1. Producers return to the book-subscription system, which is already in place, which is a well-known producer/user compatible system, and which will eliminate the clumsy practice of third-party contracts.

2. The file size presents no problems since disk capacity is very great, disks can be updated regularly, and the cumulation is done at the same time as the user acquires the current disk.

3. The package can be searched by anyone who has the hardware.

4. The disk cannot be copied, so only the owner has the rights to the material and the rights can be enforced.

5. Once delivered, the package can be searched in the user's time frame without turning on the clock for the phone company, the computer com-

pany, or the producer company. Whether turning it on, turning it off, reading it, or leaving it, it is all in the user's hands.

6. The updating of the package is as simple or as complicated as the present procedures, with the final product prepared by a disk print company just like the old book printer. The package creates a good balance with everyone's time frame and meets many of the producer/user needs.

It must be clear, however, that I am not recommending disk technology. To make such a recommendation would be to ignore the method of analysis selected for this paper. My point is that the next breakthrough in our present information systems may very likely come as a package that overcomes the growing difficulties of the present packing systems.

It can be seen from the past, present, and future that information systems have always been and always will be constrained by need and time. Progress in information system development will always be the creation of a package to better meet the expressed needs of the producer/user, and to meet these needs in optimum time frames. As long as people want to read and reread stories, look at pictures, and daydream while reading, there will be books, and libraries in which to house them. Producers need only understand the content of the information that fits the expressed needs and package it in such a way as to keep the equation of the system in balance. The need to know the weather tonight in order to determine what to wear tomorrow requires a package different from the one that allows contemplation. Television or radio is just such a package. When it comes to literature searches for research and references, I cannot help but envy Janov Pelorat, when, on his journey in search of earth, he took his library, "My library, it's indexed by subject matter and origin and I've gotten it all into one wafer" (Asimov [1982]). The package that lets me have my library with me, to be read when I want and need to read, when I want and need to search, when I want and need to do my work without clock watching, will be the breakthrough that psychohistory indicates is next for our information systems.

CHIMO: An American Indian word meaning friend, used as a greeting and a farewell. Chimo.

REFERENCES

Asimov, I., *Foundation's Edge*. Garden City, N.Y., Doubleday, 1982.
Asimov, I. *Foundations*. New York, Avon Books, 1951.
Kantor, P. B. "Evaluation of and Feedback in Information Storage and Retrieval Systems." *Annual Review of Information Science and Technology*, 17:115, 1982.

Summary

Bibliography

Publications by and About NFAIS

Summary

MALCOLM RIGBY, *National Oceanographic and Atmospheric Administration, Washington, D.C.*

During its 25-year lifetime, NFAIS has attained a number of its original objectives. For one, it has provided a forum for communication among abstracting and indexing (A&I) member services and between members and the national and international A&I community. It has helped member organizations improve services and operations and has acted as national spokesman for collective member services. Furthermore, it has undertaken specific projects of value to the member service community that no individual member could manage alone.

After a decade of responding to the challenges of standardization, elimination of duplication, reduced support for science and technology, automation, networking, repackaging, and inflation, the Federation has become independent of Federal Government support and has broadened its scope to include all disciplines and to accept international, government, foreign, and commercial organizations as members. In addition, the Federation has twice changed its name to reflect its new constituency and wider focus.

NFAIS membership has grown from fewer than 20 services during 1958 to nearly 50 by 1982, and the combined output of all services has increased 10-fold, from 350,000 to 3.4 million items.

Annual meetings have become quite successful during the past 10 years, with attendance well over 100 at each session. Workshop-type seminars have also contributed steadily to the community and the Federation, and NFAIS publications have enjoyed ever-increasing popularity. International and national exchanges and participation in advisory bodies have been notable features of the Federation's contribution to the community, and the feedback from these contacts has been even more rewarding to the member services.

The challenge of automation has been met with deliberate and intelligent foresight so that services that had only toyed with the idea of using mechanical and electronic assistance around 1957–1958 have now automated part, if not all, of their operations.

The printed page, however, is not yet obsolete, as was predicted by many authorities in the field of science information; nor is the "demise of Gutenberg" in sight, at least for this century, for in our view of the Information Age, the demand for all forms of communication and information transfer will increase logarithmically for a decade or so.

The Federation's past and its forecast for the future seem to testify in favor of a less standardized, less bureaucratic community whose members can freely test and implement any promising advances in abstracting and indexing techniques. In other words, out of seemingly chaotic current systems can evolve remarkably viable and valuable future systems. This is our faith and our motivation for staying in the game.

Bibliography

American National Standards Institute. *Guidelines for Thesaurus Structure, Construction, and Use.* New York, 1980. ANSI Z39.19-1980.
_____. *Writing Abstracts.* New York, 1979. ANSI Z39.14-1979.
_____. *Basic Criteria for Indexes.* New York, 1974. ANSI Z39.4-1968 (R-1974).
Austin, D. "The Development of PRECIS: A Theoretical and Technical History." *Journal of Documentation,* 30(1):47–102, March 1974.
Barwise, T. P. *Online Searching: The Impact on User Charges of the Extended Use of Online Information Services.* Paris, International Council of Scientific Unions Abstracting Board, 1979.
Bates, M. J. "Search Techniques." In: *Annual Review of Information Science and Technology.* Vol. 16. Edited by M. E. Williams. White Plains, N.Y., Knowledge Industry Publications, 1981, pp. 139–169.
_____. "Idea Tactics." *Journal of the American Society for Information Science.* 30(5):280–289, September 1979.
_____. "Information Search Tactics." *Journal of the American Society for Information Science,* 30(4):205–215, July 1979.
Bearman, T. C. "What's New with Secondary Services." *Bulletin of the American Society for Information Science,* 5(6):18–19, August 1979.

——. "Secondary Information Systems and Services." In: *Annual Review of Information Science and Technology.* Vol. 13. Edited by M. E. Williams. White Plains, N.Y., Knowledge Industry Publications, 1978, pp. 179-208.

Borko, H., and C. L. Bernier. *Indexing Concepts and Methods.* New York, Academic Press, 1978.

Brenner, E. H. "Descriptors, Terms, Subject Heading, Term-Indexing, Subject-Indexing: Definitions." In: *Parameters of Information Science: Proceedings of the American Documentation Institute.* Edited by A. W. Elias. Washington, D.C., American Documentation Institute, 1964, pp. 387-388.

Breton, E. J. "Why Engineers Don't Use Databases." *Bulletin of the American Society for Information Science,* 7(6):20-23, August 1981.

Byer, W. L., et al. "Building a Chemical Ingredient Data Base for Industrial and Consumer Products." *Journal of Chemical Information and Computer Science,* 16(3):137-141, August 1976.

Collinson, R. L. *Indexes and Indexing.* 3rd Edition. London, Benn, 1969.

Committee on Scientific and Technical Information. *Guidelines for the Development of Information Retrieval Thesauri.* Washington, D.C., Federal Council for Science and Technology, 1967.

Cornog, M. "A History of Indexing Technology." *The Indexer.* In press.

Costello, J. C. *Coordinate Indexing.* New Brunswick, N.J., Graduate School of Library Service, Rutgers State University, 1966.

Davis, C. H., and J. E. Rush. *Guide to Information Science.* Westport, Conn., Greenwood, 1979.

Diodato, V. P. "Author Indexing." *Special Libraries,* 72(4):361-369, October 1981.

Doszkocs, T. E. "Associative Indexing, Classification and Searching." In: *Proceedings of the 44th Annual Meeting of the American Society for Information Science.* White Plains, N.Y., Knowledge Industry Publications, 1981, p. 329.

——. "Automated Information Retrieval in Science and Technology." *Science,* 208(4):25-30, April 1980.

Fairthorne, R. A. "Content Analysis, Specification and Control." In: *Annual Review of Information Science and Technology.* Edited by C. A. Cuadra. Chicago, Encyclopedia Britannica, 1969, pp. 73-109.

Fenichel, C. H., and T. Hogan. *Online Searching: A Primer.* Marlton, N.J., Learned Information, 1981.

Foskett, A. C. *The Subject Approach to Information.* 3rd Edition. Camden, Conn., Linnett Books, 1977.

Garfield, E. *Citation Indexing: Its Theory and Application in Science,*

Technology and Humanities. Somerset, N.J., Wiley, 1979.
Hamilton, G. "How to Recognize a Good Index." *The Indexer,* 10(2):49–53, October 1976.
Harrod, L. M. *Indexers on Indexing: A Selection of Articles Published in The Indexer.* New York, Bowker, 1978.
Hawkins, D. T. "Online Information Retrieval Systems." In: *Annual Review of Information Science and Technology.* Edited by M. E. Williams. New York, Wiley, 1981, pp. 171–208.
Immroth, J. P. "Indexes to Classification Schemes." In: *Encyclopedia of Library and Information Science.* Vol. II. Edited by A. Kent et. al. New York, Dekker, 1974, pp. 305–311.
Jahoda, G. *Retrieval Systems for Individual Researchers.* New York, Wiley, 1970.
Jolley, J. C. "The Terminology of Coordinate Indexing." *Aslib Proceedings,* 28(3):120–128, March 1976.
Jones, P. K. "Towards a Theory of Indexing." *Journal of Documentation,* 32(2):118–123, June 1976.
Knight, G. N. *Indexing, The Art of.* Winchester, Mass., Allen and Unwin, 1979.
Lancaster, F. W. *The Measurement and Evaluation of Library Services.* Washington, D.C., Information Resources Press, 1977.
———. *Vocabulary Control for Information Retrieval.* Washington, D.C., Information Resources Press, 1972.
———. *Information Retrieval Systems; Characteristics, Testing and Evaluation.* New York, Wiley, 1968.
MacCafferty, M. *Thesauri and Thesauri Construction.* London, Aslib, 1977. (Aslib Bibliography 7.)
Markey, K., P. Atherton, and C. Newton. "An Analysis of Controlled Vocabulary and Free Text Search Statements in Online Searches." *Online Review,* 4(3):225–236, September 1980.
Martyn, J. "An Examination of Citation Indexes." *Aslib Proceedings,* 17(6):184–196, June 1965.
Matthews, F. W., and L. Thomson. "Weighted Term Search: A Computer Program for an Inverted Coordinate Index on Magnetic Tape." *Journal of Chemical Documentation,* 7:49–56, February 1967.
Mills, J. *A Modern Outline for Library Classification.* London, Chapman and Hall, 1960, Chapters 1–3.
Montgomery, C., and D. R. Swanson. "Machine-like Indexing by People." *American Documentation,* 13(4):359–366, October 1962.
Mulvihill, J. G., and E. H. Brenner. "Faceted Organization of a Thesaurus Vocabulary." In: *Progress in Information Science and*

Technology: Proceedings of the American Documentation Institute. Edited by D. V. Black. Woodland Hills, Calif., Adrianne, 1966.

National Federation of Abstracting and Indexing Services. *UNISIST/NFAIS Indexing in Perspective Education Kit.* Edited by E. H. Brenner. Philadelphia, 1979.

Neufeld, M. L. "The National Federation of Abstracting and Indexing Services: The Focus for Secondary Services in the U.S.A." *Reference Services Review.* In press.

———. "Abstracting and Indexing Services." In: *American Library Association Yearbook.* Vol. 7. Chicago, American Library Assn., 1982, pp. 15–16.

———. "Linguistic Approaches to the Construction and Use of Thesauri: A Review." *Drexel Library Quarterly*, 8(2):135–146, April 1972.

Neufeld, M. L., and M. Cornog. "Abstracting and Indexing." In: *New Options for Librarians.* Edited by D. Berkner and B. C. Sellen. New York, Neal-Schuman. In press.

———. *Abstracting and Indexing Career Guide.* Philadelphia, The National Federation of Abstracting and Information Services. In press.

———. "Secondary Information Systems and Services: Current Issues and Trends." In: *Annual Review of Information Science and Technology.* Vol. 18. Edited by M. E. Williams. White Plains, N.Y., Knowledge Industry Publications. In press.

Neufeld, M. L., K. L. Graham, and A. Mazella. "Machine Aided Title Word Indexing for a Current Awareness Publication." *Information Storage and Retrieval*, 10(11/12):403–410, November-December 1984.

Newberry, W. F. "Edge-Notched Cards: Prematurely Buried." *Library Journal*, 106(6):624–625, March 15, 1981.

Prywes, N. W., and A. L. Lang. "A Posteriori Indexing, Classification and Retrieval of Textual Data." *Information Storage and Retrieval*, 10(1):15–27, January 1974.

Ranganathan, S. R. *Colon Classification.* New Brunswick, N.J., Graduate School of Library Science, Rutgers University, 1965.

Robertson, C. *A Bibliography of Standards Relevant to Indexing and Abstracting and the Presentation of Information.* Ottawa, National Library of Canada, 1980.

Rothman, J. "Index, Indexer, Indexing." In: *Encyclopedia of Library and Information Science.* Vol. II. Edited by A. Kent et al. New York, Dekker, 1974, pp. 286–289.

Rush, J. E., R. Salvador, and A. Zamora. "Automatic Abstracting and Indexing. II. Production of Indicative Abstracts by Application of Contextual Inference and Syntactic Coherence Criteria." *Journal of the American Society for Information Science,* 22(4):260–274, July–August 1971.

Salton, G. "Mathematics and Information Retrieval." *Journal of Documentation,* 35(1):1–29, March 1979.

Saracevic, T. "Relevance, A Review of and a Framework for the Thinking on the Notion in Information Science." *Journal of the American Society for Information Science,* 26(6):321–343. November–December 1975.

_____. *Introduction to Information Science.* New York, Bowker, 1970.

Sharp, J. R. "Content Analysis, Specification and Control." In: *Annual Review of Information Science and Technology.* Edited by C. A. Cuadra. New York, Wiley, 1967, pp. 87–122.

Shera, J. H., and M. E. Egan. *The Classified Catalog.* Chicago, American Library Assn., 1956.

Soergel, D. *Indexing Languages and Thesauri: Construction and Maintenance.* Los Angeles, Melvill-Wiley, 1975.

Taube, M., et al. *Studies in Coordinate Indexing.* Vol. I. Washington, D.C., Documentation, Inc., 1953.

Taulbee, O. E. "Content Analysis, Specification and Control." In: *Annual Review of Information Science and Technology.* Edited by C. A. Cuadra. Chicago, Encyclopedia Britannica, 1968, pp. 105–136.

Tinker, J. F. "Imprecision in Indexing. Part II." *American Documentation,* 19(3):322–330, July 1968.

_____. "Imprecision in Meaning Measured by Inconsistency of Indexing." *American Documentation,* 17(2):96–102, April 1966.

Tritschler, R. J. "Effective Information: Searching Strategies Without Perfect Indexing." *American Documentation,* 15(3):179–184, July 1964.

United Nations Educational, Scientific and Cultural Organization. *Indexing Principles.* Paris, 1975. sc.75/ws/58.

_____. *Guidelines for the Establishment and Development of Monolingual Scientific and Technical Thesauri for Information Retrieval.* Paris, Unesco, 1970. sc/MD/20.

Vickery, B. C. . "Document Description and Representation." In: *Annual Review of Information Science and Technology.* Edited by C. A. Cuadra. Chicago, Encyclopedia Britannica, 1971, pp. 113–140.

_____. *Classification and Indexing in Science.* London, Butterworths, 1959, Chapter 1.

Wanger, J., C. A. Cuadra, and M. Fishburn. *Impact of On-Line Retrieval Services, 1974–75.* Santa Monica, Calif., System Development Corporation, 1976.

Weil, B. H., I. Zarember, and H. Owen. "Technical-Abstracting Fundamentals: I. Introduction. II. Writing Principles and Practices. III. Publishing Abstracts in Primary Journals." *Journal of Chemical Documentation*, 3:86–89, April 1963; 3:125–132, July 1963; 3:132–136, July 1963.

Weinberg, B. H. "Bibliographic Coupling: A Review." *Information Storage and Retrieval*, 10(5/6):189–196, May–June 1974.

Weinstock, M. "Citation Indexes." In: *Encyclopedia of Library and Information Science*. Vol. 5. Edited by A. Kent and H. Lancour. New York, Dekker, 1971, pp. 16–40.

Weiss, S. "Online Bibliographic Services: A Comparison." *Special Libraries*, 72(4):379–389, October 1981.

Wellisch, H. *Indexing and Abstracting; An International Bibliography*. Santa Barbara, Calif., ABC-Clio, 1980.

———. *The PRECIS Index System: Principles, Applications and Prospects*. Bronx, N.Y., H. W. Wilson, 1977.

———. "A Flow Chart for Indexing with a Thesaurus." *Journal of the American Society for Information Science*, 23(3):185–194, May–June 1972.

Whaley, F. R. "What the Indexer-Abstracter Does." *IEEE Student Journal*, 3(6):22–24, November 1965.

Williams, M. E. *Computer-Readable Bibliographic Data Bases: A Directory and Data Sourcebook*. White Plains, N.Y., Knowledge Industry Publications, 1982.

———. "Relative Impact of Print and Database Products on Database Producer Expenses and Income — Trends for Database Producer Organizations Based on a Thirteen Year Financial Analysis." *Information Processing and Management*, 17(5):263–267, 1981.

———. "Criteria for Evaluation and Selection of Data Bases and Data Base Services." *Special Libraries*, 66(12):561–569, December 1975.

Zarember, I., and E. H. Brenner. "An Alphabetic Index as a Byproduct of Computer Coordinate Indexing." In: *Parameters of Information Science: Proceedings of the American Documentation Institute*. Edited by A. W. Elias. Washington, D.C., American Documentation Institute, 1964, pp. 467–470.

Publications by and About NFAIS

Baker, D. B., et al. *Some Counterparts in Perspective: A Detailed Report on Visits to the Soviet All-Union Institute of Scientific and Technical Information, the Polish Central Institute for Documentation in Science and Technology, the Excerpta Medica Foundation, and Danish Technical Information Service.* Washington, D.C., NFSAIS, 1960.
Bearman, T. C., and W. A. Kunberger. *A Study of Coverage Overlap Among Science and Technology Abstracting and Indexing Services.* Philadelphia, NFAIS, 1977.
National Academy of Sciences/National Academy of Engineering, Committee on Scientific and Technical Communication. *Scientific and Technical Communication: A Pressing National Problem and Recommendations for Its Solution.* Washington, D.C., 1969.
National Federation of Science Abstracting and Indexing Services. *NFAIS/UNESCO Indexing in Perspective Education Kit.* Edited by E. H. Brenner. Philadelphia, 1979.
_____. *NFAIS Membership Directory.* Biennial. Philadelphia, 1979–
_____. *Science Literature Indicators Study.* Philadelphia, 1977.
_____. *Key Papers on the Use of Computer-Based Bibliographic Services.* Edited by S. Keenan. Philadelphia, 1973.

_____. *National Federation of Abstracting and Indexing Services, History and Issues, 1958–1973*. Philadelphia, 1973.

_____. *A Position Statement on the SATCOM Report Prepared by the Federation Member Services*. Washington, D.C., 1970.

_____. *National Federation of Science Abstracting and Indexing Services, 1958–1968. Ten Year Progress Report*. Philadelphia, 1968.

_____. *A Guide to the World's Abstracting and Indexing Services in Science and Technology*. Washington, D.C., 1963.

_____. *A Guide to U.S. Indexing and Abstracting Services in Science and Technology*. Prepared by the Science and Technology Division, Library of Congress, for NFAIS. Washington, D.C., 1960.

_____. "A National Plan for Science Abstracting and Indexing Services." Prepared by Robert Heller and Associates. In: *Proceedings of NFAIS Sixth Annual Meeting, March 20–22, 1963*. Washington, D.C., 1963.

_____. *NFSAIS Newsletter*. Bimonthly. Philadelphia, 1958– .

Neufeld, M. L., and M. Cornog. *Abstracting and Indexing Career Guide*. Philadelphia, NFAIS, 1982.

_____. *Energy and Environment Information Resource Guide*. Philadelphia, NFAIS, 1982.

_____. *Database Access Alternatives Study: Final Report*. Philadelphia, NFAIS, 1981.

System Development Corporation. *Recommendations for National Document Handling Systems in Science and Technology: Appendix A; A Background Study*. Santa Monica, Calif., 1965. PB-168-267.

_____. *A System Study of Abstracting and Indexing Services in the United States*. Santa Monica, Calif. 1965. TM-WD-394, PB-174-249.

United Nations Educational, Scientific and Cultural Organization and the International Council of Scientific Unions (UNESCO/UNISIST). *Study Report on the Feasibility of a World Science Information System*. Paris, 1971.

Weinberg, A. M., et al. *Science, Government and Information: The Responsibilities of the Technical Community and the Government in the Transfer of Information*. Prepared by the President's Science Advisory Committee. Washington, D.C., LEASCO Information Products, Inc., 1963. ED 048 894.

Wood, J. L., et al. "Overlap Among the Journal Articles Selected for Coverage by BIOSIS, CAS and Ei." *Journal of the American Society for Information Science*, 24(1):25–28, January–February 1973.

_____. "Overlap in the Lists of Journals Maintained by BIOSIS, CAS and Ei." *Journal of the American Society for Information Science*, 21(1):36–38, January–February 1972.